Tales of the Yankee Clipper

TALES OF THE YANKEE CLIPPER

Stories and Reflections on Joe DiMaggio

JONATHAN WEEKS

Essex, Connecticut

An imprint of Globe Pequot, the trade division of
The Rowman & Littlefield Publishing Group, Inc.
4501 Forbes Blvd., Ste. 200
Lanham, MD 20706
www.rowman.com

Distributed by NATIONAL BOOK NETWORK

Copyright © 2024 by Jonathan Weeks

Photos courtesy of Boston Public Library, Library of Congress, and Visual Hunt

British Library Cataloguing in Publication Information available

Library of Congress Cataloging-in-Publication Data
Names: Weeks, Jonathan, author.
Title: Tales of the Yankee Clipper : stories and reflections on Joe Dimaggio / Jonathan Weeks.
Description: Essex, Connecticut : Lyons Press, [2024] | Series: Yankees icon trilogy; no. 3 |
    Includes bibliographical references.
Identifiers: LCCN 2023038016 (print) | LCCN 2023038017 (ebook) | ISBN 9781493080168
    (trade paperback) | ISBN 9781493080175 (epub)
Subjects: LCSH: DiMaggio, Joe, 1914-1999--Anecdotes. | New York Yankees (Baseball team)--
    History--Anecdotes. | Baseball players--United States--Biography. | Baseball--United States--
    History–Anecdotes.
Classification: LCC GV865.D5 W44 2024 (print) | LCC GV865.D5 (ebook) | DDC
    796.357092 [B]–dc23/eng/20230816
LC record available at https://lccn.loc.gov/2023038016
LC ebook record available at https://lccn.loc.gov/2023038017

CONTENTS

INTRODUCTION

In a 1939 radio address, future British Prime Minister Winston Churchill described the intentions and interests of Russia as "a riddle wrapped in a mystery inside an enigma." He could just as well have been talking about Joe DiMaggio. DiMaggio had a talent for keeping his emotions suppressed and his innermost thoughts to himself. Few could say that they really knew him. And even the ones who did found him to be unpredictable.

One of Joe's closest friends observed that he "compartmentalized his life as a means of self-preservation. Joe's life was a jigsaw puzzle and only he had all the pieces. He believed that if no one could put it all together, he would have more freedom. His insistence on privacy is critical to understanding [him] as an icon and a man."

DiMaggio was a walking contradiction. He was quiet, but not necessarily shy. He could be both gracious and abrupt, approachable or aloof depending on the situation. Although he came across as humble, he had a tremendous sense of entitlement. He was complex, secretive, inscrutable. There were many layers to the man who came to be affectionately known as the "Yankee Clipper."

DiMaggio always felt that his actions on the field should do the talking for him. And for the most part, they did. He took over where Babe Ruth left off, providing a welcome distraction from the Great Depression and the war overseas. He helped the Yankees to nine World Series titles—a record later broken by Yogi Berra. DiMaggio's legend endured long after he took his last swing in a major-league game. Songs were composed in his honor, prestigious awards were bestowed upon him, and he was hailed as "the greatest living ballplayer" to the day he died.

To many, DiMaggio personified elegance, style, and grace. An impeccable dresser, he was married to two glamorous actresses. On the field, he glided almost effortlessly, never having to dive for a ball and rarely (if ever) making a mistake on the basepaths. He became the living embodiment of the American dream and a symbol of the country's so-called greatest generation. In later years, he remained a throwback to an era when baseball truly meant something to the masses—long before commercial endorsements and seven-figure salaries became the primary focus of players.

As time marched on, DiMaggio grew increasingly distrustful of the people around him. It was understandable—inevitable even. Everyone wanted a piece of him—to meet him, talk to him, acquire his autograph. He tried his best to maintain a polite façade, but the weight of being Joe DiMaggio was cumbersome. He was hounded by fans wherever he went—even in restrooms and Catholic churches. Whenever he avoided someone in an effort to maintain his personal space, he risked being labeled rude, ungrateful, or antisocial.

. . . A heavy burden indeed.

Many have tried to analyze him, to understand his behavior and get inside his head. He remains a murky figure nonetheless. A careful examination of his life reveals only small pieces of the whole—fleeting glimpses of the man who grew from a quiet, self-conscious boy to a national hero. In later years, he was seen as a lonely figure, shaken and embittered by the loss of his second wife. One thing holds true: There has never been anyone quite like him. And there never will be again.

PLAYERS, MANAGERS, AND WRITERS ON DIMAGGIO

"I don't think anyone can put into words the great things that Joe DiMaggio did. Of all the stars I've known, DiMaggio needed the least coaching."—**Joe McCarthy**

"Joe DiMaggio batting sometimes gave the impression, the suggestion that the old rules and dimensions of baseball no longer applied to him, and that the game had at last grown unfairly easy."—**Donald Hall**

"There was an aura about him. He walked like no one else walked. He did things so easily. He was immaculate in everything he did. Kings of state wanted to meet him and be with him. He carried himself so well. He could fit in any place in the world."—**Phil Rizzuto**

"Joe made you feel confident. If another player got too emotional about an umpire's call or something like that, Joe would simply gaze in his direction or mumble a few words and the other guy knew it was time to relax."—**Billy Johnson**

"He came to play and was a bear-down, no-nonsense player all the way. Not just on the field, but in his whole life. He had a lot of pride in himself. He always looked like the part he played—he was all class in everything he did."—**Gene Woodling**

"He just was never a guy who could let down in front of strangers. He was a guy who knew he was the greatest baseball player in America and he was proud of it. He knew what the press and the fans and the kids expected of him, and he was always trying to live up to that image. That's why he couldn't be silly in public like I could or ever be caught without his shirt unbuttoned or his shoes shined. He knew he was Joe DiMaggio and he knew what he meant to the country. He felt that obligation to the Yankees and to the public."—**Lefty Gomez**

"He was the antithesis of the iconoclastic, mind-expanding, authority-defying '60s, which is why I think he suspected a hidden meaning in my lyrics. The fact that the lines were sincere and that they've been embraced over the years as the yearning for heroes and heroism speaks to the subconscious desires of the culture. We need heroes, and we search for candidates to be anointed."—**Paul Simon**

"Do you believe the great DiMaggio would stay with a fish as long as I will stay with this one? he thought. I am sure he would and more since he is young and strong."—**Excerpt from Ernest Hemingway's *The Old Man and the Sea***

DIMAGGIO ON DIMAGGIO

"I can remember a reporter asking me for a quote and I didn't know what a quote was. I thought it was some kind of soft drink."

"I'm just a ballplayer with one ambition, and that is to give all I've got to help my ballclub win. I've never played any other way."

"Baseball didn't really get into my blood until I knocked off that hitting streak. Getting a daily hit became more important to me than eating, drinking, or sleeping."

"You ought to run the hardest when you feel the worst. Never let the other guy know you're down."

"A person always doing his or her best becomes a natural leader, just by example."

"I like to be popular, who doesn't? But I don't pay much attention to the fans. While I give them all I have, and I hope I can make good for them, primarily I am out there playing ball for the club—and for myself. You have got to do the best you can while you last in this game, and I want to make what I can while I last."

PART I

A Chronological Journey through DiMaggio's Life and Career

BREAKING WITH TRADITION

Joseph Paul DiMaggio was born in Martinez, California, on November 25, 1914. He was the eighth child (and fourth son) of Giuseppe and Rosalie DiMaggio. His father came to America in 1898 from the fishing community of Isola delle Femmine (literally translated as "The Island of Women"), which is located on the Sicilian coast. The town itself is situated on the mainland and takes its name from a small island that lies just off the shore in the Tyrrhenian Sea. A fisherman by trade, Giuseppe settled in the San Francisco Bay area in search of better commercial prospects. He left Rosalie (who was pregnant with their first child) behind, promising to send for her once he had established himself in America. After working for multiple railroads, Giuseppe was able to purchase a boat and return to fishing. It took him several years to save enough money to bring his wife and their daughter, Nellie, to the United States.

During Joe's preschool years, the family (which included nine children by then) moved to North Beach. Giuseppe expected all five of the DiMaggio boys to work on his crab boat once they came of age, but Joe loathed the smell of dead fish and avoided chores whenever possible. Giuseppe was less than pleased with Joe's work ethic, sometimes referring to him as "lazy" or "good for nothing." In later years, the Yankee icon confessed that the game of baseball held no initial attraction for him aside from providing a welcome escape from his fishing duties.

Professional baseball arrived in California at the beginning of the twentieth century with the establishment of the Pacific Coast League. The circuit began with six clubs located in three states. By the 1930s, the league had expanded to eight teams. The San Francisco Seals were among the most successful franchises, capturing seven championships between 1909 and 1928. Because there was no major-league baseball on the West Coast in those days, PCL teams developed sizeable fan bases. Some clubs were actually able to persuade highly talented players to remain in the minors by offering competitive salaries.

Tom and Mike—the oldest DiMaggio brothers—played on the local sandlots but ultimately caved to family pressure, joining their father on the boat. Vince, Joe, and Dominic had other ideas, aspiring to the major leagues. Rosalie often covered for her younger sons, keeping their baseball activities hidden from Giuseppe, who considered the game to be a pointless distraction.

No one seems to know precisely when Joe first learned the rudiments of baseball. According to one story, he and his buddies took turns swinging a boat paddle at a cloth ball held together with string. At Hancock Elementary School, he played a modified version of the game in the recess yard. In place of bats, the boys would swat at the ball with their bare hands. Joe later became a regular at the North Beach and Funston playgrounds. The North Beach field was smaller, and Joe's pals would encourage him to try to hit the Powell Street cable car if it approached while he was at bat. Legend has it that he accomplished the feat more than once.

Because Joe's family didn't have money for unnecessary items and his father was not a proponent of the sport, Joe had to borrow gloves from teammates. He caught bare-handed when none were available. Although he was always an exceptional hitter, he had occasional trouble with ground balls and his relays across the diamond were erratic. "I had a strong arm, but I made a lot of throwing errors," he told one biographer. "My teammates kidded me that it was dangerous to sit behind first base when I played shortstop." Given his defensive shortcomings and lack of passion for the game in the early days, few if any could have predicted that he would become one of the greatest players in baseball history.

ONE DOOR CLOSES, ANOTHER OPENS

DiMaggio may have not been motivated by a love of baseball, but he developed a competitive spirit early on. In his *New York Times* best-selling biography *Joe DiMaggio: The Hero's Life*, author Richard Ben Cramer asserts, "It was the way [DiMaggio] was in a game. He had to win. That was the reason he'd play—he wanted to win something."

There were rules against smoking on the local playgrounds, but Joe would secretly puff on cigarettes, hiding them from his friends, who would inevitably try to bum off of him if they knew he had them. When they weren't engaged in games of baseball, the boys would often play cards. Joe and his buddy Niggy Marino rigged the decks and worked in tandem, using furtive signals to hustle pocket change from opponents. Joe was required to help support his family financially and he sold newspapers on the corners of Sutter, Sansome, and Market Streets. His younger brother, Dominic, worked the opposite corners.

Joe wasn't much of a student and rarely kept up with the assignments. He was extremely quiet in class, afraid to speak up for fear of appearing ignorant. Self-conscious from an early age, he was prone to blushing—a symptom of social anxiety. His family spoke Sicilian at home, but he was clumsy with the language, making it somewhat difficult for him to communicate. Though he wasn't academically inclined, he developed a knowledge of the streets. In addition to hawking newspapers and cheating at cards, he made extra cash stripping the copper wires from crumbling buildings and selling them to local junk dealers.

Joe made it through middle school and moved on to Galileo High. Listless and bored, he took to cutting classes with his pal Frank Venezia. The two spent their weekdays at Marina Park, watching older men wager on card games. After several months of continuous absences, the school finally sent a truancy notice home. Displeased with their brother's behavior, Tom and Mike roughed Joe up. When it became apparent that the school did not want him back, Joe dropped out at the age of sixteen. He worked at several menial jobs, but the pay was poor and he disliked the work immensely. Baseball eventually became his primary focus.

Joe's older brother Vince was next in line to join the family business. But he had no intention of pursuing a career as a fisherman. With a melodic tenor voice, he had aspirations of becoming a musical performer. Singing wasn't his only talent. His powerful bat and slick glove made him a standout in the local baseball leagues.

As word of Vince's skills on the diamond spread, he received an offer to play in the Northern California League—a semipro circuit composed of teams sponsored by lumber and mining companies. Because Vince was still legally a minor, his father's signature was required on the contract. Giuseppe refused, but Vince would not be deterred. He lied about his age and signed the document himself. While playing up north, he fell head over heels for a girl named Madeline Cristani. When Giuseppe learned that Vince intended to propose to her, he denounced the marriage and informed his son that he was no longer welcome at the family home.

In 1932, Vince signed with the San Francisco Seals and was sent to the club's Class-D affiliate in the Arizona-Texas League. He was vying for a batting title when the circuit abruptly folded. Summoned to play for the Seals, he paid an unannounced visit to his family's Taylor Street flat. He was carrying a stack of cash he had earned while playing ball. "I didn't bring [a] check," he later recalled. "I brought it in cash so [my father] could see it was more than a piece of paper. . . . And the first thing he [said] when he saw [it] was 'where'd you steal that money?'" The next day, Vince introduced Giuseppe to Seals' owner Charley Graham, who assured the elder DiMaggio that the money had been rightfully earned. It was an important moment for Vince and his younger brothers. From that point on, Giuseppe understood that his sons could make a decent living playing ball.

Vince got into 59 games with the Seals that year, hitting .270 with 21 extra base hits. Meanwhile, Joe became a sensation on the local scene. He played for several different teams during the 1932 slate, establishing himself as one of the best hitters in the city. The games drew fairly large crowds and a hat was passed around after each match to collect donations. It wasn't unusual for players to walk away with five to ten dollars apiece.

The Seals had a mediocre year in 1932, falling out of contention with a handful of games still remaining. Realizing there was very little at stake, manager Ike Caveney allowed shortstop Augie Galan to participate in a series of exhibition games overseas. Galan later forged a successful major-league career, playing in three World Series and three All-Star Games. His absence created a golden opportunity for Joe.

With a roster opening, Vince told Caveney how his younger brother had been tearing up the local circuit and could serve as a reliable substitute for Galan. Caveney spoke to Graham, who had already heard about Joe through an acquaintance. They agreed to give the kid a shot. Joe logged his first professional appearance on a Saturday afternoon at Seals Stadium. After tripling in his first at-bat, he reportedly made a pair of fine running catches in shallow left field. Vince later joked, "Maybe if I'd kept my mouth shut, I'd be remembered as the greatest DiMaggio."

A HOME IN THE OUTFIELD

In later years, Joe claimed that he was never paid for the three PCL games he appeared in near the end of the 1932 campaign. But he made out pretty well in '33. To prepare for the season ahead, he joined a winter league. When it came time to negotiate a contract with the Seals, he enlisted the help of his brother Tom. Considered by family members to be the smartest of the DiMaggio clan, Tom brokered a pact worth roughly twice as much as the average PCL rookie salary. Included in the agreement was a clause entitling Joe to a pair of new suits, which Tom claimed for himself as a form of repayment. "Tom did pretty well on the deal," Joe later said. "I didn't even get reimbursed for cab fare to the stadium and back. It cost me 30 cents."

In 1933, the United States was in the throes of the Great Depression. Unemployment was at an all-time high and attendance at ballgames was on the decline. Most people stayed away from the ballpark unless there was something of particular interest going on. Believing that the stock market slump was only temporary, Charley Graham had built a brand new stadium in San Francisco's Mission District. The cost of construction was over $1 million and the ambitious Seals owner was heavily in debt by the time the '33 campaign arrived. He figured a local Italian kid with a hot bat might help boost attendance a bit. In addition to Galan and the DiMaggio brothers, the Seals began the season with another future star: Curt Davis, a right-handed pitcher who would win 10 or more games during 11 big-league seasons and help the Dodgers to a long overdue World Series berth in 1941.

While "Joe D." impressed everyone with his hitting, his defense still left something to be desired. During a spring training infield drill, one of his throws sailed into the stands past Graham's head. "I'll say one thing about the kid," Graham joked. "He's got a hell of an arm." In the last exhibition game of the year, Galan sat out with an injury. Taking his place, DiMaggio committed several errors. One reporter remarked that he looked "bewildered" at shortstop.

Seals' skipper Ike Caveney had spent four years with the Cincinnati Reds during the early '20s. Though he fashioned a commendable .283 batting average over 21 professional seasons, he was shaky on defense, leading the National League with 49 errors in 1923. Still, he knew the game and had an eye for talent. It was clear that the younger DiMaggio could hit. But Caveney needed to park him in a spot where his marginal defense would cause minimal harm. An experiment at first base failed miserably when Joe couldn't get the footwork down. Caveney tried talking to the struggling rookie afterward to relax him, but it seemed to have little effect. At the end of spring training, Joe was listed as a utility player and placed on the bench, joining his brother Vince, who was nursing a sore arm.

During the first week of the regular season, Joe was summoned by Caveney to pinch-hit for the Seals' starting right fielder. When the inning was over, Caveney assigned DiMaggio to the outfield—a position he had never played before. The learning curve was steep in the weeks that followed, but Joe was up to the challenge, recording 407 putouts and 32 assists by season's end. He did so without the support of his brother, who ended up being cut from the team. Vince was recalled in April and officially released a couple of weeks later. He ended up playing for the Hollywood Stars—a rival PCL club.

A GLIMPSE OF THINGS TO COME

In the absence of his older brother, Joe isolated himself. His quiet nature negatively impacted his relationships with teammates and adversely affected the way he was perceived by sportswriters. Before games, he could be found smoking in the corner of the clubhouse—alone and virtually unapproachable. He made little effort to establish friendships. One reporter described him as "awkward" and "surly." Teammate Steve Barath observed, "He was just backward. . . . I lived with him for weeks and we never even had a conversation."

It took a while for DiMaggio's bat to heat up. A slump during the month of May drove his average below .250. By then, the Seals were floundering near the bottom of the standings. On May 28, Joe cracked a double in the second game of a doubleheader. It was the beginning of something extraordinary as he went off on a historic tear, breaking the PCL record of 49 consecutive games with a hit, which had been set by Oakland Oaks first baseman Jack Ness in 1915.

DiMaggio's streak drew little attention at first. But by the time it reached 40 games, fans were flocking to the stadium, prompting newspapers in Pacific Coast League cities to report on Joe's daily activities. Journalists trying to interview San Francisco's rookie sensation found it to be a maddening experience as DiMaggio offered mostly nonverbal responses, grunting, shrugging, and staring impassively into space. Off the record, press members took to calling him "Dead Pan Joe."

Newspapers had been inaccurately printing Joe's name as "DeMaggio" all year and he never corrected them. After signing an endorsement deal with the Hillerich & Bradsby Company (makers of the Louisville Slugger), Joe wrote his name with a deliberate space between the "i" and the capital "M." When the streak reached 49, Charley Graham asked DiMaggio about the spelling of his name so it could be properly engraved on a commemorative watch. Joe told him he could spell it any way he liked.

As the story goes, even DiMaggio's father took an interest in the streak. Though Giuseppe could scarcely read a word of English, he learned how to find Joe's name in the boxscores and determine his hit totals for the day. If it was more than one, Giuseppe would promptly relay the news to Joe's mom, often waking her from a sound sleep. At one point during the streak, Vince—by then with the Hollywood Stars—was asked by a reporter what he would do if his brother needed a hit and the ball was heading in his direction. "I would stand on my ear to try to get the ball," he responded dutifully.

The ceremony honoring DiMaggio for breaking the record was held before the game actually took place. Joe's parents were there along with San Francisco mayor Angelo Rossi. In addition to the engraved watch, Joe received a leather traveling bag, a bonus check, and a bouquet of flowers. Once the game was underway, he avoided an awkward situation by officially claiming the record for himself with a first-inning single off of Bobo Newsom. Newsom would go on to win more than 200 games over 20 major-league seasons. DiMaggio would gather at least one hit in his next 11 PCL games.

Observers said that DiMaggio looked fatigued and under pressure on the day the streak ended. Ike Caveney moved Joe from the clean-up slot to the lead-off position to get him an extra plate appearance that afternoon. It didn't help as he grounded out twice, flied out twice, and hit into a force play. But one of his outs chased the winning run across the plate.

Even when he failed, he succeeded.

"I'm glad it's over," he admitted in a rare display of verbosity after the game. "The strain was getting a bit tough."

Years later, after he had survived a similar ordeal in the majors, he remarked that the PCL streak was much easier to endure. "No pressure, no big crowds, no reporters following me around," he asserted.

ALMOST A YANKEE

The Pacific Coast League was on shaky footing at the beginning of the 1934 campaign. With the US economy in the dumps, owners were forced to purge their rosters of high-salaried players. There had been talk of a temporary shutdown the previous spring, but baseball commissioner Kenesaw Mountain Landis had nixed the idea by threatening to make every player in the PCL available to clubs outside the circuit. Despite the hype surrounding DiMaggio's 61-game hitting streak, the Seals had averaged just 1,200 paid admissions per home game in 1933 (still better than half the teams in the league). With a hefty mortgage on his hands, Charley Graham sought to lure fans through the turnstiles any way he could. One strategy was to sponsor Ladies' Day promotions.

Commenting on DiMaggio's meteoric rise to stardom, one biographer remarked, "It was an odd way to become a man—instantly and in the public view—but by the time Joe DiMaggio turned nineteen and signed for a second year with the Seals, he was the man of that club, a big man for the league." In many ways "Dead Pan Joe" was still a boy—bashful, self-conscious, and ill at ease around members of the opposite sex. Although he became an object of desire to many of the women who attended games, he strenuously avoided them—just as he had avoided his sisters' friends while growing up. He found plenty of girls attractive, but if he allowed himself to appear interested, he might be forced to hold a meaningful conversation. And that could expose the embarrassing truth—that he had absolutely no idea what to say.

Eventually, with the help of a good friend, Joe did meet a nice young lady. Her name was Violet Koski—a local San Francisco girl who worked in a drugstore. On her days off, she got in the habit of going to the ballpark. Joe made her fight for his attention, ignoring her initial attempts to engage with him, but he eventually agreed to accompany her on a double date. He became reasonably comfortable around her and the two began seeing each other on a regular basis for a while.

Even in the early stages of his professional career, women considered DiMaggio to be quite a catch. He was handsome, talented, and moving up in the world. The Yankees and Red Sox had both expressed interest in him near the end of the '33 campaign. Joe was the biggest gate attraction in the PCL, and Charley Graham knew that a deal with either club would net him a small fortune. If Babe Ruth could earn $35,000 per year with his skills in obvious decline, Graham was certain he could get twice as much for DiMaggio.

In late May 1934, the Seals were wrapping up a home stand against the Hollywood Stars. Newspapers had been playing up the alleged rivalry between Joe and his brother Vince. Both players collected a pair of hits as the two clubs split a doubleheader on "Family Day" at the stadium. After the game, there was a dinner at one of the DiMaggio sisters' homes. Joe attended the gathering and opted to take a cab back home.

The events that followed have been a source of debate over the years. Though some of the details raise further questions, the simplified version (told by Joe himself) is as follows: On the ride home, his foot fell asleep. As he got out of the cab, he put his full weight on the numb leg and crumpled to the pavement. He heard a series of sharp cracks in his knee as he fell. Unable to straighten the leg, he was driven by an acquaintance to a local hospital, where it was determined that he had torn some cartilage.

It was an unmitigated disaster for DiMaggio and Graham. As word of the accident spread, major-league scouts labeled Joe as damaged property. Graham's hopes of a blockbuster deal evaporated. And Joe's path to the majors was temporarily blocked.

Sports medicine was still in its infancy during DiMaggio's days. Players were encouraged to keep on going until their bodies literally broke down—or at least until the pain reached an intolerable level. DiMaggio was used sparingly over the next week. In a game against the LA Angels, he blasted a pinch-hit homer and was forced to walk around the bases. The next day, he delivered a clutch double and barely made it to second. It was clear he needed more rest in order for the leg to heal.

At least one scout had the presence of mind not to bail on DiMaggio. Bill Essick, who covered the San Francisco territory for the Yankees, arranged to have an orthopedic specialist examine Joe's knee. The prognosis was good. Given his youth and body type, DiMaggio was expected to make a full recovery. The Yankees kept the information hidden from other teams and quietly followed Joe's progress.

In July, the Seals rushed DiMaggio back into the lineup on a full-time basis. It proved to be a grievous mistake. During a game in early August, he raced in to grab a sinking line drive and fell down hard. He stayed in the game but came up limping after a ground out in his next at-bat. While heading out to his defensive post as the teams were changing sides, he collapsed in the dugout. It marked the end of his season. He sat out more than 80 games. The team crumbled without him, falling below .500 for the year.

COMING BACK STRONG

With DiMaggio's health in question, Charley Graham was anxious to cut a deal. The Yankees had mined the Pacific Coast League for talent in the past and fared pretty well, adding Tony Lazzeri, Lefty Gomez, and Frankie Crosetti to their ranks. But Yankee GM Ed Barrow was hesitant to gamble on a kid with a bum knee, even if he was being touted as the next megastar.

In November 1934, Graham squeezed all he could out of his prized slugger, negotiating a trade with the Yankees. The final arrangement was beneficial to both clubs. The Yankees sent several minor leaguers of modest value to San Francisco. They allowed the Seals to retain DiMaggio's services for one more year. A small wrinkle in the plan developed when Doc Farrell—a utility infielder who had played in portions of eight major-league seasons—refused to report to the Seals' training camp. Barrow coughed up enough cash to complete the transaction, which he later referred to as the best deal he ever made.

With DiMaggio's presence in San Francisco assured, Graham sought to boost attendance even further by hiring Lefty O'Doul as manager. O'Doul was a living legend in San Francisco, where his star power rivaled that of Babe Ruth. Having grown up in Butchertown—the city's meat-packing district—he began his Pacific Coast League career as a pitcher, winning 25 games for the Seals in 1921. When chronic arm trouble set in, he was moved to the outfield. He spent part of eleven seasons in the big leagues, capturing batting titles in 1929 and 1932. In the former campaign, he fell two base hits short of the hallowed .400 mark. Wherever he went in the city, he found himself surrounded by admiring fans. He was everything an idol should be: handsome, charismatic, generous, and accommodating to his supporters.

. . . A perfect role model for DiMaggio.

DiMaggio had a deep respect for O'Doul, who recognized Joe's vast potential and went out of his way to nurture the budding superstar. The two developed a bond that extended beyond the confines of the field and lasted for many years. Joe also developed an amicable relationship with Ty Cobb, who was a friend of O'Doul's. Cobb lived in Burlingame, which is located in the Bay Area about 16 miles from San Francisco. When O'Doul took over as manager, Cobb began showing up at Seals Stadium. He took an active interest in DiMaggio's development, offering advice (most of it unsolicited) and even helping Joe negotiate his first Yankee contract.

DiMaggio was not the only one to benefit from the departure of Ike Caveney. O'Doul's friendly, approachable manner kept players loose and upbeat. There were no curfews and few restrictions. He allowed his men to do as they pleased during off hours as long as they showed up at the ballpark ready to play.

Feeling relaxed and confident, DiMaggio made spectacular catches in the outfield while hovering near the .400 mark at the plate all season long. In the end, he missed out on a batting title by one point. As a collective unit, the Seals enjoyed one of their finest campaigns, winning 103 regular season games and defeating Los Angeles in the championship playoff.

O'Doul remained at the San Francisco helm for 16 more seasons. By the time he retired with the Seattle Rainiers in 1957, he was the most successful manager in PCL history. In later years, he refused to accept credit for DiMaggio's success. "I was smart enough to leave him alone," he humbly insisted.

THE FRICASSEED FOOT

On the strength of his performance in 1935, DiMaggio was invited to attend Yankee training camp the following year. Because Tony Lazzeri and Frankie Crosetti both lived in San Francisco, Bill Essick (the scout who had convinced the Yankees to stick with DiMaggio) suggested that they accompany the kid to Florida. Essick assumed that their shared Italian heritage and San Francisco roots would lead to some male bonding, but he was wrong. DiMaggio was extremely uncomfortable around strangers and tended to become virtually mute. Lazzeri was also a man of few words, prompting one sportswriter to complain that obtaining a useable quote from him was like "mining for precious ore with a nail file."

Rather than travel to St. Petersburg by train, the two Yankee veterans decided they would make the trip in Lazzeri's newly acquired sedan. Crosetti recounted the 2,900-mile odyssey as follows:

> We each put up so much money for meals and gas and headed to Florida for spring training. There were no superhighways in those days. We had to go up hills and on winding roads and through towns. The trip took us about a week, with me and Tony doing all of the driving. None of us talked a lot, so on the whole drive we probably didn't say more than three words to each other in a week. Just as we were reaching Florida, Tony said to me, "Let's make the kid drive." And the kid, Dimag, said, "I don't know how to drive."

According to DiMaggio, Crosetti threatened to throw him out of the vehicle before cooler heads prevailed.

Crosetti's nickname of "Crow" was not only a shortened version of his last name, but it was an accurate description of what his shrill voice sounded like as it carried across the diamond. A Yankee lifer, he played and coached for the club from 1932 to 1968, winning a total of 17 World Series titles. He collected so many rings over the years that the Yankees started giving him engraved shotguns instead. As a player, he was known for his superb defense at shortstop. As a coach, he was renowned for his ability to steal signs from opposing teams.

Among the greatest second basemen of Lively Ball Era, Lazzeri was an integral part of seven pennant-winning Yankee squads. In 1925, he set the Pacific Coast League single-season record for home runs with 60. He suffered from epilepsy—an affliction that prevented most major-league teams from bidding on his services. But savvy New York executive Ed Barrow decided it was worth the risk, shelling out $50,000 to acquire Lazzeri's contract. "As long as he doesn't take fits between three and six in the afternoon, that's good enough for me," Barrow asserted. Lazzeri proved to be a good investment, averaging 96 RBIs per year during his 12 seasons in the Bronx.

Lazzeri, Crosetti, and DiMaggio arrived in camp ahead of schedule. Joe was assigned to a room with Crosetti. When practice games began, he received a nickname that stuck with him for many years. In the politically incorrect climate of the 1920s and '30s, players were saddled with all kinds of inappropriate monikers—often based on their ethnicity or physical characteristics. Hall of Fame catcher Ernie Lombardi was known as "Schnozz" on account of his bulbous nose. Outfielder Bob Fothergill, who stood 5'10" and weighed more than 230 pounds, was called "Fats" (although he grew to despise the handle and would sometimes come to blows with those who invoked it in his presence). DiMaggio was labeled

DiMaggio and Tony Lazzeri look dapper in street clothes as they pose with Red Sox manager Joe Cronin at Fenway Park. Lazzeri and DiMaggio played together for two seasons before Lazzeri signed with the Cubs.
(COURTESY OF THE LESLIE JONES COLLECTION/BOSTON PUBLIC LIBRARY)

"Dago" by teammates, following in the mold of Lazzeri and Crosetti, who were often referred to as "Big Dago" and "Little Dago" (respectively). Commenting on the racial insensitivity within baseball in the early days of the twentieth century, Hall of Fame pitcher Lefty Gomez commented, "It wasn't meant to be fresh or to run down a guy's nationality. It was just a way of kidding each other, of developing a sense of closeness. It was something to tie us together. . . . I'm Spanish and Irish and they called me 'Spic' and 'Mick.' It didn't mean anything."

DiMaggio's Italian background was conspicuously mentioned in nearly every article written about him that spring. One journalist actually referred to him as "The Big Wop"—a comment that would inevitably generate major controversy in the current era. Regardless of how Joe's name appeared in print, Italian Americans were proud of their affiliation with him and turned up at the ballpark in large numbers to cheer him on.

Although Lou Gehrig was the driving force of the Yankee offense, sportswriters still mourned the loss of Babe Ruth, who had joined the Boston Braves in 1935 and retired shortly into the season when it became apparent that he couldn't cut it at the major-league level anymore. Garrulous, accessible, and larger than life, "The Babe" was always good for a story or quote. DiMaggio's enigmatic personality paled in comparison, but it became clear from the onset that he would be a valuable asset to the club. In his first exhibition game, he hammered a triple and three singles. Over the next few games, his batting average leveled off at .600. And then something unfortunate occurred.

While sliding into second base in a game against the Boston Bees, DiMaggio's foot got stepped on. "I thought I was spiked," he told a biographer, "but there was no blood, just a bruise. The next morning, the foot was swollen, so I went to see Doc Painter." The veteran Yankee trainer placed Joe's foot in a diathermy machine. (For the record, diathermy increases blood flow to injured parts of the body by applying heat generated with a high frequency current.) "I felt [my foot] burning, but I thought that's what it was supposed to feel like," DiMaggio recalled. "Then it really began to hurt, but I didn't want to complain."

He should have spoken up. His foot was seriously scalded, bringing about an abrupt end to his exhibition season. Outfielder George Selkirk remembered the incident vividly. "I was in and out of the training room myself a couple of times and DiMaggio was sitting with his foot in that thing. Somebody had changed the gears or fooled with the dials and it was hotter than it was supposed to be. DiMaggio just sat there with his foot burning up. I guess he was too shy to ask why it was getting so hot. . . . That foot was really burned badly. It was a sickening sight." The unfortunate but preventable accident kept Joe out of action for well over a month.

RETURN TO GLORY

When DiMaggio arrived in New York for the '36 campaign, the Yankees were not as dominant as they had been during the "Roaring Twenties." After capturing six pennants and three World Series titles between 1921 and 1928, the Bombers fell into a slump, claiming one championship over the next seven seasons.

With the untimely death of manager Miller Huggins in 1929, Jacob Ruppert and Ed Barrow had installed Bob Shawkey—a former pitcher of note—at the helm. The team stumbled on his watch, prompting Yankee executives to find a more suitable replacement. They settled on Joe McCarthy, who had led the Cubs to a World Series berth in 1929. Describing McCarthy's on-field persona, a *New York Times* writer colorfully observed, "he was a stocky, five-foot-eight inch Philadelphian with a strong Irish face, an inexpressive manner, a conservative outlook—the master of the non-committal reply and a devotee of the 'set lineup.'" It took some time for McCarthy to find his footing, but he eventually led the Yankees to eight pennants and seven World Series titles—an accomplishment that landed him in the Hall of Fame. DiMaggio was a vital component of McCarthy's success.

A crowd of 25,000-plus turned up at Yankee Stadium to see Joe D.'s regular season debut on May 3. It was one of the largest gatherings of the year (to that point). DiMaggio hit out of the third slot in the batting order—a position that had been occupied by Ruth for the better part of 15 seasons. Proving that he had fully recovered from his early season mishap, Joe banged out three hits (two singles and a triple) while scoring three runs. He kept up the pace in the weeks that followed, reaching base safely in 28 of his first 30 games. By the end of May, he was carrying a batting average of .381.

As DiMaggio continued to prove himself on a daily basis, he received deferential treatment from management. McCarthy, who was somewhat strict, had imposed a smoking ban during games. But he allowed Gehrig and DiMaggio to puff away in the tunnel that led from the dugout to the clubhouse. By some reports, Joe had a three pack per day habit. Pete Sheehy—longtime Yankee clubhouse attendant—said of DiMaggio's vices, "He must have [drunk] thirty half-a-cups of coffee a day. Joe was a nervous sort. It was all inside of him. He was intense. He would smoke a pack of Camels every day before the game. Sometimes, during the game, he would sneak under the stands and smoke between innings."

The emergence of DiMaggio allowed the Yankees to finally rid themselves of their resident problem child, Ben Chapman. A productive hitter with exceptional speed, Chapman had led the American League in stolen bases for three consecutive seasons (1931–1933). But his mercurial temper and flagrant bigotry had brought shame to the Yankees on multiple occasions. The most notorious episode occurred at Griffith Stadium in 1933, when Chapman deliberately spiked Senators' infielder Buddy Myer, who was mistakenly believed to be Jewish. During the ensuing brawl, Chapman stormed the Washington dugout and attacked pitcher Earl Whitehill. A series of anti-Semitic slurs issued by Chapman prompted more than 15,000 New York residents to sign a petition calling for his removal from the roster in 1934. The Yankees finally pulled the trigger in June of '36, sending Chapman to Washington in exchange for Jake Powell. Powell eventually settled in left field, while DiMaggio assumed full-time responsibilities in center. On an interesting side note, Powell ended up making a racially insensitive remark about Blacks during an interview at Comiskey Park in 1938. His comment caused a public outcry and helped increase awareness of the prejudice in baseball.

The Yankees got significant contributions from the usual sources in 1936 as Gehrig smashed a league-leading 49 homers and drove in 152 runs. Other players to reach the century mark in RBIs that year included Lazzeri and Bill Dickey—a Hall of Fame catcher who was perennially overshadowed by his high-profile teammates. Dickey's

The starting 1936 Yankee outfielders strike a throwing pose. From left to right: Myril Hoag, Ben Chapman, and DiMaggio. Chapman ended up being traded to the Washington Senators that year.
(COURTESY OF THE LESLIE JONES COLLECTION/BOSTON PUBLIC LIBRARY)

low-key personality and habitual absence from the spotlight led to his enduring nickname of "The Man Nobody Knows." His remarkable ability to bring out the best in pitchers led one writer to flatteringly remark, "He isn't just a player, he's an influence." The year 1936 was Dickey's finest offensive campaign as he compiled a .362 batting average—third highest in the American League behind Luke Appling of the White Sox and Earl Averill of the Indians.

Had there been a Rookie of the Year Award in 1936, it's a safe bet that DiMaggio would have won it. He finished among the top 10 in more than half a dozen offensive categories, leading the American League with 15 triples. His efforts helped the Yankees build a 19.5 game lead over the Tigers by season's end. After three consecutive second place finishes, Jacob Ruppert's crew was back on top.

SUBWAY SERIES: PART IV

The 1936 Fall Classic was the fourth installment of New York's ongoing "Subway Series" drama. It was the first October showdown between the Yankees and Giants since the opening of Yankee Stadium in 1923. More significantly, it was the Bombers' first World Series without Babe Ruth.

The Giants of 1936 had a completely refurbished lineup that featured several Hall of Famers. Carl Hubbell—a hard throwing left-hander with a wicked screwball—was the ace of the pitching staff. Outfielder Mel Ott, with his trademark leg kick at the plate, was one of the most prolific home run hitters of the era. Travis "Stonewall" Jackson, nicknamed for his sparkling defense, was a steady presence at third base, while Bill Terry—the last NL player to hit .400—served double duty as a player and manager.

After spending most of July out of pennant contention, the Giants went off on an incredible 24–3 tear in August. Highlights from the month included a 15-game winning streak that lasted from August 11 to August 28. The Cardinals and Cubs made the stretch run interesting, but in the end, the two clubs wound up in a second place tie—five games behind Terry's Giants.

Supremely confident, the Yankees entered the Series as odds-on favorites. But they didn't look the part in Game 1. On a soggy afternoon at the Polo Grounds, Hubbell methodically subdued the Yankee offense, gathering eight strikeouts and scattering seven hits. The only Yankee run came on a third-inning homer by George Selkirk—the man who had been faced with the unenviable task of replacing Babe Ruth in right field. The Giants didn't need to bat in their half of the ninth as they breezed to a 6–1 victory.

Game 2 was among DiMaggio's best efforts. He went 3-for-5 at the plate with a pair of RBIs and two runs scored. The rest of the Yankee regulars were in top form as well, battering five Giants hurlers for 18 runs in a lopsided win. After taking two of the next three games, the Bombers hoped to clinch the Series on the road to avoid facing Hubbell again in a Game 7.

More than 38,000 fans jammed the Polo Grounds on October 6 to see Freddie Fitzsimmons of the Giants square off against Lefty Gomez.

"Fat Freddie" had been brilliant in his last start, while Gomez (known as "Goofy" to some for his offbeat behavior) had come away with a win in a mediocre outing. Neither pitcher was terribly effective in Game 6 as the Yankees carried a 6–5 lead into the ninth inning. Once again, it was DiMaggio who took center stage. After leading off with a single, Joe D. moved to third on a subsequent single by Gehrig. Dickey followed with a hot grounder to Terry at first base. Realizing that DiMaggio was hung up between third and home, Terry threw to Eddie Mayo at the hot corner. As the ball was in transit, DiMaggio broke for the plate. Mayo gathered Terry's relay and fired to catcher Harry Danning. It appeared as if DiMaggio would be cut down at home, but the All-Star rookie surprised everyone by leaping into the air. He sailed clear over Danning's tag and crashed down behind the Giants' second-string catcher with his hand on the plate.

Safe!!

The Yankees batted around in the inning, tacking on six more runs. In his second at-bat of the frame, DiMaggio delivered an RBI single. It was his third hit of the afternoon. After the Series-clinching Yankee victory, Terry was asked by a reporter to evaluate DiMaggio's contributions. "I've always heard that one player can make a difference between a winner and a loser," said the Giants' skipper. "Now I know it's true."

When DiMaggio's train arrived in San Francisco, there were thousands of fans lined up to greet him. He was promptly escorted to City Hall, where Mayor Rossi gave him a ceremonial key to the city. At 21 years of age, Joe D. had become a superstar.

BABY BOMBERS

One factor that kept the Yankees in contention throughout the 1930s and beyond was a bountiful farm system. During the years preceding World War II, the International League was considered the highest level of play outside the majors. Established in the nineteenth century, the circuit underwent a number of changes in its early days. By the end of the 1920s, there were eight teams in the loop with some having direct ties to major-league affiliates. Looking to expand the Yankee talent base, Jacob Ruppert purchased the Newark Bears in 1931. Within six years, the franchise had become the most dominant force in the International League. Nearly every player on the 1937 roster appeared in the majors at least briefly. Several became key contributors in New York during DiMaggio's heyday. The most prominent are listed here.

CHARLIE KELLER

LEFT FIELD

Keller was saddled with the nickname "King Kong" on account of his power at the plate, but he actually found the moniker insulting and rarely responded to it. Lefty Gomez, the pithy Yankee southpaw, once joked, "Keller wasn't scouted, he was trapped." A left fielder, Keller drew more than 100 walks in five seasons. From 1939 to 1946, he was one of the Yankees' top run producers, averaging 90 RBIs per year.

JOE GORDON

SECOND BASE

During the 1930s and '40s, middle infielders rarely displayed home run power. But Gordon broke the mold, slamming 20 or more homers in seven seasons while reaching the century mark in RBIs four times. Defensively, he had excellent range and a powerful, accurate arm. Named AL MVP in 1942, he was posthumously elected to Cooperstown in 2009. Before the 1941 World Series, Dodger manager Leo Durocher commented, "We're not afraid of DiMaggio or Keller. The man we fear is Gordon."

SPUD CHANDLER

PITCHER

An ultracompetitive right-hander with a bit of a mean streak, Chandler led the AL in hit batsmen during the 1940 campaign. He enjoyed a pair of 20-win seasons with the Yankees and posted a stellar .717 lifetime winning percentage—a mark that placed him among the top five in major-league history. There was no Cy Young Award in Chandler's day, but he captured MVP honors in 1943.

TOMMY HENRICH

RIGHT FIELD

A powerful slugger, Henrich earned the nickname "Old Reliable" for his ability to drive in runs when they were most needed. He gathered 80 or more RBIs in six seasons, losing three years in his prime to military service. One of his teammates remarked that he "was an intense player who used to tell younger players, 'If you don't want to hustle with this club, there's no use playing.'"

Chandler and Henrich both made their Yankee debuts in May 1937. Chandler posted a 7–4 record in 12 games, while Henrich hit .320 in 242 plate appearances. The Bears did just fine without them, building a 25.5 game lead in the standings by season's end. After capturing the International League pennant, they swept both rounds of the playoffs and faced the Columbus Red Birds of the American Association in the Junior World Series. The talent-laden Bears got off to a rocky start, dropping the first three games, but rallied for four straight wins, establishing themselves as undisputed champions of the minor leagues. Many historians still consider the '37 Newark squad to be the greatest in minor-league history.

Meanwhile, in New York, all eyes were on DiMaggio. In spite of his remarkable rookie performance, the Yankees failed to offer him a raise before the '37 campaign. After a bit of haggling, Ruppert and Barrow increased the bid to $15,000, which was below the slugger's asking price but miles above the average American salary. Joe reluctantly agreed.

During spring training, DiMaggio came down with a sore arm. A subsequent medical exam revealed that he was suffering from tonsillitis along with an infected tooth. A procedure was performed and he didn't play in his first regular season game until April 30.

In many ways, 1937 was a coming out year for DiMaggio. Not only had he become a bona fide celebrity, but he was introduced to the New York nightlife by Joe Gould (manager of heavyweight champion James Braddock) and George Solotaire (an influential Broadway ticket broker). DiMaggio's new friends arranged for him to mingle with the city's top businessmen, actors, and theater icons. On any given night during a

Yankee home stand, he was likely to be found hanging with the Manhattan elite in New York's most exclusive venues.

Joe had his own foray into acting during the '37 slate, landing a cameo role in the film *Manhattan Merry-Go-Round*—a musical comedy that received an Academy Award nomination for Best Art Direction. The Yankee idol was given three lines of dialog, flubbing them so badly that a dozen reshoots were required to get a useable take. On the set, he laid eyes on showgirl Dorothy Olson for the first time. A blonde bombshell with a shapely figure, Olson went by the stage name of Dorothy Arnold. She had no idea who Joe was and, when she learned what he did for a living, she wasn't terribly impressed. Upon hearing that he wanted to meet her, she came around for a polite introduction. Two years later, she ended up marrying him.

Though he would go on to win three MVP Awards in other campaigns, 1937 was arguably DiMaggio's best season from a statistical perspective. He set career-high marks in several categories, leading the AL in runs (151), homers (46), and slugging percentage (.673). In the end, he was a runner up for Most Valuable Player, yielding the title to Charlie Gehringer of the Tigers, who captured the American League batting crown with a lofty .371 mark.

The Yankees repeated as AL champs, winning 102 games and spending a total of 148 days in first place. There was some resistance from the White Sox, Indians, and Tigers during the first half, but by the end of September, all three clubs were well out of contention. Over the course of the season, the Yankees won 39 games by five or more runs and shut out opponents on 15 occasions.

The World Series was a rematch from the previous year, but it wasn't as hotly contested this time around. The Yankees jumped out to a 3–0 Series lead before falling to the Giants at the Polo Grounds in Game 4. DiMaggio drilled his first career World Series homer in the finale, a third inning shot off of left-hander Cliff Melton. He finished the Series at .273 with 4 RBIs. Gomez and Red Ruffing (another eventual Hall of Famer) carried the bulk of the pitching responsibilities, combining for three wins and 16 strikeouts as the Yankees came away with their third championship of the decade.

THE HOLDOUT

In one of the most defining measures of President Roosevelt's "New Deal" domestic policy, Congress passed the Fair Labor Standards Act in 1938, creating a national minimum wage and setting the maximum work week at 40 hours. The news would have been better for American laborers had the country not fallen into a massive recession that drove unemployment up to 19 percent—a significant increase from the previous year. Meanwhile, dark clouds of war were gathering over Europe as Germany forcibly annexed Austria and engaged in a series of aggressive persecutory actions against Jewish citizens.

Trouble of a less serious nature was brewing in the Bronx. Acting on advice from members of his inner circle, DiMaggio asked Yankee management for a substantial pay raise, elevating his price tag to $40,000. Although Joe had enjoyed one of his finest seasons in '37, his demand was somewhat unreasonable given the fact that none of the other veterans on the New York roster (Hall of Famers included) were earning that much.

As could only be expected, Yankee GM Ed Barrow was floored by the proposal. "You know, young man, it took Lou Gehrig fifteen years to earn the salary you are asking and you have been with the Yankees only two seasons. What would you say if I told you that Lou Gehrig is not making $40,000?"

Without missing a beat, DiMaggio replied, "I would say Lou Gehrig is highly underpaid."

When Barrow countered with a $25,000 offer, negotiations stalled out. Joe had invested a significant amount of capital in a restaurant overlooking San Francisco's Fisherman's Wharf. He named it "Joe DiMaggio's Grotto" and brought his brothers in to help. The oldest of the clan, Tom, was left in charge of the business. While waiting for the Yankees to meet his demands, Joe worked in the restaurant and publicly remarked that he was prepared to spend the entire season there if necessary. Newsreel footage was taken of Joe clad in a chef's hat toiling over a stove. Behind the scenes, the Yankee All-Star had reached a tentative agreement with Charley Graham allowing him to work out with the Seals to stay in shape. Graham figured he could get some extra fans in the seats by allowing them to come early and watch DiMaggio take batting practice.

When the season opened on April 18, DiMaggio was not in uniform. The Yankees were also without Tony Lazzeri, who had been released the previous October and signed by the Chicago Cubs. Joe Gordon performed capably in Lazzeri's stead, but the Bombers stumbled out of the gate, dropping three of four games to the Red Sox at Fenway Park.

Hoping to capitalize on the situation in New York, St. Louis Browns' president Don Barnes reached out to Yankee executives about a possible deal for DiMaggio. The *New York Times* reported that Barnes extended a cash offer of $150,000, which Jacob Ruppert declined. "The deal isn't dead as far as the Browns are concerned," Barnes asserted. "I would certainly like to get DiMaggio for the Browns. I don't know whether our price was wrong or whether Colonel Ruppert wouldn't consider losing DiMaggio." Clarifying the matter, Ruppert stated unequivocally that his star center fielder was "not for sale at any price."

As the holdout dragged on, sportswriters took to coloring DiMaggio as spoiled and greedy. Even Joe McCarthy weighed in on the topic, commenting bluntly, "The Yankees can get along without DiMaggio." In the days that followed, events on the field contradicted that statement. By the end of play on April 29, the team was sitting in fourth place with a mediocre 6–6 record.

Joe was stung by McCarthy's words. In spite of his obvious value to the club, he began to doubt himself and worry that the Yankees would move on without him. On April 20, he gave in to the mounting pressure, accepting Barrow's offer. "There won't be any chance of argument over salary next year," he assured members of the press. "Naturally, I thought I was worth more this year, but I'd rather play ball than hold out. I can't get back quick enough and I'm rarin' to go." When he returned to action on April 30, he made it clear that he intended to earn his pay, hitting safely in 12 of his first 14 games while running his batting average up to .418. This included eight multihit performances along with six homers and 13 runs batted in.

Fans in New York refused to let DiMaggio off the hook so easily. They booed him, composed hate mail, and threw garbage at him from the stands. "All I was trying to do is to get as much as I could. Is that so terrible?" he said in his own defense. "I had a great season and some of my friends said I ought to be worth $40,000 to a team like the Yankees. I guess they were wrong. I know I was wrong holding out as long as I did. I hear the boos and I read in the papers that the cheers offset them, but you can't prove that by me. All I ever hear is boos—and the mail. You would have thought I kidnapped the Lindbergh baby the way some of the letters read."

The entire ordeal was critical in shaping Joe's future attitudes. He had come to understand that, no matter how hard he tried, the fans, the press, and the executives in the Yankee front office would never be his true allies. Although he continued to pose for pictures, offer cordial responses to questions, and give 100 percent on the field, part of him remained closed off from the public forever. From that point on, he kept his true feelings insulated from everyone outside his elite inner circle.

At least one New York reporter saw through Joe's façade. A few days before the 1938 World Series began, Jimmy Powers of the *Daily News* wrote, "I think I understand Joe DiMaggio. He and Bill Terry are alike in many respects. They frankly look upon baseball as a business. They believe their batting and fielding averages should speak for themselves. . . . I think both are shortsighted in this, for the extra effort is slight and it reaps fat dividends. Lately, both have made belated attempts to appease 'the mob,' but it is evident their hearts are not in the handshakes."

ALL'S WELL THAT ENDS WELL

There were a number of notable happenings beyond the Big Apple in 1938. On June 11, Johnny Vander Meer of the Reds—a virtually unknown southpaw playing in his first full season—got his name on the map with a no-hitter against the Boston Bees. Four days later, he made baseball history by repeating the feat against the Brooklyn Dodgers. At the end of the twentieth century, he was still the only major-league player to have tossed consecutive no-hitters. On an interesting side note, Vander Meer's second masterpiece came in the first night game played at Ebbets Field in Brooklyn.

Hank Greenberg of the Tigers came close to establishing a record of his own as he slammed his 58th home run of the season on September 27. With five games left to go, he seemed destined to break or at least tie Babe Ruth's record of 60 home runs (set in 1927). A majority of Greenberg's homers were hit at Briggs Stadium in Detroit. With three of the remaining games taking place on the road, "Hammerin' Hank" was held to a double and four singles in his last few plate appearances.

Greenberg wasn't the only player to come up short. Lou Gehrig fell shy of the team lead in a number of statistical categories during the 1938 campaign. Though he distinguished himself as the first player to collect no fewer than 100 RBIs in 13 straight seasons, his annual total of 114 was his lowest mark in over a decade. Additionally, his batting average dropped below .300 for the first time since 1925. With Gehrig showing signs of decline, DiMaggio carried the Yankee offense, slamming 77 extra-base hits and driving in 140 runs. (Both marks were third best in the AL.) DiMaggio's .324 batting average was the highest among Yankee regulars.

Jacob Ruppert's Bombers won fewer games in 1938 but still managed to hold off the second place Red Sox by a fairly wide margin. In the National League, Cubs executives became dissatisfied with the performance of manager Charlie Grimm and replaced him with more than 70 games remaining. Mired in third place, the club made a gradual climb to the top that was capped off by a 10-game winning streak in late September. Gabby Hartnett—the Hall of Fame catcher who replaced Grimm as a player-manager—delivered a clutch homer on September 28 against the Pirates. The memorable shot, known forever after as "The Homer in the Gloamin,'" broke a 5–5 tie and lifted Chicago into first place. The Cubs clinched the NL crown a few days later.

The improbable pennant run—completed without the benefit of a single 20-homer or 100-RBI man in the lineup—was all the magic the Cubs had left in them as the Yankees executed a businesslike sweep in the World Series. It was a reunion of sorts for Lazzeri, who had hit .267 in 54 games with the Cubs that year. He played a limited role in the Fall Classic, going hitless in a pair of pinch-hitting appearances. It was the only World Series in which he failed to reach base during his distinguished career.

Joe Gordon and Bill Dickey were the primary offensive weapons for New York against Chicago, combining for 12 hits and eight RBIs. DiMaggio hit safely in three straight games after going 0-for-4 against starter Bill Lee in the opener. His most memorable shot was a two-run homer off of a sore-armed Dizzy Dean in Game 2. For DiMaggio, it was the fourth straight year that he had helped his team to a championship. After the Series, McCarthy declared, "I believe we are the best ballclub ever assembled . . . we have the pitching, the power, the defensive play." John Drebinger of the *New York Times* was in agreement, commenting, "The Yanks still top the baseball world, their position more impregnable than ever. Three years running they have stomped all competition out of their own American League and, in three successive tries, the National League certainly has shown it has nothing to match this remarkable machine, which many contend is the mightiest ballclub of all-time. At all events, if there are still any disbelievers, it is quite certain that they are keeping in hiding today."

A SOMBER PRELUDE

At the end of the 1938 campaign, 71-year-old Yankee owner Jacob Ruppert fell seriously ill with circulatory issues. Confined to his bed for most of the winter, he suffered a heart attack. When word spread that his condition was grave, friends and former players began showing up at his Fifth Avenue apartment to offer their farewells. Babe Ruth paid a visit on January 13 and tried to cheer his former boss by telling him he would pull through. Ruppert passed away a few hours later.

Four thousand people attended Ruppert's funeral services at St. Patrick's Cathedral in New York. Gehrig, Ruth, and manager Joe McCarthy were among the mourners. The following day, Ed Barrow was appointed president of the Yankees, taking over the club's daily operations. In the wake of the previous year's contract dispute, he wasn't feeling particularly charitable toward DiMaggio when salary negotiations arrived. The Yankee center fielder, who had vowed not to cause a public stir this time around, quietly settled for a modest pay increase. "I didn't like being called a sourpuss," he said years later. "I wanted to put the holdout and the boos behind me."

On another sour note, it became glaringly obvious during spring training that something was wrong with Gehrig. Although no one is certain precisely when the veteran first baseman was afflicted with ALS (a crippling neurological disease that causes catastrophic loss of motor skills), sportswriters had seen indications of impairment in 1938. They had attributed his statistical decline to advancing age. Dan Daniel of the *New York World Telegram* was among the first to write about it, commenting, "[Gehrig] cannot get the old swing, he cannot put the old driving force on the ball." John Drebinger of the *New York Times* was of the same mindset. "'The Iron Horse' is getting old," he observed. "He is always doing his best and it isn't exactly sporty to ride a fellow merely because the years have caught up with him."

DiMaggio poses with Yankee Manager Joe McCarthy (center) and Lou Gehrig (right). He looks a bit tired in the photo.

It was clear that age wasn't the only thing affecting Gehrig. DiMaggio claimed that he saw the veteran first baseman swing through more than half a dozen straight fastballs during batting practice—something that would never have occurred a couple of years earlier. Even worse, Gehrig struggled to field routine ground balls and hobbled around the base paths. Entering the 1939 campaign, the sport's reigning Iron Man had played in a record 2,122 consecutive games. He had accomplished the feat in spite of a broken toe, a torn muscle in his leg, bone chips in his elbow, and multiple fractures of his pinky finger. Though there were rumblings from sportswriters that he should take a break, he had brushed off the criticism. "I have given my best to the club and the game," he asserted, "and I deserve the chance to work out my current difficulties."

When the regular season began, Gehrig collected just one hit in his first 17 at-bats. Though he would hit safely three more times over the next few days, the game of baseball had become an uphill battle for him. While putting on his uniform one afternoon, he lost his balance and fell flat on his back. Pitcher Wes Ferrell claimed that Gehrig remained on the clubhouse floor in a daze for nearly a full minute.

Realizing that he couldn't continue in his current state, Gehrig approached McCarthy on the night before a matinee in Detroit. "I'm not helping the team any," he admitted sadly. "I know I look terrible . . . it isn't fair to the boys for me to stay in there. I want you to take me out of the lineup."

Gehrig's Iron Man streak ended on May 2, 1939. McCarthy instructed the Yankee icon to carry the lineup card to the plate before the game began. Tigers' announcer Ty Tyson promptly informed fans that Gehrig would not be playing that day. The two-time American League MVP tipped his cap as the crowd offered him a rousing ovation. Commenting on Gehrig's difficult decision, McCarthy said after the game, "I told him it would be as he wished. Like everybody else, I'm sorry to see it happen. I told him not to worry. Maybe the warm weather will bring him around. We'll miss him. You can't escape that fact. But I think he's doing the right thing."

Just like that—Gehrig was out and DiMaggio was in as the de facto leader of the Yankees.

But DiMaggio would experience his own problems during the spring of '39. After agreeing to a salary he felt was beneath him, he suffered another serious leg injury. In the third inning of a game against the Senators on April 29, he was chasing a flyball hit by left fielder Bobby Estalella. His spikes got caught in the turf and he tore a calf muscle. It seemed as though things couldn't possibly get worse for the Yankees.

FOUR IN A ROW

During the five weeks it took for DiMaggio's leg to heal, the Yankees proved what they were made of, going off on a 24–4 rampage during the month of May. The Bombers didn't just beat opponents, they pulverized them. On May 2, they dismantled the Tigers 22–2. Five days later, they roughed up the White Sox 15–4. In a May 14 game against the A's, they romped to a 10–0 win. And then, on the last day of the month, they victimized Red Sox hurlers for 17 runs on 17 hits.

The Yankees got strong performances from Dickey, Gordon, and George Selkirk in 1939 as each player reached the 100-RBI plateau. Charlie Keller, promoted from Newark, hit .334 in his major-league debut. Red Rolfe, a talented third baseman who never seemed to get the attention he deserved, enjoyed the finest offensive season of his career, leading the American League in runs (139), hits (213), and doubles (46). A product of Dartmouth University, Rolfe formed a personal bond with Joe McCarthy and was said to be next in line for the manager's position in New York. But it never happened. He ended up serving as head coach at Yale University before managing the Detroit Tigers for three full seasons.

Staked to a boatload of runs day in and day out, seven members of the Yankee pitching staff finished with double digit win totals in 1939—more than any team in the majors. Red Ruffing, who led the club with 21 victories that year, had worked in a coal mine as a teenager and lost several of his toes in a horrible accident. He learned how to compensate for the handicap, ascending to the majors with the cellar-dwelling Red Sox in 1924. A trade to New York altered his career trajectory. He retired with 273 wins—a total that would undoubtedly have been much higher had he not floundered in Boston for portions of seven seasons.

Returning to action on May 27, DiMaggio hovered around the .400 mark all summer. He made his fourth consecutive All-Star appearance on July 11. The game, which featured more than a dozen Hall of Famers, was held at Yankee Stadium. Fulfilling a promise to Dorothy Arnold, who he had been seeing regularly since they met on the set of *Manhattan Merry-Go-Round*, Joe D. drilled a fifth inning homer off of Cubs' ace Bill Lee.

In mid-September, DiMaggio developed an infection in his left eye, which became inflamed and painful to the touch. By then, the Yankees had already clinched the pennant and were more or less just playing out the string. Though DiMaggio figured McCarthy would take him out of the lineup, the Yankee skipper urged him to tough it out. A mini-slump from September 10 through September 16 dropped his batting average from .401 to .388. He finished the season at .381 and later remarked that he probably would have fared better had the infection not been in the eye directly facing opposing pitchers (Joe was a right-handed hitter).

The Reds, making their first World Series appearance since the controversial 1919 affair, didn't know what hit them. Keller and Dickey combined for five homers and 11 RBIs as the Yankees bowled over Cincinnati in four games. DiMaggio was at the center of a memorable Series moment, which became known to many as "Lombardi's Snooze."

After being outscored by a 13–4 margin in the first three games, the Reds fought back in the finale, carrying a 4–2 lead into the top of the ninth at Crosley Field. The Yankees staged a rally that sent the game into extra innings. In the tenth, Frankie Crosetti led off with a walk and moved to second on a sacrifice by Rolfe. Keller followed with a grounder to short that was botched by Cincinnati's Billy Myers. With runners on the corners, DiMaggio dropped a single into right field. Crosetti scored easily as the ball was mishandled by outfielder Ival Goodman. Recognizing a golden opportunity, Yankee third base coach Art Fletcher waved Keller home. The throw arrived on time and there was contact between Keller and catcher Ernie Lombardi. Accounts of the play vary widely. Some claim that Lombardi took a knee to the head. Others maintain that it was a shot to the groin. After Keller had scored the insurance run, Lombardi lay on the ground with the ball resting in the dirt nearby.

Taking advantage of the situation, DiMaggio completely circled the bases. Lombardi, who later claimed he was feeling dizzy from the heat, recovered in time to attempt a tag, but Joe executed an evasive hook slide, crossing the plate safely. "He gave us one of the greatest pieces of sliding I've ever seen," said Fletcher. "He had to slide over Lombardi's hand and then dig down and touch the plate, and he did it to perfection. Lombardi found out that you can't sit down with those Yankees on the basepaths, hey?"

The runs delivered by Keller and DiMaggio proved to be inconsequential when the Reds failed to score off of closer Johnny Murphy in their final at-bat. It was the fourth straight World Series title for New York—a new major-league record. In the clubhouse after the game, DiMaggio proudly showed off the bruises he had acquired during the four-game sweep. His legs and hips were covered with them. In spite of having missed more than 30 games during the regular season, his impressive numbers earned him American League MVP honors.

DOROTHY AND JOE TIE THE KNOT

While Joe was busy cementing his status as the greatest all-around player in the majors, Dorothy Olson was slowly making a name for herself in Hollywood. Born in Duluth, Minnesota, Dorothy was a self-proclaimed tomboy in her younger years, often playing football and baseball with local boys. Her interests turned to singing and dancing when she reached teenhood.

During her high school years, she took dancing lessons and performed as an amateur in various local venues. She graduated from Denfeld High School in 1935 and joined a performing arts troupe that toured the Chicago area. Her travels eventually landed her in New York City, where she attended classes at the Paramount School of Acting. On the side, she did some modeling and appeared in a handful of movie shorts. It was during this period that she created the stage name of Dorothy Arnold.

In 1937, Dorothy appeared on the cover of *True Romances* magazine. Her encounter with DiMaggio on the set of *Manhattan Merry-Go-Round* led to a long distance relationship. Having signed a contract with Universal Studios, the budding actress made four film appearances in 1938, two of which were uncredited. She had a breakout year in 1939, participating in nine movie projects. This included a major role in a twelve-part horror serial starring movie icon Bela Lugosi (who was renowned for his role as Count Dracula). Dorothy also had a significant part in a mystery-crime drama titled *House of Fear.*

Joe and Dorothy were married on November 19, 1939. The wedding, which took place at Sts. Peter and Paul Cathedral in San Francisco, created a national sensation. More than 20,000 well-wishers jammed the streets of North Beach to get a glimpse of the couple as they entered and exited the church. *Time* magazine reported that the wedding party had to battle the crowd on the way in. One woman actually fainted in a crush near the doorway. It took the ensemble half an hour to get out of the church and across the street afterward as cameras rolled and flashbulbs popped.

According to one of DiMaggio's friends, the couple had their first argument as man and wife during the reception. Dorothy wanted to stay and enjoy the party. Joe was anxious to depart for their honeymoon. By the time they left the reception hall, they weren't speaking.

Unlike Joe, Dorothy didn't mind the attention. She was comfortable around photographers, reporters, and assorted hangers-on. She adored fancy restaurants and nightclubs. Her outgoing personality served as an effective counterbalance to Joe's social awkwardness. She made a number of concessions for Joe, converting to Catholicism and learning enough Italian to have meaningful conversations with his parents. Even so, Joe never fully appreciated her.

After exchanging vows, the couple took up residence in Manhattan. Like most men of the era, Joe expected his wife to stay at home. In an attempt to appease him, Dorothy put her acting career on hold. One researcher remarked of the arrangement, "Since she'd met DiMaggio, the arc of her life zipped like a Bob Feller fastball. After the wedding, it moved like a Tommy Bridges curveball."

The marriage was strained from the onset as Joe proved to be jealous, moody, and emotionally unavailable. The couple eventually split—twice—once in 1942 and again the following year. They were finally divorced in 1944, although they continued to be involved romantically (on and off) for quite some time. In 1946, Dorothy married a stockbroker named George C. Shubert. Out of the spotlight for more than a decade, she was never able to completely revive her acting career. She settled for a handful of scattered TV roles during the 1950s.

THERE'S NO CRYING IN BASEBALL!

Following his MVP season, DiMaggio was more confident than ever that he deserved a raise. Though he settled for less than his asking price, he remained one of the highest paid players in the game. Only Hank Greenberg of the Tigers made more money that year.

DiMaggio brought Dorothy with him to spring training but kept her all to himself, booking a hotel about ten miles away from camp. Upon reporting for duty, he told reporters that he hadn't engaged in any baseball-related activities since the previous October. This may or may not have contributed to a preseason injury. During an exhibition game against the Dodgers, he hit a double and wrenched his knee sliding into second. He was out of action until early May.

The year 1940 was an off year for many of the Yankee regulars. Red Rolfe's batting average dropped by more than 70 points. Frankie Crosetti failed to reach the .200 mark at the plate, and Bill Dickey had the worst offensive season of his career. If Lou Gehrig was the luckiest man on the face of the earth (as he had proclaimed in his farewell speech), then his replacement—Babe Dahlgren—was quite possibly the most unfortunate. With big shoes to fill and all eyes upon him, Dahlgren managed just 73 RBIs and 40 extra-base hits all year (numbers typically reached by Gehrig before the All-Star break). In February 1941, Dahlgren's contract was sold to the Boston Braves.

DiMaggio enjoyed another fine season in 1940, compiling an on-base streak of 40 consecutive games and capturing his second straight batting title with a .352 mark. His efforts weren't enough to carry the team as the Yankees failed to spend a single day in first place. Although they finished just two games out of the race, most of the drama was provided by the Tigers and Indians.

A former member of the Yankee organization, Cleveland manager Ossie Vitt had guided the 1937 Newark Bears to a Junior World Series title. With the manager's position capably filled in the Bronx, he accepted an offer to manage the Indians. Vitt was a difficult man to play for—quick to place blame, slow to offer support, and prone to berating his players in front of teammates. With a powerful lineup that included Hall of Famers Lou Boudreau and Bob Feller, Vitt's crew contended for the AL pennant throughout the 1940 campaign. But things took an ugly turn in June, when players attempted a coup.

During a miserable 13-game road trip, Vitt made a series of cutting remarks to Feller and his staff mate Mel Harder. After a lengthy debate, players decided to bring their grievances to owner Alva Bradley. Harder—a 12-year veteran—was appointed spokesman. Accompanied by a dozen teammates, Harder openly advocated for Vitt's dismissal. Bradley promised to investigate the matter thoroughly and instructed players to keep the meeting under wraps. But details were leaked to a local sportswriter. Incredibly, the article that appeared in the *Cleveland Plain Dealer* took up more newspaper space than Hitler's invasion of Paris. As it turned out, Vitt was allowed to keep his job. In subsequent reports, the Indians were referred to as "Vitt's Crybabies," "The Bawl Team," and the "Half Vitts."

Meanwhile, in Detroit, the Tigers were slowly clawing their way into first place. Massive efforts from Greenberg (41 HR/150 RBI/.340 BA) and Rudy York (33 HR/134 RBI/.316 BA) helped Detroit take over the AL lead by late July. It was up and down from there. A doubleheader win over the A's on September 19 put the Tigers back on top. The Indians had a chance to claim the pennant with a sweep of the Tigers in the last three games of the regular season. But a fourth inning homer by York off of Feller in the series opener allowed the Tigers to clinch their first American League championship since 1935.

Detroit ended up losing to Cincinnati in the World Series. Vitt left the Indians after the season was over, signing with the Portland Beavers of the Pacific Coast League. Years later, Alva Bradley drafted a memo revisiting the topic of the "Crybaby Indians." Published in the *Cleveland*

News, the document stated that the complaints lodged by players against Vitt were completely justified.

THE GLORIOUS SUMMER OF '41

The Yankees' performance in 1940 prompted a few necessary changes. Phil Rizzuto, who had been named MVP of the American Association, was promoted to New York and thrown into a starting role at shortstop. Frankie Crosetti, an indispensable member of the Yankee lineup for nearly a decade, became a utility man. Rizzuto's teammate in Kansas City—Johnny Sturm—took over for Babe Dahlgren at first base. In a brief experiment, Sturm was benched and Joe Gordon was used to fill the vacancy. But in the end, Gordon couldn't master the position and he was moved back to his primary post.

The pitching corps were strengthened considerably with the return of Lefty Gomez, who had made just nine appearances in 1940 due to a variety of ailments. Known for his quirky behavior and wry humor, Gomez was one of the most entertaining characters of the era. He once held up a World Series game watching a plane fly overhead. And during a postretirement speaking engagement, he memorably remarked, "I was the worst hitter ever. I never even broke a bat until last year when I was backing out of the garage." Healthy again in 1941, Gomez led the American League with a .750 winning percentage.

Annual contract negotiations went well for DiMaggio. He asked for another raise and got one, bumping his salary up to $37,500. Had the Tigers not shelled out $55,000 for Greenberg (who appeared in just 19 games before leaving to serve in the Army for the better part of four seasons), DiMaggio would have commanded the highest salary in the game. By way of comparison, the average annual salary among ordinary Americans was a little over $1,200 in 1941.

Joe D. got off to a typical hot start, hitting safely in his first eight games while elevating his batting average to .528. But the worries of domestic life may have affected his performance on the field to some extent. On May 15, he went 1-for-4 against the White Sox in a disheartening 13–1 loss at Yankee Stadium. His average had dipped to .304 by that point. No one would have guessed that he was on the verge of a 56-game hitting streak—the most celebrated record in baseball.

On the 50th anniversary of his crowning achievement, DiMaggio was invited to attend multiple dinner celebrations. Put off by the unwanted attention, he wrote in his journal, "Had I known this would be happening on account of the streak, I would have stopped hitting at 40 games." He almost didn't make it that far, extending the skein in his last at-bat on several occasions. He got a little help from outside sources as well. In a game against the Browns on May 18, the official scorer credited him with two hits on a pair of obvious defensive lapses. He received another "gift" that afternoon on account of catcher's interference.

The streak failed to attract significant attention until May 28, when Dan Daniel of the *New York World-Telegram* reported that DiMaggio had hit in 13-straight. By the time he reached the 40-game mark on June 28, the Yankee Clipper's daily exploits were a matter of public record. Asked if the pressure was getting to him, he responded coolly, "Why should I worry? The only time to worry is when you're not hitting. I'm not worried now—I'm happy."

On June 2, Lou Gehrig died from complications of ALS. Joe McCarthy and Bill Dickey left the club to attend the funeral in New York while the rest of the team traveled to Detroit to take on the Tigers. Gehrig's death struck a dissonant chord as the Yankees lost three in a row, falling to fourth place. They nearly dropped their fourth straight against the humble Browns on June 7. After squandering a 6–1 lead, they came storming back for an 11–7 victory. The remarkable rally kicked off an eight-game winning streak that moved the club into second place. By the end of the month, the Bombers had taken over the AL lead.

DiMaggio and the Yankees offered a welcome escape from the harsh realities of war. Overseas, German air raids of Britain continued until early May, killing 40,000 civilians and damaging more than a million residential homes. In June, Nazi forces invaded Russia with more than 3 million troops. It was the largest military operation in history and it would bring about the highest death toll. Describing the effect DiMaggio's streak had on the American public, one researcher pointed out, "Joe gave America just what it needed—something apart from woe and war

DiMaggio is pictured here in the prime of his career. Few players have been as revered and respected. The popular Yankee icon reportedly turned down offers to have a New York City street named after him and a statue erected in the city. (COURTESY OF THE LESLIE JONES COLLECTION/BOSTON PUBLIC LIBRARY)]

to talk about—a summer craze." At one point during the streak, students taking a summer history class in Cincinnati were polled to determine the greatest Americans of all time. George Washington and Abe Lincoln finished second and third (respectively) to DiMaggio.

Prior to the 1941 campaign, the New York press had not always been flattering in their reports about the Yankee Clipper. But as his hitting streak continued, all was forgiven. Russell Owen of the *New York Times* offered glowing praise before game #54: "It has been said that [DiMaggio] is shy and inarticulate. He may have been once, but he had plenty of poise on this day. He is a good-looking chap, with black curly hair, sparkling eyes, and a rather long nose, which gives him a sort of Cyrano de Bergerac profile. One can imagine that, had he lived long ago, Joe might have been quite a boy with a rapier. He is usually quiet, but smiles easily, if a smile can be called a slight brightening of the features and a bit of light behind the eyes. Altogether a likeable fellow."

The hero worship of DiMaggio proved to be hazardous at times. After the final out of a doubleheader sweep over the A's in early July, fans streamed onto the field to congratulate him for hitting safely in both games. A photo taken that afternoon shows Joltin' Joe bolting for the safety of the clubhouse with frenzied fans surging toward him on all sides.

The streak finally came to an end on July 17 at Cleveland Stadium. In an oft-repeated tale, DiMaggio was on his way to the ballpark in a cab with Lefty Gomez when the driver recognized his famous passengers. "I got a feeling if you don't get a hit in your first at-bat today, they're gonna stop you," the cabbie said to DiMaggio. Irritated by the comment, Gomez retorted, "Who the hell are you? What are you trying to do, jinx him?" The jinx appeared in the form of Indians' third baseman Ken Keltner, who made a pair of spectacular plays to prevent DiMaggio from extending his streak to 57. The Yankee idol claimed to have crossed paths with the anonymous cab driver again in the early '70s. "Now this [was] thirty years later and the guy said he was that cab driver," DiMaggio asserted. "He apologized and he was serious. I felt awful. He might have been spending his whole life thinking he had jinxed me, but I told him he hadn't. My number was up." After being thwarted by Keltner, DiMaggio rattled off another 16-game streak. Had Cleveland manager Roger Peckinpaugh started a less capable player at third base, Joe might have hit in 73 straight games!

Aided tremendously by DiMaggio's monumental efforts, the Yankees built a 12-game lead over their closest rivals—the Indians—by the end of July. They continued to pull ahead in the months that followed, clinching the pennant in early September. As had been the case so many times before, luck would be on their side in October.

RIGHT THROUGH THE WICKETS

After capturing three National League titles during the Dead Ball Era, the Dodgers fell on hard times. Weak hitting, poor fielding, and sloppy baserunning became staples in Brooklyn during the 1920s and '30s. During that barren period, the team came to be known to fans as "The Daffiness Boys" or (more popularly) "The Bums" in reference to a famous caricature created by illustrator William Mullin. In 1938, Larry MacPhail—the club's new vice president and GM—began importing a steady stream of talent. The addition of several key players, including Hall of Famers Pee Wee Reese, Joe Medwick, and Billy Herman, lifted the Dodgers back into contention. By 1941, they weren't so "Daffy" anymore, capturing their first pennant in over twenty years.

Commenting on the Yankees' 1941 World Series opponents, researcher Bill James remarked that the Dodgers were among the first teams to assemble a lineup of eight legitimate stars. Even so, the Dodgers entered the Series as underdogs. Because Yankee Stadium had twice the seating capacity of Ebbets Field, Yankee executives suggested that all of the games be held in the Bronx to maximize ticket sales. MacPhail promptly declined the offer.

It was a relatively quiet Series for DiMaggio, who gathered five singles and a pair of walks. But the Yankees didn't need him to be brilliant as Charlie Keller and Joe Gordon combined for 14 hits and 10 RBIs. The first three games were tight, low-scoring affairs. The Yankees won the opener 3–2 at Yankee Stadium, and the Dodgers returned the favor the following day. Game 3 featured a showdown between aging knuckle-baller Freddie Fitzsimmons and Yankee southpaw Marius Russo—a 14-game winner during the regular season. "Fat Freddie" turned in one of his finest efforts of the year, holding the Yankees scoreless through six innings. With two outs in the seventh, Russo hit a line drive that struck Fitzsimmons on the knee. Pee Wee Reese caught the ball in the air to retire the side, but Fitzsimmons, who had been cruising to that point, was unable to continue due to injury. Hugh Casey—one of the most reliable Brooklyn hurlers—crumbled in relief, allowing a pair of runs on four consecutive singles as the Yankees won a 2–1 nail-biter.

The Bombers caught another big break in Game 4. Trailing 4–3 in the top of the ninth, Tommy Henrich came to the plate with two outs and Casey on the mound. Henrich worked the count full before swinging through a breaking ball for strike three. Game over!

Or was it?

Fate intervened as the pitch dipped under catcher Mickey Owen's glove and rolled to the backstop, setting off a series of unfortunate events for the Dodgers. Henrich reached base safely. DiMaggio singled, and Keller followed with a two-run double, giving the Yankees the lead. Completely rattled, Casey walked Bill Dickey and surrendered another two-run double to Gordon. The rally finally ended when Yankee closer Johnny Murphy grounded out. The Dodgers went quietly in their half of the ninth, completing a demoralizing 7–4 loss.

Commenting on the offering that eluded Owen, Henrich later said, "It was a bad pitch—I mean a ball—but it had me fooled completely. I admit that." Casey was flabbergasted by the sudden turn of events. "I've lost a lot of ball games in some funny ways," he said, "but that is the first I've lost by striking out a man."

The ill-fated play sparked an ongoing debate as to whether or not Casey should have been charged with a wild pitch. Owen—a dependable defensive catcher who made four straight All-Star appearances beginning in 1941—offered no excuses. Speaking to a correspondent from the *New York Times*, he said, "It wasn't a strike. It was a great breaking curve that I should have had. But I guess the ball hit the side of my glove . . . I [deserved] an error on it."

Dixie Walker, the Dodgers' hard-hitting right fielder, groused, "I tell you, those fellows have got all the luck on their side. Never saw a team get so many breaks as they have." Jimmy Wasdell—a utility outfielder—was in agreement, joking, "There are angels flying around those Yankees, I tell you." Divine intervention or not, the Yankees breezed to a 3–1 win at Brooklyn in the finale, clinching their fifth World Series title in six years.

On an interesting final note, Owen was the goat of the World Series during a season in which he had set a defensive record for catchers by accepting 476 consecutive chances without an error. "Nobody knows that," he said. "I made a boo-boo after setting the record. Now they'll never forget me."

THINNING OF THE TALENT POOL

In response to the escalating crisis overseas, Congress passed a series of Neutrality Acts in the 1930s aimed at preventing US involvement in foreign conflicts. On December 7, 1941, the Imperial Japanese Navy Air Service brought war to America's doorstep with a surprise military strike on the US naval base at Pearl Harbor. Shortly before 8 a.m., the Japanese attacked with 353 aircraft, inflicting heavy damage on the unsuspecting US forces. More than 2,400 American casualties were reported. A day later, President Franklin Delano Roosevelt referred to the assault as "a date which will live in infamy" and officially declared war on Japan.

In the years following America's entry into World War II, more than 400 ballplayers traded their major-league uniforms for military attire. The A's, Phillies, and Dodgers were hit the hardest as each franchise lost more than thirty players to the armed forces by 1945. The Yankee lineup became virtually unrecognizable with the departure of the entire Hall of Fame corps. Ruffing, Gordon, and DiMaggio joined the Army Air Force. Rizzuto and Dickey enlisted in the Navy. Gomez—upon receiving a 4-F classification that disqualified him from serving—went to work in a General Electric defense plant. He was released by the Yankees in 1943.

A couple of weeks after winning his fifth World Series ring, DiMaggio celebrated the arrival of his son, Joe Jr. As he was adjusting to life as a father, the Yankees came to terms with him on a contract worth more than $43,000. They drove a hard bargain as usual, leaving him with the distinct impression that he had been taken for granted. His bitterness toward Yankee executives persisted for the remainder of his career and beyond. In spite of his misgivings, he entered the 1942 campaign as baseball's highest paid player.

Dorothy and Little Joe accompanied DiMaggio to training camp, but an ongoing rift in the marriage made things extremely uncomfortable for everyone involved. Joe performed poorly in spring training and carried his slump into the regular season. Before long, fans began booing him. "I'd rather hear the cheers, of course. Who wouldn't?" he said to a reporter. "I give the fans all I have. But, I'm out there playing for the club and myself. That's how I make my living."

War had not yet changed the face of the Yankees in 1942. Strong performances from the usual contributors lifted the club into first place on May 6. They never relinquished the lead, compiling their highest regular season win total since 1939.

It was an excellent season for pitchers as the Yankee staff posted the lowest ERA in the American League. Tiny Bonham had a banner year on the mound, assembling a 21–5 record while leading the AL in shutouts. Spud Chandler was another dependable member of the starting rotation, gathering 16 wins against 5 losses. During one remarkable stretch in May, Chandler allowed just one earned run in 30 innings.

DiMaggio was sluggish in the first half, but he did get going eventually. During an Independence Day doubleheader at Fenway Park, he went 3-for-9 with a homer and a pair of RBIs. He hit safely in the next 16 games, raising his batting average by 20 points. He finished the year at .305 as the Yankees finished nine games ahead of the second place Red Sox.

Meanwhile, in the National League, the Cardinals relied heavily on pitching to sneak past the Dodgers on the way to their first World Series appearance in eight years. Mort Cooper and Johnny Beazley combined for 43 wins, while Max Lanier—among the best of the wartime hurlers—chipped in with 13 victories of his own. Playing in his first full big-league season, Stan Musial finished second on the club to Enos Slaughter in runs, extra-base hits, and RBIs. Slaughter was the prime offensive catalyst for St. Louis, posting a .315 average with runners in scoring position and a .333 mark with the bases loaded.

Dating back to the "Murderer's Row" squad of 1927, the Yankees had compiled a 32–4 overall record in postseason play. But they weren't prepared for the dynamic Redbirds, who won four in a row after dropping the opener at home. Many observers felt that the Cardinals' speed was the deciding factor. Watching Game 5 from the stands, Braves' manager Casey Stengel quipped, "It isn't a ballclub, it's a track team." Interestingly, it was a different St. Louis squad that had handed the Yankees their last World Series defeat in 1926. The 1942 Fall Classic was one of DiMaggio's best as he rang up a .462 batting average before cooling off in the last two games. Commenting on the surprising outcome of the

Series, Dick McCann of the *New York Daily News* wrote, "The team that wouldn't be beaten beat the team that couldn't be beaten. And so, those amazing Cardinals of St. Louis this morning are champions of all the baseball world. And the once-proud Yankees are ex-champions, thoroughly thumped, utterly routed."

IN THE ARMY NOW

DiMaggio played the entire 1942 season under 3-A status—a military classification assigned to married men with children who were in no immediate danger of being called to active duty. In addition to the annual All-Star Game between the AL and NL, another game was held that year pitting stars from both leagues against a team composed of players who had enlisted in the armed forces. Joe D. participated in both games and was booed every time he took the field. He told reporters he didn't understand why fans were on his case, but it was actually quite obvious. He was performing well below standards in spite of his extravagant salary. And he was content to hide behind his 3-A classification while other men were joining the military. More than sixty players exchanged bats for rifles in 1942, including Indians' pitching great Bob Feller and Brooklyn's star third baseman Cookie Lavagetto. Dorothy kept telling Joe that the boos would continue until he signed up, but that wasn't an accurate prediction. Fans finally left him alone when he started hitting in the second half.

Prior to the opening of Yankee camp in 1943, DiMaggio cryptically told a reporter that spring training would not be a concern for him that year. The media had a field day with the comment, speculating that he intended to enlist. Joe debunked the story and then made a liar of himself. On February 17, 1943, he sacrificed his Yankee salary for a $50 per month job as an Army recruit. In an article written for *Baseball Magazine*, Dan Daniel gushed, "[DiMaggio] has the temperament for the soldier. He has gone into the Army looking for no favors, searching for no job as a coach. He wants to fight, and when he gets his chance, he will prove a credit to himself and his game and the Yanks and his family."

Joe never got anywhere near a battlefield. It has been said that FDR and General George Marshall (chief of the US armed forces) felt that the morale of soldiers would be seriously damaged if DiMaggio ended up being killed in action. Assigned to an Army Air Force base in Santa Ana, California, the Yankee Clipper joined the ballclub in residence there. The team was composed mainly of college, semipro, and minor-league players, but DiMaggio quickly transformed them into world beaters. He assembled a 27-game hitting streak at one point as his new team won 20 games in a row.

While Joe's AAF squad was tearing up the military circuit, Santa Ana commanders began spoiling their star outfielder. Joe was invited to eat with his superiors and attend their parties. They furnished him with cigarettes, liquor, and weekend passes. Dorothy and Joe had temporarily worked out their differences and were renting a house not far from the base. Dorothy brought Little Joe to some of the games and, although DiMaggio enjoyed his son's company, he continued to butt heads with his wife over a variety of topics. Dorothy eventually proceeded with the divorce, claiming cruelty on Joe's part. The split was finalized in May 1944. The settlement included a cash payment of $14,000 and monthly stipends of $150 for the care of Joe Jr.

Although his personal life was falling apart, DiMaggio rose to the rank of sergeant. In June 1944, he was transferred to Honolulu, Hawaii, where he served in the Seventh Air Force. It was there that he was reunited with Yankee teammates Red Ruffing and Joe Gordon. Cardinals' hurler Johnny Beazley also played for the Honolulu squad. Around the same time, the Navy began exporting players to Hawaii, among them Hall of Famers Phil Rizzuto, Pee Wee Reese, and Johnny Mize. In September 1944, the Service World Series was played between the Army and Navy. Joe's little brother Dominic (by then a star center fielder for the Red Sox) was flown in from Australia along with Rizzuto to play for the Navy squad. The epic clash proved to be no contest as the Navy won most of the games with one ending in a tie. Joe's health had taken a turn for the worse by then and he didn't appear in any of them.

Dorothy and Joe continued to associate with one another after the divorce, spending Christmas together in 1945. When newspapers began reporting that an official reunion was imminent, Dorothy set the record straight, commenting, "It seems that every time we turn around, somebody has us reconciled and we're getting a little bit stupid and jerky about it." She claimed that Joe was only maintaining ties with her for the purpose of spending time with their son. But the truth of the matter was that he had been trying to win her back for quite some time. The stress of the situation was literally eating him up inside. He complained of chronic abdominal pain and ended up being shipped to a California hospital for evaluation.

In February 1945, DiMaggio pulled a few strings, arranging a transfer to a Special Services unit in Atlantic City, New Jersey. The Yankees had won a World Series without Joe in 1943 before plummeting to third place the following year. Although a handful of prewar veterans returned to the majors in 1945, DiMaggio was not among them (in spite of swirling rumors that he might be). It was too late to save the team anyway. With a roster full of imposters, the Yankees dipped to fourth place—their lowest order of finish since 1925. Joe received an official discharge from the service in September 1945. He later commented that he couldn't wait for his stint in the military to end.

HAIL, HAIL, THE GANG'S ALL HERE

While DiMaggio was fulfilling his obligation to Uncle Sam, the team fell under new ownership. In 1945, a syndicate composed of Dan Topping, Del Webb, and Larry MacPhail purchased the Yankees for $2.8 million. Ed Barrow continued to serve as chairman while MacPhail began to assert his authority as GM and president.

Before the war, MacPhail had helped rebuild the Dodgers and turn the Cincinnati Reds into a marketable commodity. But according to researcher Glenn Stout, "MacPhail's talents came with a price, for he was also a drunk, a boor, and a bully who took delight in spending other people's money. He was a micromanager who didn't recognize any barrier between the front office and the field. He was not above giving his manager suggestions, even in the midst of a game." Conflict between MacPhail and Joe McCarthy was inevitable.

With most of his stars lost to military duty, McCarthy had his hands full assembling a competitive lineup. In 1945, he was forced to rely on players who were merely competent at best. To fill DiMaggio's shoes that year, he employed a center field platoon consisting of Johnny Lindell, Tuck Stainback, and Russ Derry. Lindell—a former pitcher—was the best of the three, but after a multihit performance against the Senators on June 5, he was summoned to serve in the Army. The Yankees ultimately finished just 10 games above .500.

By the time the 1946 campaign arrived, McCarthy had lapsed into chronic alcoholism. Most of his best players returned to action, including the outfield tandem of DiMaggio, Keller, and Henrich, but the Yankees got off to a lukewarm start anyway. MacPhail publicly criticized the team for not hustling, and McCarthy let his emotions get the best of him, shouting drunkenly at pitcher Joe Page (who was being groomed as a replacement for closer Johnny Murphy) on a flight from Cleveland to Detroit. In the aftermath, McCarthy returned to his farm in Tonawanda, New York, and sent a telegram to MacPhail that read, "It is with extreme regret that I must request that you accept my resignation as manager of the Yankee Baseball Club effective immediately. My doctor advises that my health would be seriously jeopardized if I continued. This is the sole reason for my decision, which as you know, is entirely voluntary on my part."

While it's true that McCarthy suffered from chronic gallbladder issues in addition to his drinking problem, it's obvious that physical health was not his sole reason for leaving New York. MacPhail had a talent for turning any clubhouse into a hostile work environment. In his famous autobiography *Nice Guys Finish Last*, former Dodger manager Leo Durocher asserted, "When I say that Larry MacPhail was half madman and half genius, I am not trying to say that he was two separate persons. Not at all. It was two different sides of the same personality. . . . He fired me sixty times if he fired me once, and I was still there when he left. He even fired me on the night we won Brooklyn's first pennant in twenty-one years."

McCarthy's departure upset DiMaggio, who later referred to the Hall of Fame skipper as one of his favorites. "Never a day went by when you didn't learn something from Joe McCarthy," he asserted. DiMaggio wasn't alone in his admiration of Marse Joe. "I owe everything to McCarthy," said Frankie Crosetti. "I wasn't much of a ballplayer when I came up.

Most managers wouldn't have stayed with me as long as he did. He had a wonderful way with players. He had the knack of giving you confidence and bringing out the best in you."

With the team in flux, DiMaggio's performance suffered. By the end of June, his batting average was down to an uncharacteristic .267. Things would get worse before they got better. During a July 7 game against the A's at Shibe Park, he launched a shot into the left-center field gap and slid awkwardly into second, spraining his ankle and tearing cartilage in his knee. He was out of action for nearly a month. Though he hit .317 in the second half, he finished the season with the lowest average of his career (to that point) at .290.

Other Yankees seemed to have lost their swing as well. Keller and Henrich combined for a middling .263 batting mark. Snuffy Stirnweiss—a wartime stand-in who had won the AL batting crown in 1945—slipped to .251. Joe Gordon had the worst offensive season of his career and ended up being traded to Cleveland. As the Red Sox continued to pull ahead in the standings, replacement manager Bill Dickey worried about his future with the club. When MacPhail refused to make a commitment to him, Dickey resigned from his post with 14 games remaining in the season. Asked about the decision, he answered plainly, "I have no hard feelings about not managing. I didn't enjoy it." Coach Johnny Neun didn't enjoy it either—at least not in New York. Taking the reins from Dickey, he guided the Yankees through the final two weeks of a lackluster third place finish. He left the Big Apple the following year to manage the Reds.

THE UNDESERVING MVP

At some point during the 1946 campaign, DiMaggio began experiencing chronic pain in his heel. Doctors told him he would need an operation in the offseason to remove a bone spur. Believing that the discomfort would subside with some rest, Joe avoided medical intervention until after the winter holidays. The procedure went poorly and he was forced to check into Johns Hopkins Hospital to have the original incision site repaired with a skin graft taken from his hip. He missed the entire exhibition schedule.

Though DiMaggio's doctors didn't expect him to be back on the field until June or July, he felt a pressing need to return sooner. "I've got to get going," he told sportswriter Dan Daniel. "I've got to make good—otherwise where will I be? Where will I stand when it comes time to sign a contract for 1948? If it's up to me, you'll see me in there before May 1." True to his word, DiMaggio made his first regular season appearance on April 19. He remained a regular in the lineup throughout the year, sitting out just 14 games.

It was a year of sweeping changes in New York as Bucky Harris took over the Yankee helm. Harris had gained lasting acclaim in 1924 with the Senators, guiding the club to its only Washington-based World Series title. Just 27 years old at the time, he had been dubbed a "boy wonder" by sportswriters. When he arrived in the Bronx for the 1947 slate, he had 20 years of big-league managerial experience to his credit. Renowned as a master strategist, he took the time to learn the strengths and weaknesses of his players while emphasizing the little things that helped win ballgames.

To replace weak-hitting first baseman Nick Etten, the Yankees acquired George McQuinn. Originally a product of the Yankee farm system, McQuinn had helped the St. Louis Browns to an improbable World Series berth during the war-torn season of 1944. An excellent defensive first baseman, he posted the highest fielding percentage among players at his position three times. The year 1947 was one of his finest all around campaigns as he hit .304 and made his sixth All-Star appearance. On a personal level, he was quiet and mild mannered. His Yankee teammates called him "Si," which was short for "silent."

With the departure of Joe Gordon, Harris installed the versatile Snuffy Stirnweiss at second base. Stirnweiss had led the AL in stolen bases twice during the war years, but the Yankees weren't doing much running in 1947. A patient hitter and strong defensive presence, Stirnweiss served as an adequate replacement for Gordon in many respects. But Gordon's 29 homers with Cleveland (tops among major-league second basemen) must have stung Yankee executives to a great extent.

In exchange for Gordon, the Yankees acquired pitcher Allie Reynolds, who would be one of the club's most dependable performers for nearly a decade. With a variety of weapons in his arsenal—including a fastball, curve, and slider—he was lights-out in postseason play, compiling a 7–2 record in six World Series with the Yankees. He immediately assumed the title of staff ace in 1947, winning 19 games that year.

The Yankees were a bit slow out of the gate, posting a 20–17 record through May. But a 19-game winning streak from June 29 to July 17 put them ahead of the pack the rest of the way. It was one of DiMaggio's most productive stretches as he hit .355 with 15 runs scored and 17 RBIs. Things took an unfortunate turn for the Yankees in the first half, when Charlie Keller wrenched his back while swinging at a pitch. By the end of June, Keller was experiencing shooting pain down his leg. He ended up undergoing surgery for a slipped disc and missing the remainder of the season. It was the end of his days as a full-time player. During the 1947 World Series, someone suggested that he carry the lineup card to home plate. "Not for me," he said. "The next time I go [onto] the playing field, I'm going out to play, not to get sympathy."

In a surprising decision, the Baseball Writers Association of America handed the AL MVP Award to DiMaggio in spite of the fact that he failed to lead the league in any major offensive category (he wasn't even a team leader in some departments). The choice was especially mystifying considering the effort put forth by Ted Williams. The talented Red Sox slugger captured his second Triple Crown in 1947. At the close of the twentieth century, Williams and Rogers Hornsby were the only players to have turned the trick twice.

The debate over whether or not Williams was a better player than DiMaggio has continued to the present day. DiMaggio once publicly referred to "The Splendid Splinter" as the best left-handed hitter he had ever seen. But in private, the Yankee idol was far less charitable, commenting, "He throws like a broad and runs like a ruptured duck." Williams, who was never shy about expressing his opinions, was quite flattering in his remarks about the Yankee Clipper. In his autobiography *My Turn at Bat: The Story of My Life*, Williams wrote, "In my heart, I have always felt I was a better hitter than Joe, which was always my first consideration, but I have to say that he was the greatest baseball player of

DiMaggio was one of the most popular players of his time—even outside of New York. Here he is greeted by a throng of autograph seekers in Boston.
(COURTESY OF THE LESLIE JONES COLLECTION/BOSTON PUBLIC LIBRARY)

our time. He could do it all." DiMaggio certainly didn't do it all in 1947, but he did enough to steal the MVP Award from his Boston rival.

BATTLE FOR THE BIG APPLE

Prejudice was not the only reason for the exclusion of Black players from major-league baseball. It was assumed by many that the integration of the majors would lead to the collapse of the Negro Leagues and the loss of income for team owners (a scenario that eventually became a reality). Dodger GM Branch Rickey had two primary motives for breaking the color barrier in Brooklyn. First and foremost, he wanted to win pennants. Second, he viewed segregation as an unethical practice. Rickey knew it would be a rough road for the first pioneer and he weighed his options very carefully. In the end, he chose Jackie Robinson—an exceptional all around athlete who had competed at UCLA before rising to the rank of second lieutenant in the US Army. As the story goes, Rickey told Robinson that he was looking for someone who had the strength not to fight back. Robinson was up to the task, making his major-league debut on April 15, 1947. In the years that followed, the major-league talent pool was strengthened considerably.

Jackie Robinson's saga was not the only excitement in Brooklyn during the spring of 1947. When Larry MacPhail lured Charlie Dressen away from a coaching position with the Dodgers, manager Leo Durocher accused the Yankee executive of consorting with gamblers. Durocher was already under suspicion of doing the same. Outraged by the claim, MacPhail filed a libel suit with the commissioner's office. As a consequence, Durocher was suspended for the entire season. Dressen ended up with a 30-day suspension for violating a verbal agreement with the Dodgers, and both teams were slapped with fines for engaging in public feuding. The incident served to intensify the growing rivalry between the two clubs.

Owing much to strong pitching, patient hitting, and speed on the basepaths, the Dodgers—led by former Philly skipper Burt Shotton—survived a late season collapse to claim their first pennant since 1941. The primary focus of the World Series was, of course, Robinson, who later wrote of his experience, "I was proud . . . and yet I was uneasy. There I was—the black grandson of a slave, the son of a black sharecropper, part of an historic occasion, a symbolic hero to my people."

Had Robinson not made a landmark appearance in the Series, it would still be considered a classic. Not only did it go the distance, but five of the seven games were decided by two runs or fewer. Rendering it even more thrilling, the Dodgers staged a pair of Series-tying rallies.

Game 4 was the most dramatic by far as Yankee hurler Bill Bevens—owner of a substandard 7–13 record during the regular season—came within one out of a no-hitter. Bevens' control was suspect that afternoon and it got him into trouble in the fifth as the Dodgers capitalized on a pair of walks, bringing Spider Jorgensen home with a sacrifice and a fielder's choice. With his club trailing 2–1 in the bottom of the ninth, Shotton called upon Cookie Lavagetto to pinch hit for Eddie Stanky with two outs and two runners on base. A star in Brooklyn prior to

World War II, Lavagetto sacrificed four full seasons to military duty and returned as a utility man. In the most defining moment of his career, he delivered a walk-off double, spoiling Bevens' no-hitter and tying the Series at two games apiece.

The Yankees won a tight pitching duel in the next meeting and almost clinched the Series the following afternoon in the Bronx. After the Dodgers had taken an 8–5 lead in the top of the sixth, the Bombers got a pair of runners aboard with two outs in the bottom of the frame. DiMaggio smashed a long drive toward left field. There was a low fence that bordered the Dodger bullpen, and the ball appeared to have the velocity to clear it. But Al Gionfriddo—a mediocre outfielder who had seen limited action that year—raced into the corner and made a stupendous running catch to end the inning. A famous clip of the play shows Joltin' Joe kicking the dirt in disgust after Gionfriddo robbed him of what might have been (at the very least) an RBI double or triple. The catch made all the difference as the Yankees came up two runs short. Once again, the resilient Brooklynites had rallied to even things up. The following day, DiMaggio refused to autograph a picture of Gionfriddo's catch, barking irritably at the photographer who asked him to do it.

The Dodgers jumped out to a 2–0 lead in the Series finale, but it was as close as they would get as the Yankees pecked away at five different pitchers for a 5–2 win. Though DiMaggio managed a modest .231 average during the Series, he scored 4 runs and drove in 5. His solo homer off of Rex Barney in the fifth meeting held up as the game-winning blast. He launched another home run (a solo shot off Joe Hatten) in Game 3. He was the only player on either team to go deep more than once.

The year ended on a sour note for DiMaggio when he became embroiled in a family dispute. Joe had lost a great deal of revenue while serving in the Army and he was in trouble with the IRS. To bail him out, Tom arranged for Dominic to buy out Joe's share of the family restaurant on Fisherman's Wharf in San Francisco. While the agreement allowed Joe to escape a potentially disastrous situation, the Yankee slugger believed he should have received more for his share of the business. In a retaliatory gesture, he made his brothers remove his first name from the restaurant's title. From that point forward, it was known simply as "DiMaggio's Grotto."

LAUNCHINGS AND LANDINGS

The Yankees' 1947 World Series victory brought about an unexpected departure. As teams were headed off the field after Game 7, Larry MacPhail caught up with Dodger executive Branch Rickey and attempted to console him. Rickey, who was still upset over the early season feud between MacPhail and Durocher, treated the Yankee co-owner to a verbal lashing. The conversation ended with Rickey telling MacPhail that he never wished to speak with him again.

MacPhail, who was severely intoxicated, proceeded to spoil the Yankee victory party by unleashing a torrent of insults and punching a reporter. His behavior prompted co-owners Dan Topping and Del Webb to buy out his share of the ballclub. When the 1948 season arrived, MacPhail was gone and George Weiss was the new GM.

Weiss had joined the Yankees in 1932 as head of player development. He would remain with the team through the 1960 campaign, presiding over 19 pennants and 15 World Series titles. Although his unprecedented success ultimately landed him in the Hall of Fame, he was a notorious penny-pincher who was not above hiring private detectives to dig up dirt that could be used against players during salary negotiations. The low point of Weiss' Yankee tenure came in 1957, when he threatened to go public with evidence of Mickey Mantle's extramarital affairs. Feeling that the miserly executive had finally crossed a line, Topping and Webb intervened with a generous contract offer, nearly doubling Mantle's pay. Behind his back, players referred to Weiss as "Lonesome George" because he had no friends on the ballclub. He didn't need any to build multiple dynasties in New York.

The end of World War II ushered in a period of economic prosperity for America. Feeling unusually generous before the 1948 campaign, Weiss negotiated a deal with DiMaggio that included a pay increase of more than 30 percent. The Yankee Clipper earned every penny that year, enjoying his finest offensive season in more than a decade. Not only did he lead the American League in homers (39), RBIs (155), and total bases (355), but he hit at a combined .363 clip against New York's closest rivals—the Indians and Red Sox. Despite his efforts, the Yankees couldn't keep up with either club, finishing two and a half games out of first place.

In addition to DiMaggio, the Yankees got significant contributions from Yogi Berra, who had a breakout season. When Berra arrived on the scene in September 1946, the Bombers already had several catchers in residence. Yogi served as a second-string outfielder while making occasional appearances behind the plate. The departure of catcher Aaron Robinson in 1948 gave Berra a chance to prove himself as a full-time player. He finished third on the club in extra-base hits (48) and RBIs (98) while hitting .305. By 1949, he was New York's first-string backstop.

Describing Berra's approach to hitting, Eddie Joost of the A's once remarked, "As a hitter, [Yogi] was impossible to explain. If you'd bounce a ball to the plate, throw it over his head, or throw it at him, he'd hit it solidly." Elaborating on his personality, teammate Gene Woodling (who joined the Yankees in 1949) asserted, "For the public, Berra built an image of being a dumb, funny guy. He did make the absurd, nonsensical statements he was famous for—I'd say 'Jesus, Yogi, what are you talking about?' But he was a serious player. He wasn't dumb. . . . Yogi got good mileage out of the publicity."

Carried by DiMaggio, Berra, and Henrich (who reached career-high marks in multiple offensive categories), the 1948 Yankees remained in contention throughout the second half of the season, posting a 40–19 record in August and September. They had a chance to capture the pennant with a sweep of the Red Sox in their last two games but couldn't get it done. Tommy Byrne faltered on the mound in the first meeting, giving up 4 runs in 2.1 innings of work. BoSox right-hander Jack Kramer improved his record to 18–5 with a five-hit victory, eliminating New York from the postseason.

Cleveland and Boston ended up in a first place tie, necessitating a one-game playoff to determine the AL championship. The game was held on October 4 at Fenway Park and featured appearances by five Hall of Famers. American League MVP Lou Boudreau went 4-for-4 at the plate with a pair of homers as the Indians breezed to an 8–3 win. They moved on to a World Series victory over the Boston Braves. As of 2024, it remained the last championship in franchise history.

THE TURNING POINT

In 1946—the year Jackie Robinson broke the minor-league color barrier with the Montreal Royals—at least six Blacks were lynched in the South. Restrictive covenants barring people of color from buying homes were still legal. And only a handful of Black students were attending white colleges. While the verbal and physical abuse encountered by Robinson (on and off the field) helped draw national attention to the issue of racism in America, baseball was slow to embrace change.

By the end of the 1948 campaign, only seven Black players had entered the big leagues. The Dodgers, Indians, and Browns all jumped on the bandwagon early, but other clubs waited much longer. The Yankees weren't integrated until 1955 with the arrival of Elston Howard. The Tigers delayed the inevitable until 1958 and the Red Sox ended their long holdout the following year.

Teams that were willing to accept integration benefited greatly—especially the 1949 Dodgers. Don Newcombe—a big right-hander with a lively bat and explosive fastball—won 17 games while leading the league in shutouts. Roy Campanella established himself as one of the top catchers in the majors. And Jackie Robinson had an MVP season. The combined efforts of all three helped guide the Dodgers to their third pennant of the decade.

Across town, change of a different sort was taking place. Prior to the hiring of Bucky Harris, Casey Stengel had been mentioned as a possible replacement for Joe McCarthy. The deal had been nixed by Larry MacPhail, who didn't feel that Stengel was a suitable alternative. During his nine seasons with the Dodgers and Braves, Stengel had posted a winning record just once. And his reputation as a clown was well established. Casey had a habit of making comical but absurd statements that defied conventional logic (a manner of speaking that came to be known as "Stengelese"). Eccentricity aside, he was a likeable guy (at least reporters thought so) and an innovative tactician. "Casey knew baseball," said one contemporary. "He only made it look like he was fooling around. He knew every move that was ever invented and some that we haven't even caught on to yet."

When the Yankees finished third in 1948, Harris' head ended up on the chopping block. Recognizing Stengel as a diamond in the rough, George Weiss handed him the job in New York. To convince members of the media that the decision was no joke, Bronx executives asked DiMaggio to stand beside his new field boss during a press conference in a gesture of support. Casey got off on the wrong foot with Joe from the start. Asked how he felt about managing one of the all-time greats, the new Yankee skipper answered dismissively, "I can't tell you much about that being since I have not been in the American League so I ain't seen the gentleman play, except once in a very great while." His answer prompted a scowl from Joltin' Joe, who rarely spoke to Casey after that. "So what if he doesn't talk to me?" Stengel once grumbled to reporters. "I'll get by and so will he."

During spring training, Stengel tried to assert his authority by holding two workouts per day and reeducating veterans on the fundamental aspects of the game. This insulted the established players, who felt that such things were beneath them. When DiMaggio was asked what he thought about the new Yankee manager, he kept his comments brief but offered nothing positive.

During an exhibition game in Beaumont, Texas, DiMaggio was rounding second base when he felt a searing pain in his heel. He was transported to Dallas to have the old injury reevaluated. Though his foot felt as if it were on fire, doctors couldn't pinpoint the precise cause. Whatever the reason, he was unable to play when the regular season began. On May 3, he received more bad news—his father had passed away. He left New York to attend the funeral and found that, wherever he went, people kept hounding him about his ailing foot. Irritable and feeling sorry for himself, he began refusing phone calls and visits from friends.

In DiMaggio's absence, Stengel implemented a platoon system. Nine different players spent time in the outfield while seven appeared at first base that year. Stengel's juggling act seemed to work. With the exception of three days in September, the Yankees spent the entire season in first place. The key to their success was pitching as four hurlers gathered at least 15 wins. Joe Page—by then the premier closer in the American League—saved 27 games and won 13 in relief.

DiMaggio didn't take the field until June 28. When he did, he played like a man possessed. Though he missed 79 games, he finished third on the club in homers and RBIs. His .346 average would have won him the batting title had he logged enough plate appearances to qualify for it.

In late September, Joe came down with a case of the flu and wound up with pneumonia. He was still ailing when the Bombers celebrated "Joe DiMaggio Day" at the Stadium on October 1. Trailing the Red Sox by a game in the standings, the Yankees moved into a first place tie with a dramatic 5–4 win over Boston. DiMaggio had lost close to 20 pounds by then and was unable to fully exert himself without gasping for breath. Showing the resilience that had come to characterize him throughout his career, he somehow managed to pound out a pair of hits and score a run. With the pennant on the line the following day, the Yankees survived a ninth-inning Red Sox rally for a 5–3 victory.

The season ended on a down note for DiMaggio as his bat went dead in the World Series. In fact, it was the worst October of his career as he managed just two hits and three walks. The fact that he was able to play at all in his weakened state was a triumph in itself. The Series lasted five games, with each of the first three meetings decided by a single run. Once again, the Dodgers were snake-bitten as the Yankees outhit and outpitched them at every turn. The real hero for New York was a versatile utility man named Bobby Brown. During his seven full seasons in the Bronx, Brown spent time at almost every position on the diamond. The 1949 Fall Classic was his finest hour as he reached base in 8 of 14 plate appearances and drove in five runs—more than any player on either team. The highly educated Brown later became a practicing cardiologist. He also served ten years as president of the American League.

DiMaggio waited until Game 5 to make a contribution, driving in a pair of runs with a sacrifice fly and a homer—the sixth of his postseason career to that point. Although the Yankees would go on to win each of the next four World Series, the writing was on the wall. At thirty-four years of age, the Yankee Clipper appeared to be past his prime.

THE LAST REMARKABLE SEASON

By 1950, the Great Depression was becoming a distant memory to the people who had lived through it. Folks were moving away from cities into the suburbs and the average family income was on the rise at $3,300 per year. A house cost around $8,500, while a new car could be bought for roughly $1,500. Television sets were gradually becoming staples in American homes, though less than 10 percent of the population owned them at the beginning of the decade. Western heroes like the Lone Ranger and Hopalong Cassidy attracted a significant portion of the existing viewership.

The World Series was nationally televised for the first time in 1947 and remained an annual tradition every year after that. But radio was still the most dominant medium for baseball coverage. In his book *Real Grass, Real Heroes*, Dominic DiMaggio fondly recalled the pretelevision era. "If your town had a major-league or minor league team, you could walk down your neighborhood street and hear the home team's game being broadcast over the radio with the crowd noise and the announcers play by play descriptions coming through the screen doors and open windows. . . . Every house had the baseball game on the radio and you could walk down the street to the corner store and keep up with the game almost as well as you could sitting at home."

Prior to the 1950 campaign, members of the Yankee roster received questionnaires from the front office asking, "Who is your baseball model, and which player do you admire the most?" More than half of the active players put down DiMaggio's name. Some answers were more descriptive than others. Billy Johnson wrote, "He puts his heart into every inning more than any player I have ever seen." Jerry Coleman provided an almost poetic response: "He is grace, strength, power, all of it effortless."

DiMaggio's ex-wife took him to court for more money in the off-season. Keeping his son's best interests in mind, Joe didn't even protest. Contract negotiations went smoothly as well with Weiss agreeing to match his $100,000 salary from the previous year. At the beginning of spring training, the Yankee Clipper told reporters he was healthier than ever and hoped to play in every game.

The Dodgers and Yankees were poised to dominate their respective leagues throughout the decade. In the Bronx, DiMaggio and Henrich were fading, but Rizzuto was in his prime and Berra was on the verge of becoming the most productive catcher in Yankee history. Acquired from the Giants in August 1949, Hall of Famer Johnny Mize became a valuable member of the Yankees' first base tandem. The pitching corps were solid with the ultrareliable Allie Reynolds at the top of the rotation followed by flame thrower Vic Raschi and breaking ball specialist Eddie Lopat.

In Brooklyn, the Dodgers had assembled a team for the ages with five Hall of Famers taking the field on a typical day. Any pitcher lucky enough to dispose of Pee Wee Reese, Duke Snider, and Jackie Robinson at the heart of the order had to contend with Gil Hodges and Roy Campanella further down the lineup. Don Newcombe and Preacher Roe formed a potent one-two punch on the mound, while staff mates Carl Erskine and Ralph Branca seemed well on their way to greatness.

Although Brooklyn was expected to run away with the pennant, the Phillies took everyone by surprise. Led by Hall of Famers Richie Ashburn (a perennial .300 hitter) and Robin Roberts (winner of at least 20 games in six consecutive seasons), the youthful Philly squad—dubbed "The Whiz Kids" by sportswriters—kept the Dodgers at bay from the third week of July until season's end.

The American League pennant race took an unexpected turn when the Tigers—managed by former Yankee great Red Rolfe—hung on to first place through July and August. A nosedive in mid-September put them behind the Yankees. Reynolds, Raschi, and Lopat combined for 55 wins, but relief ace Joe Page suffered a hip injury that drastically reduced the movement on his pitches. By season's end, he had 7 losses and 5 blown saves to go with a bloated 5.04 ERA—the worst of his career to that point. Tom Ferrick, acquired from the Browns in June, picked up the slack, winning eight games while saving nine.

DiMaggio hit .319 in April but slumped mightily after that. By July, his batting average was hovering around the .260 mark. Hoping to shake things up, Stengel hatched a crackpot plan, putting Joe at first base. It wasn't a total disaster. He made 13 putouts without committing an error. But there was one awkward play in which he stumbled and fell while scrambling back to the bag. He nearly got run over. When newspapers published photos of his clumsy footwork, Joe was furious. But as fate would have it, Hank Bauer sprained his ankle during the game and DiMaggio ended up back in center field. Describing his experience at first base, the Yankee Clipper later admitted, "I was in a cold sweat every minute. . . . I was never so nervous in my life."

Determined to stay where he belonged, Joltin' Joe rattled off a 13-game hitting streak. He followed with a 19-game streak in September. By season's end, his average was above the .300 mark. And his power numbers were on point as well. He finished among the American League leaders in homers (32), RBIs (122), and doubles (33). His slugging percentage was tops in the circuit.

It took the Yankees exactly 10 hours and three minutes to execute a sweep in the World Series. The Phillies led only once during the four games and hit just .203 as a collective whole. Reynolds came up huge for the Yankees, allowing one earned run in 10.1 innings of work. A sign of things to come, rookie Whitey Ford pitched a gem in the finale. Called up from the American Association in July, the future Hall of Famer won 10 of 11 decisions (including the postseason) and finished second in Rookie of the Year voting. By the time he retired, he was the winningest pitcher in World Series history.

DiMaggio performed exceptionally well against the Phillies. His tenth-inning homer off of Roberts in the second meeting held up as the game-winner. His RBI double in the deciding match staked the Yankees to a 2–0 lead. He reached base safely in all four games while hitting .308. There was little indication that the next season would be his last.

NEW BLOOD

DiMaggio wasn't fully aware of it in 1950, but his job was in jeopardy. While the Yankees were working toward their second consecutive AL pennant, an 18-year-old phenom named Mickey Mantle was tearing up the Western Association. After capturing a minor-league batting title with a .383 average, Mantle was summoned to New York as a nonroster invitee. He arrived as a shortstop, but wouldn't remain at the position for long. His manager at Joplin—Harry Craft—had sent along a scouting report recommending that he be moved to the outfield. After observing Mantle during workouts, Stengel was inclined to agree. In fact, Casey couldn't say enough good things about the kid. "He has more speed than any slugger I've ever seen, and more slug than any speedster, and nobody has ever had more of both of 'em together," gushed the Ol' Perfessor. "This kid ain't logical. He's too good. It's very confusing."

Though DiMaggio had finished the 1950 campaign strong, he ruminated over his first half struggles. His shoulders and knees were ailing and it was clear that he was no longer the player he had once been. Before leaving New York at season's end, he told reporters he was uncertain about playing for the Yankees the following year.

At that point in his career, DiMaggio had plenty of other irons in the fire. He had a radio show and a variety of endorsement deals. He had also signed a contract with MGM studios to appear as himself in a full-length comedy feature titled *Angels in the Outfield*. A biopic film about Joe's life was discussed, although it never actually materialized.

In June 1950, the North Korean People's Army attacked their neighbors to the south, touching off the first full-scale conflict of the Cold War. In November of that year, DiMaggio went to Korea with his old friend, Lefty O'Doul, on a goodwill mission. Joe and Lefty visited a number of hospitals, sharing anecdotes and signing autographs. Their travels eventually landed them in Japan, where DiMaggio was treated like royalty. Bad news arrived over the winter as Joe's mom was diagnosed with cancer. She died a few months later at the age of 73.

By the time spring training arrived, Mantle was being hailed as the second coming of Babe Ruth. DiMaggio quickly grew tired of the hype. Before the team broke camp, he called a group of reporters to his hotel and announced that 1951 would be his last season as a player. When the story exploded in the newspapers, manager Casey Stengel remarked, "I haven't heard anything about it, but if that's the way he feels, that's his prerogative. I can't hold a gun to his head and say 'you've got to play ball.' Of course I'd hate to see it happen, but that's a decision the player makes himself." Pitcher Eddie Lopat was skeptical about the announcement, commenting that he would believe it when it actually happened. But veteran slugger Johnny Mize knew exactly where DiMaggio was coming from. "As you get along in years, this training gets to be a trial with its aches and pains and the torture of stiff, creaky joints," he said. "Sometimes I feel the ballplayers should be paid for spring training only and let them play the season for the love of the game." GM George Weiss was taken completely off guard by the news. "DiMaggio has not discussed this with any official on the club," he informed the press. "We regret to hear anything like this, and we hope he will have the sort of season that will cause him to change his mind."

He didn't.

Neck problems, shoulder issues, and back misery kept Joltin' Joe out of action for more than a month. He finished the year with a .263 batting average, which was more than 60 points below his lifetime mark. During a July game against the Red Sox, Stengel conspicuously tried to replace DiMaggio in the middle of an inning. Joe waved the substitute off, grumbling that he would be the one to decide when it was time to come out of a game. After the third out had been recorded, he went straight to the clubhouse without a word to anyone. Relations had been somewhat strained between Stengel and DiMaggio before then, but there was no relationship left to repair afterward. Stengel's insensitive stunt drew scathing criticism from the New York press.

The season didn't go much better for Mantle. Overwhelmed by the high expectations placed upon him, he began striking out with alarming regularity and throwing tantrums in the dugout. In mid-July, he was sent to the Yankees' affiliate in Kansas City. He considered quitting baseball altogether before his father sternly lectured him about a life of drudgery in the Oklahoma lead mines. Mantle hit .361 during his minor-league stint and returned to New York in August.

The combined efforts of Reynolds, Raschi, and Lopat kept the Yankees in contention throughout the season. The trio gathered 59 wins while posting a collective 3.08 ERA. Stengel's platoon system worked fairly well as Mize and Joe Collins drove in 97 runs from the first base position. Splitting time at second and third base, Gil McDougald captured Rookie of the Year honors. Yogi Berra—in his third campaign as a full-time catcher—emerged as the driving force of the offense, leading the club in homers and RBIs.

The Red Sox and Yankees played each other eight times during the last 10 days of the season. The Bombers came away with seven wins, eliminating Boston from pennant contention. The Indians, who had spent most of August on top of the American League standings, fell into a September swoon, finishing in second place.

THE FINAL OCTOBER

In one of the tightest pennant races of the twentieth century, the Dodgers and Giants ended up in a first place tie on the final day of the regular season. Unlike the American League, which relied on a winner-take-all single-game tie-breaker, the NL employed a best-of-three format. The 1951 playoff became an instant classic as the teams split the first two meetings. Things looked bleak for the Giants in Game 3 as Brooklyn carried a 4–1 lead into the bottom of the ninth at the Polo Grounds. Defying the odds, the Giants staged an incredible rally, knocking starter Don Newcombe out of the game. With one out and a pair of runners aboard, Bobby Thomson crushed a three-run homer off of reliever Ralph Branca, lifting the Giants to a dramatic 5–4 win. On WMCA Radio, announcer Russ Hodges came unglued, shouting repeatedly, "The Giants Win the Pennant!!"

The 1951 Fall Classic was the last of six Subway Series between the Giants and Yankees. Although the teams would meet again in October 1962, the Giants had moved to San Francisco by then. Entering the 1951 October Showcase, the Yanks held a 3–2 lifetime edge.

In spite of DiMaggio's aloofness, he cared deeply about his public image. He had appeared in nine prior World Series and, although he enjoyed a few shining moments, he had never actually carried the club in the postseason—not even in his MVP years. This particular Series, which would be his last, meant everything to Joe. He wanted to be remembered as one of the all-time greats, not as a player who choked when the stakes were high.

The Giants had momentum on their side in the early going, breezing to a 5–1 win in the opener. Although the Yankees responded with an efficient 3–1 victory in the second meeting, the game is best remembered for a mishap that altered the trajectory of Mickey Mantle's career. The Bombers were leading 2–0 in the fifth when Willie Mays hit a pop-up to right-center field. DiMaggio was not as mobile as he had once been, and Mantle sprinted toward the ball to help out. When he arrived on the scene, he found the veteran ball hawk poised to make the catch. In order to avoid a collision, Mickey was forced to come to an abrupt stop. There was a loud snap before his knee blew apart and he crumpled to the turf in agony. DiMaggio calmly instructed the rookie not to move and assured him that a stretcher was on the way. It was one of only a handful of conversations that transpired between the two men that season. Mantle's knee was never right afterward, costing him hundreds of appearances over the years.

By the time Game 4 rolled around, DiMaggio was 0-for-11 at the plate and his presence in the lineup seemed to be doing the club more harm than good. With Mantle out of commission, there were few options. Stengel had no choice but to keep penciling Joe into the lineup and hoping for the best. The Yankee Clipper finally earned his keep in the last three games. His two-run homer in the fourth meeting gave the Yankees all the insurance runs they would need. His 3-for-5 performance the following day helped the Bombers grab a 3–2 Series lead. In the finale, the Giants wanted no part of a red-hot DiMaggio, intentionally walking him twice. He doubled and flied out to deep center field in his other two plate appearances. The Series-clinching victory earned Joe his ninth championship ring—a record later broken by Yogi Berra.

DiMaggio might have ended his career on a high note had *Life* magazine not published scouting reports compiled by the Dodgers prior to the 1951 Series. Their assessment of DiMaggio was harsh. "He can't stop quickly and throw hard. You can take an extra base on him. . . . He can't run and won't bunt. . . . His reflexes are very slow and he can't pull a good fastball at all."

When the *Life* story hit newsstands, Joe was on his way to Japan with fifteen other players for a series of exhibition games. In spite of the hero's welcome they received, DiMaggio wasn't feeling celebratory. He left the tour early and arranged a meeting with Yankee owners. Dan Topping was prepared to offer him $100,000 to play as often or seldom as he liked, but Joe wasn't interested. "I'm never putting on that monkey suit again," he allegedly said.

Topping called a press conference the following day to make it official. In front of an army of press men, the Yankee idol professed, "I have had more than my share of setbacks during my career. In recent years, these have been much too frequent to laugh off. When baseball is no longer fun, it's no longer a game. And so, I've played my last game of ball."

And with that, Joltin' Joe's days as a Yankee were over.

FIRST DATE WITH MARILYN

Just a few days after his retirement as a player, DiMaggio began to cash in on his enduring fame. He signed a lucrative contract to conduct televised interviews before and after Yankee home games during the 1952 campaign. He was already doing a weekly segment on NBC. Many observers noted that Joe was clunky on camera, fumbling his lines and coming off as unnatural. But he was the biggest name in baseball and people were willing to forgive his shortcomings.

Because DiMaggio wasn't a movie buff, he got his first look at Marilyn Monroe in a magazine. During spring training in 1951, the iconic starlet had done a photo shoot with assorted members of the Chicago White Sox. Dressed in white shorts and high heels, she clowned around with pitcher Joe Dobson, third baseman Hank Majeski, and outfielder Gus Zernial. Like most red-blooded American males, Joe found Marilyn to be quite fetching.

Shortly after viewing the photos, DiMaggio bumped into Zernial at a charity fundraiser and asked him how he had come to work with Monroe. Zernial—one of the most prolific sluggers of the 1950s—put Joe in touch with PR man David March, who had organized the photo session. March arranged for Joe to meet Marilyn on a double date at a fancy LA restaurant.

Monroe reportedly showed up two hours late, and, although DiMaggio would normally have been insulted by the gesture, he was awed by her beauty. The actress later admitted that, when she heard Joe was an athlete, she worried that he might be loud and ill-mannered. On the contrary, she found him to be a perfect gentleman. Joe didn't blow Marilyn away with his conversational skills, but she was highly impressed when actor Mickey Rooney sat down at the table and made a big fuss over the Yankee icon. She compared the experience to "sitting next to a peacock with its tail spread."

Monroe's real name was Norma Jean Baker. Born and raised in LA, her mother suffered from schizophrenia and was unable to reliably care for her. She spent most of her childhood in foster homes and an orphanage. At some point during her upbringing, she was sexually abused by one of her caretakers. At Van Nuys High School, she began dating a 21-year-old factory worker named Jim Dougherty. Looking to escape her living situation, she got married at the age of 16. Dougherty joined the Merchant Marines during World War II while Marilyn took a job in a munitions factory. It was there that she met a photographer named David Conover, who worked for the 1st Motion Picture Unit of the Army Air Force. Conover helped jumpstart a successful modeling career for Marilyn. By 1946, she had appeared on the covers of more than 30 magazines. Dougherty didn't approve of his wife's new vocation and the couple split.

Marilyn landed a series of minor movie roles with 20th Century Fox and Columbia Pictures during the late '40s. In 1950, she signed again with Fox and gained acclaim for her appearance in the John Huston film *The Asphalt Jungle*. This led to larger roles in multiple 1951 features, including *Love Nest* and *Let's Make It Legal*. One reviewer ranked her among the top up-and-coming actresses of the year.

Shortly after meeting Joe, Marilyn made headlines when she publicly admitted that she had posed for a nude calendar in 1949. She said that she had been broke and desperately in need of money at the time. The public confession invoked a wave of public sympathy and enhanced interest in her films. There were several new releases in 1952, making her a bona fide star and a sex symbol—qualities that drew DiMaggio to her but ultimately led to an unhappy ending.

A MATCH MADE IN HOLLYWOOD HELL

DiMaggio and Monroe were inseparable in the months following their first date. While the 1952 baseball season was underway, Marilyn visited

Joe in New York as often as she could. She appreciated how he always seemed to be looking out for her and respected his need for privacy. The couple spent a majority of their evenings at home. It was a refreshing change for Marilyn, who was accustomed to putting on a Hollywood façade for the public.

Joe had earned his fame with raw athletic ability. But Marilyn had been forced to manufacture her image, undergoing plastic surgery, dying her hair blonde, and changing her name. On the way to stardom, she had been taken advantage of by numerous studio executives and typecast as a bimbo. DiMaggio loathed Hollywood and truly believed in his heart that Marilyn would leave her acting career behind if he asked her to. But he was gravely mistaken. She had worked very hard to get where she was and actually craved the attention.

The courtship was far from blissful even in the beginning. Marilyn developed a close relationship with Joe's son, who had been shuffling back and forth between parents for nearly a decade while struggling to capture his father's attention. When DiMaggio's ex-wife read in the papers that Little Joe had been lounging around a hotel pool in Bel Air with a bikini-clad Monroe, she took Big Joe to court in an attempt to restrict his visitation rights. Not only was the petition denied, but Dorothy was chastised by the presiding judge.

There were plenty of arguments between Marilyn and Joe. In September 1952, Marilyn flew to New York for the premiere of her film *Monkey Business* and to act as Grand Marshal for the Miss America Pageant in Atlantic City. She showed up at the pageant in a black gown with a plunging neckline. One ambitious photographer took a shot of her while standing on a balcony above. When the revealing photo of Marilyn (and her cleavage) appeared in newspapers, Joe literally screamed at her to dress more appropriately in public. It was just one in a long line of ugly spats. While Joe was sweet and doting at times, he could also be ultrapossessive and verbally abusive.

There were two events that negatively impacted DiMaggio in 1953. After his retirement, existing rules required suitable candidates to wait a full year before appearing on the Hall of Fame ballot. Eligible for the first time in 1953, the Yankee Clipper received just 117 of

264 possible votes—well below the 75% needed for induction. Seven players received more consideration than Joe, including former teammate Bill Dickey (who would gain entry the following year). Dizzy Dean and Al Simmons were the only two hopefuls enshrined.

A few months later, Joe's brother Mike fell overboard while warming up the engine of his fishing boat—likely due to a heart attack. He drowned in the waters of Bodega Bay, which is located north of San Francisco. Marilyn stayed by Joe's side throughout the tragic ordeal and the two grew closer than ever.

While working on a movie called *River of No Return*, Marilyn butted heads with her director. She called Joe in tears and, although he loathed being on movie sets, he traveled to the Canadian Rockies (where the film was being shot) to offer his support. Once the project had wrapped, the studio wanted Marilyn to begin work immediately on a new film titled *The Girl in Pink Tights*. Marilyn thought the script was silly and didn't want to do it, but the executives kept pressing, saying she was in breach of contract. Joe stuck by her during the ongoing dispute and, shortly after the holidays, asked her to marry him.

She said, "yes."

Three days later, they went to City Hall and tied the knot. Though it was supposed to be a secret, someone (probably Marilyn herself) tipped off the publicity department at 20th Century Fox. The newlyweds were mobbed by a throng of reporters as they emerged from the judge's private chambers. One journalist asked Joe if the marriage would be good for him and he joked, "It's got to be better than rooming with Joe Page." Marilyn said she planned on continuing her acting career while balancing her duties as a housewife. Joe didn't like that at all and promptly ushered her out of the building.

THE BITTER END

The marriage between Joe and Marilyn lasted just nine months. Evaluating what went wrong, one biographer candidly wrote, "He was neat. She was sloppy. He was repressed. She was hyperactive. Each was willful. Each had a temper. Each was a star. Stars in collision. Marilyn liked older men, successful older men. DiMaggio liked younger women, blonde younger women. But when it came time to play house, reality came crashing all about them, shattering dreams into so much shrapnel."

Shortly after the wedding ceremony, Marilyn accompanied Joe on an exhibition tour of Japan, where she was warmly embraced by fans. Marilyn went on a side trip to South Korea with Lefty O'Doul's wife to entertain US troops. Upon returning, she reportedly said to Joe, "You've never heard such cheering." He assured her that he had—many times. Marilyn's issues with 20th Century Fox were resolved by mid-April and she went back to work on a musical titled *There's No Business Like Show Business*. When filming wrapped, she jumped straight into another project—a Billy Wilder comedy called *The Seven-Year Itch*.

Joe was beginning to test Marilyn's patience by that point. He preferred not to venture out in public, avoiding Hollywood parties like the plague. He despised the attention she received from men and would often brood over it. The arguing increased as sightings of the couple together became less frequent.

In the fall of 1954, Marilyn was in New York working on *The Seven-Year Itch*. One scene required her to stand over a subway grate while blasts of air lifted up her dress. Joe was at Toots Shor's that night—a popular restaurant and bar owned and operated by one of the most famous proprietors in the city. Everyone who was anyone on the New York sporting scene had enjoyed a meal or a drink there at some point in time. One of Joe's acquaintances, a Broadway columnist named Walter Winchell, convinced him to watch the filming of Marilyn's sidewalk scene, which was being shot on Lexington Avenue.

Joe arrived to find a huge crowd of spectators assembled. It took several takes to get it right, and each time Marilyn's dress blew up, Joe grew increasingly angry. He eventually stormed off the set. As the story goes, he went back to the restaurant and vented his frustrations to Toots Shor, who responded with a vulgar reference to Marilyn. DiMaggio was none too happy about the comment and left abruptly.

Later, when filming was done, there was a hellacious argument between Joe and Marilyn in the couple's suite at the Hotel St. Regis. Joe lost his composure and allegedly hit her. It was the last straw for Marilyn. Making sense of the whole mess years later, Joe's brother Dominic said, "[Marilyn's] career was first. Joe could not condone the things that Marilyn had to do. Joe wanted a wife he could raise children with. She could not do that."

At Marilyn's request, Joe was prohibited from entering the 20th Century Fox studio lot. He apologized for his behavior and begged her to reconcile, but she wanted no further part of the marriage. Joe moved out of the couple's LA home, telling reporters he was headed back to San Francisco. The divorce was expedited with remarkable efficiency. Tortured by the loss, Joe ended up in a New York hospital with an ulcer. He would continue to pine over Marilyn in the years that followed, hoping to win her back. In the end, he almost did.

AMONG THE STARS

In 1954, the Baseball Writers Association of America changed the eligibility rules for the Hall of Fame, announcing that a player would have to be retired for five years before gaining entry to Cooperstown. An exception was made for candidates who had received at least 100 votes the year before. Because Joe was among that group, he returned to the ballot only to be snubbed again. He was much closer this time (falling just 5.6% short), but the results were disappointing given the fact that Rabbit Maranville—a light-hitting shortstop with a lifetime .258 batting average—received more votes than anyone on the ballot.

DiMaggio finally got what he deserved in 1955, garnering 88.8% of the vote. On January 27, Joe Trimble of the *Daily News* reported, "Yesterday's selectees comprised the largest number to be named in one year since 1947, when Frank Frisch, Mickey Cochrane, Carl Hubbell, and Lefty Gomez made it. The shrine now contains 77 honored greats. DiMaggio incidentally will be the last one to gain the Hall of Fame so soon after retirement."

Later in the year, DiMaggio had a widely publicized "date" with Monroe. Though the two were no longer married, Marilyn still turned to Joe when the chips were down. And he went running to her every time the opportunity arose. In November 1954, Marilyn had been admitted to the Cedars of Lebanon Hospital for a gynecological procedure. She had been diagnosed with endometriosis—a disorder that left her incapable of bearing children. In need of support, she had called Joe. He drove her to the hospital, sat by her bedside, and had roses delivered to the room. Honoring her request, he even kept reporters at bay.

In a poetic example of sheer irony, it was Joe who escorted Marilyn to the premiere of *The Seven-Year Itch* on her birthday in June 1955. Her boyfriend at the time—playwright Arthur Miller—was married and unable to attend. Joe and Marilyn made a very conspicuous entrance on the red carpet at Loew's State Theater in Times Square, New York. After enduring the blowing dress scene (perhaps with his eyes closed), Joe took Marilyn to Toots Shor's for a birthday celebration. Asked about the nature of their relationship, he told reporters, "We're just good friends. We do not plan to remarry. That's all I care to say."

On July 26, Joe was officially inducted to Cooperstown along with Ted Lyons, Gabby Hartnett, and Dazzy Vance. The 45-minute ceremony was presided over by commissioner Ford Frick. According to newspaper reports, DiMaggio received the loudest ovation. When it was his turn to speak, he recounted the long trip to his first spring training with Tony Lazzeri and Frankie Crosetti. He said that he had tried to model himself after Gehrig, who he had watched closely both on and off the field. After a few words of thanks to Joe McCarthy, he concluded the speech by saying, "The last chapter has been written. I can now close the book."

Less than a week later, the Yankees honored Joe at their annual Old-Timers' Day celebration. In addition to DiMaggio, a number of other living legends made appearances, including Ty Cobb, Cy Young, Jimmie Foxx, and Burleigh Grimes. DiMaggio told reporters he had been informed of his Hall of Fame selection by an anonymous truck driver. He was on his way from Boston to New York when the unidentified trucker leaned out of his cab and shouted congratulations.

It ended up being a pretty good year for the Brooklyn Dodgers. After seven losing appearances in the World Series, the club finally captured a championship, beating the Yankees, 4 games to 3. Duke Snider was the star of the show for Brooklyn, slamming four homers and driving in seven runs. Describing the mood in Flatbush, John Drebinger of the *New York Times* wrote, "In Brooklyn there was wholesale delirium. It rose hoarsely in bars and in pool rooms and even passed contagiously to lady shoppers downtown . . . motorcades raced up and down 86th Street, Fourth and Flatbush Avenues, Ocean Parkway and the other main thoroughfares, ringing the welkin with the clang of cowbells, the tootle of horns and the pop-off of toy cannons. . . . At the same time, stuffed pillows and bolsters, hastily molded into the form of human effigies, were strung from lampposts bearing crude signs, 'Yankees!'"

THE DARK SIDE OF DIMAGGIO

After his split with Monroe, DiMaggio became a serial dater. His association with America's most glamorous actress gave him a kind of sexual magnetism that women could not resist. One biographer described Joe's allure as such: "Every female of a certain age in America had wondered what it might be like to be Marilyn Monroe. . . . But it was something about Joe, too—because he had been so publicly, famously hurt, it gave him a softer edge, a vulnerability that drew women in, like bears to honey—a lot of volunteers to fix his broken heart." Joe was seen in public with a number of Miss America Pageant winners, including Yolanda Betbeze (who took the crown in 1951), Lee Meriwether (the 1955 selectee), and Marian McKnight (the 1957 queen).

Sexual conquests aside, Joe spent his free time golfing and playing cards. He was a regular at the 500 Club—a popular lounge and dinner theater in Atlantic City. "The Five" (as it came to be known) was run by a notorious racketeer named Paul "Skinny" D'Amato, who was a friend of DiMaggio's longtime Newark pal Abner "Longy" Zwillman. Having earned a fortune through rum-running, prostitution, and gambling, Zwillman was even more crooked than D'Amato.

DiMaggio accepted an off-the-books job entertaining high rollers in the back room at The Five. He was paid handsomely to play cards with D'Amato's friends. A round of golf was even more profitable. The problem with the arrangement was that few of D'Amato's acquaintances were reputable businessmen. This eventually landed DiMaggio in hot water.

On October 25, 1957, a friend of D'Amato's brought Joe to the Warwick Hotel to meet some Cuban gangsters who wanted him to serve as a front man for a gambling ring. On their way to the meeting, they stopped by the suite of Albert Anastasia, who was the most powerful crime boss in New York at the time. Later that day, Anastasia (aka "The Mad Hatter" or "Lord High Executioner") was shot and killed at the Park Sheraton Hotel in Midtown Manhattan. There was an investigation and Joe was questioned by detectives. Realizing the kind of trouble it could bring, he denied ever having met Anastasia and invented a story about the Cubans being baseball fans who wanted to talk to him about the 1957 World Series.

Looking to sever his ties to organized crime, Joe landed a public relations position with the V. H. Monette Company, which was based in Smithfield, Virginia. The company was a leading supplier of goods to US military exchanges worldwide. Joe and his boss Val Monette would drum up new contracts by playing golf with high-ranking officials at assorted military posts in the United States and abroad. DiMaggio made appearances at officers clubs and coached kids living on the bases. He was paid more than $30,000 per year and given a permanent suite at the Lexington Hotel in New York.

Joe worked with Monette for several years but could have gotten by without the additional income. Zwillman, who was being watched closely by tax investigators, couldn't legally explain all the money he had in his possession. And so he would stuff large portions of it into suitcases and leave them with his most reliable associates. Because DiMaggio had proven his loyalty on multiple occasions, Zwillman reportedly entrusted Joe with three separate deposits. A member of the "Big Six" mafia ruling commission, Zwillman was subpoenaed to testify before a Senate Committee investigating organized crime in 1959. Shortly before his scheduled appearance, he was found hanged in his West Orange, New Jersey, home. The death was ruled a suicide, but suspicious bruises on his wrists led many to believe that it had been a mob hit. DiMaggio still had Zwillman's money, which he had allegedly stashed in his San Francisco home. No one came to claim it and, because he couldn't hand it over to authorities without incriminating himself, the cash remained at his disposal for years.

After retiring from baseball, DiMaggio did some PR work for a company that sold supplies to US military bases. In this photo, he is teaching a young boy how to handle a bat. Judging by the troubled expression on Joe's face, it's clear that the youngster needs a bit more instruction.
(COURTESY OF STATE LIBRARY AND ARCHIVES OF FLORIDA ON VISUAL HUNT)

GOODBYE, NORMA JEAN

Following her 1956 marriage to Arthur Miller, Monroe miscarried multiple times and fell into a deep depression. She turned to alcohol and barbiturates to ease her suffering. Though her performances in *Bus Stop* and *Some Like It Hot* earned her critical acclaim, she proved to be difficult to work with on the latter project, demanding dozens of retakes and arguing with director Billy Wilder over how her character should be portrayed.

In a gesture of affection, Miller began working on a script called *The Misfits*, which was intended to showcase Marilyn's true talent. While waiting for the screenplay to be completed, Monroe starred in a feature called *Let's Make Love*, which was a commercial and critical flop. Filming of *The Misfits* began in July 1960. By then, Marilyn was suffering from painful gallstones and her addiction was so severe that production had to be halted briefly so she could undergo detox. Before filming wrapped, Miller and Monroe announced that they would be seeking a divorce. The movie received mixed reviews upon its release, but future generations of critics would find merit in Marilyn's work.

In a familiar pattern, Monroe turned to DiMaggio for support during this difficult period. Consumed by health problems, she had her gallbladder removed and underwent another procedure to address her gynecological issues. In February 1961, her frequent mood swings landed her in a psychiatric ward. She used the one phone call they allowed her to contact Joe. He showed up the next day, referring to Marilyn as his wife and assuring the on-duty staff that, if she wasn't released immediately, he would tear the facility apart with his bare hands. They promptly complied, transferring Marilyn to Columbian Presbyterian Hospital, where she was placed in a private room.

Joe received a welcome invitation that spring. Casey Stengel had left the Yankees and Ralph Houk—the club's new manager—wanted DiMaggio to serve as a batting instructor during training camp. This pleased Joe greatly. He flew Marilyn down to St. Petersburg and looked after her while attending to his duties with the team. They were together for the entire spring and the relationship—though not clearly defined—seemed to work this time around.

When the regular season began, Marilyn flew back to New York to stay with Joe at his suite in the Lexington Hotel. She was eating healthier and drinking in moderation. She looked better than she had in many months. Things went very well until August, when Joe had to go on a business trip. In his absence, Marilyn traveled to LA to be with Frank Sinatra, who had at one time been a close friend of DiMaggio's. The affair was kept secret because the two men were no longer on speaking terms and Marilyn knew there would be trouble if word got out.

DiMaggio learned about the whole ordeal, of course—how Marilyn had lapsed back into drug abuse and how Sinatra, feeling that she was too much to handle, had left her for another woman. In time, Joe would also learn about Marilyn's affairs with two very powerful politicians—both of whom happened to be members of the Kennedy clan.

Still, Joe wanted her. He had always wanted her.

Marilyn moved back to California permanently and won a Golden Globe Award. She began work on a film called *Something's Got to Give*, which was a remake of a 1940s rom-com titled *My Favorite Wife*. Shooting was delayed when she developed a sinus infection. The studio said she was exaggerating her illness and eventually fired her, but not before she had filmed a nude scene. She was the first major actress to be filmed nude at the height of her career.

When Joe found out that the studio had dumped her, he flew to LA and asked Marilyn to marry him. Her rejection led to a horrible fight and he allegedly hit her (again). In spite of his volatile temper, she knew that he cared for her deeply—more than anyone else in her life. And she recognized that she had given him good reason to be angry with her at times (although it failed to justify any physical abuse). Marilyn truly loved him. And she needed someone to take care of her. No one knew how to do that better than Joe. And so she made up with him. When he popped the question a second time, she said, "yes."

The wedding never took place.

20th Century Fox reopened negotiations with Monroe in late June 1962. A new agreement was reached, which included the completion of *Something's Got to Give* and a starring role in *What a Way to Go!* (a comedy that ended up being released in 1964 with Shirley MacLaine in the lead). The studio had tarnished Marilyn's public image and, in an attempt to repair it, she did interviews for multiple magazines along with a photo shoot for *Vogue*.

On August 5, 1962, Marilyn's housekeeper—a woman named Eunice Murray—awoke at 3 a.m. and noticed that the light was on in the actress's bedroom. Unable to get a verbal response, she tried the door and found it to be locked. Murray immediately phoned Ralph Greenson—the psychiatrist Marilyn had been working with. Greenson arrived promptly and gained access through a bedroom window. Marilyn had been dead for several hours. There were empty prescription bottles next to her bed. A toxicology report confirmed that she had died of a barbiturate overdose. Because the amount she had ingested was well over the lethal limit, it was considered a probable suicide.

THE CLIPPER'S REVENGE

On the day of Marilyn's death, Joe played in a charity old-timers' game in San Francisco with his brothers Vince and Dom. He stayed out late that night with Lefty O'Doul and a group of Lefty's friends. In the morning, he received a phone call from the doctor who had pronounced Marilyn dead. The news was devastating.

Joe flew to LA to identify the body. He then asked for permission from Marilyn's half-sister, Berniece Baker Miracle, to begin making funeral arrangements. News of Marilyn's death was all over the radio by then, and as DiMaggio took in the details, he became convinced it was the Kennedys who had killed her.

Joe drove to her house in Brentwood to have a look around. The police granted him access, and upon checking the contents of her bedroom, he discovered that her personal notebook was missing along with a set of pearls he had given her as a wedding gift. He asked police if any papers had been removed, but was told that they hadn't. However, Marilyn's address book had been found with a letter folded inside. It was intended for him.

Dear Joe,

If I can only succeed in making you happy, I will have succeeded in the biggest and most difficult thing there is—that is, to make one person completely happy. Your happiness means my happiness and . . .

(It ended abruptly there.)

Angry with everyone who had ever taken advantage of her, DiMaggio made an agreement with Berniece to keep the funeral completely private. Those who were without an invitation were turned away. While this gesture was made out of love, respect, and deep sorrow, it also served as a form of revenge for DiMaggio.

The memorial service was held on the same day that Marilyn and Joe had planned to be married a second time. She had maintained a close relationship with DiMaggio's son, who rode with his dad to the chapel at Westwood Memorial Park. Marilyn's Hollywood contacts, including studio heads and assorted stars, were forced to stand outside the cemetery gates. According to multiple reports, Sinatra and Sammy Davis Jr. tried to force their way in with the help of their bodyguards, but they were ultimately denied access. As the story goes, lawyer Mickey Rudin (who was there by invitation) complained to Joe that he was excluding a lot of very important people. The grieving DiMaggio snarled, "Tell them if it wasn't for them, she'd still be here."

DiMaggio had roses delivered to Marilyn's crypt for many years. He refused to talk about her publicly and would not permit her name to be mentioned in his presence.

DONNING THE GREEN AND GOLD

Joe retreated into private life after Marilyn's death, but he was not a hermit. He remained an avid golfer until various ailments made it physically uncomfortable for him. His favorite course was the Presidio in San Francisco. He would often hit the links with Louis Almada—a former Pacific Coast League outfielder. Almada was careful not to offer Joe advice even if he asked for it. "I would never tell him how to play it," Almada said, "because if it went wrong, he wouldn't talk to you for the rest of the game."

Joe participated in a number of charity golf tournaments over the years but always kept his distance from the general public. Hall of Famer Ralph Kiner recalled, "Joe was so aloof, you couldn't really get to him. He always had a gopher with him—some guy on hand to send on errands and look out for him. Joe always sat alone. . . . At any event, he always had to be the man. He had to be the last guy announced, even at Shea Stadium. . . . Joe did not want the glare, but he did want the glory."

When Joe reached his 50th birthday in 1964, more than a thousand people showed up at the Sheraton Palace Hotel in San Francisco to help him celebrate. Broadcaster Mel Allen served as master of ceremonies. Joe was flanked at the head table by a number of baseball luminaries, including Willie Mays, Mickey Mantle, and Lefty Gomez. He gave a humble speech, thanking everyone for spending the evening with him and declaring that he was proud to have been a Yankee.

DiMaggio was still a Yankee—sort of. He participated in old-timers' games every year and served as a special instructor at Yankee training camp from 1961 through 1967. At the time of Joe's retirement in 1951, he was two years short of the requirements for a full major-league pension. When the A's moved to Oakland in 1968, owner Charlie Finley saw it as a golden opportunity to bring DiMaggio aboard.

A former insurance salesman, Finley had earned a reputation as an eccentric over the years. He assumed ownership of the A's while the team was in Kansas City. In an effort to boost attendance, he resorted to all kinds of wild stunts, dressing the team in tacky green and yellow uniforms with white shoes. He placed sheep with dyed wool in a pasture beyond the outfield fence and also installed a children's zoo. He even mounted a mechanical rabbit named "Harvey" behind home plate. With the press of a button, the rabbit would pop up out of the ground and supply umpires with fresh baseballs.

DiMaggio lived on Beach Street in San Francisco, which was just a few miles from the A's new home (the Oakland-Alameda County Coliseum). Finley convinced Joe that a two-year contract with the club would be beneficial to both parties because it would satisfy his pension requirements while allowing the A's to tap his expansive knowledge of the game. Joe recognized the merit of such a deal, signing on as executive vice president. A few weeks later, he agreed to work as a full-time coach. There were conditions, of course (there always were with DiMaggio). He refused to be stationed at first or third base and retained the right to decline invitations to public appearances. Asked by reporters why he had never taken a job of this sort with the Yankees, he said he had never been offered one. In fact, the Yankees had never actually paid him for his annual spring training appearances (although his room and board were covered).

DiMaggio admitted that it felt strange to be wearing an A's uniform, but he was excited about the team's prospects. "The Oakland A's are coming," he told one reporter. "They will never finish last again. There are too many good young ballplayers here." He was on target with that statement. When DiMaggio joined the club, the A's had Reggie Jackson, Catfish Hunter, and Bert Campaneris on the roster. They were just a few years away from establishing a dynasty.

DiMaggio's observational skills proved useful to the club on more than one occasion. While walking around the Coliseum prior to Opening Day, Joe allegedly noticed that the views of home plate were obscured in portions of the upper deck. Responding to his discovery, team officials moved the infield farther away from the backstop.

Throughout the year, Joe worked tirelessly with outfielders to enhance their defensive skills. In particular, he spent a lot of time with left fielder Joe Rudi, who became one of the best in the majors. Rudi later gave DiMaggio a lot of credit for the three Gold Glove Awards he received during his career.

Joe also proved helpful to third baseman Sal Bando, who had failed to reach the .200 mark at the plate in 1967. DiMaggio noted that Bando was getting jammed on nearly every pitch. A simple adjustment was all it took to raise Bando's batting average by 59 points. Recognizing Jackson's untapped home run potential, DiMaggio convinced the young slugger to use heavier bats. Although he continued to strike out often, Reggie launched 29 bombs in 1968—fourth most in the American League.

The A's won 82 games during DiMaggio's brief stint as a coach—their highest total since 1948. Joe moved to the front office full time in 1969. The A's made several useful upgrades that year, acquiring starting pitcher Vida Blue and assigning Hall of Famer Rollie Fingers to the bullpen. Manager Bob Kennedy was replaced with Hank Bauer as the team remained in serious contention for most of the year. Bauer was fired by Finley when the A's collapsed in September, but DiMaggio—now eligible for a full major-league pension—left the club on good terms.

THE GREATEST LIVING BALLPLAYER

The year 1969 was considered baseball's centennial year. In celebration of the occasion, sportswriters voted to determine the greatest players of all-time in multiple categories. The results were announced on the night before the 1969 All-Star Game, which took place while the Apollo 11 space mission was in progress. As Neil Armstrong and Buzz Aldrin were taking giant leaps for mankind, Babe Ruth was judged by sportswriters to be the greatest ballplayer among the living or dead. In the realm of the living, DiMaggio was selected.

Though he commented humbly, "I never dreamed it would be me," Joe eagerly embraced the title, insisting on having it attached to his name at future Old-Timers' Day games. This helped add to the mystical aura already surrounding him. It also sparked an ongoing debate among journalists and fans. Years later, NBC Sports correspondent Joe Posnanski wrote of the questionable honor bestowed upon Joe, "It was—like a Supreme Court justiceship—a title that would last until death. Even after superior players like [Willie] Mays and [Hank] Aaron and [Frank] Robinson stopped playing, even after his career was equaled by remarkable players like Barry Bonds and Rickey Henderson and Joe Morgan and Mike Schmidt, DiMaggio remained 'The Greatest Living Ballplayer.' He would come to Yankee Stadium, give that two-handed wave he made famous, and (stadium announcer) Bob Sheppard would say those three words: 'Greatest . . . Living . . . Ballplayer.'"

The 1969 vote also included a pair of dream teams. DiMaggio was assigned to the outfield on both squads alongside Ty Cobb, Babe Ruth, Ted Williams, and Willie Mays. Only two other players appeared in both fantasy lineups—Lefty Grove (a left-handed pitcher) and Pie Traynor (a third baseman).

In 1999, more than two million fans voted for MLB's "All-Century Team." When the ballots were counted, DiMaggio was among the top 10 vote-getters. At the turn of the twenty-first century, Bill James—a recognized statistical authority—employed various sabermetric strategies to evaluate the game's best and brightest across the eras. He published his results in a 1,000-page tome titled *The New Bill James Historical Baseball*

DiMaggio's monument at Yankee Stadium was added shortly after his death in 1999. Many Yankee greats have been honored with plaques, but few have had monuments dedicated to them. Joltin' Joe shares that distinction with Miller Huggins, Lou Gehrig, Babe Ruth, Mickey Mantle, and George Steinbrenner.
(COURTESY OF MADE IN COPENHAGEN ON VISUAL HUNT)

Abstract. Players were ranked by position. DiMaggio appeared at number five among center fielders behind Mays, Cobb, Mantle, and Tris Speaker.

BEING JOE DIMAGGIO

Long after he took his last swing in a major-league game, DiMaggio made a comfortable living off of his name. During the 1940s and '50s, he served as spokesman for Buitoni pasta products. In 1973, he went to bat for Mr. Coffee.

Until then, coffee was made at home in percolators manufactured by appliance giants such as General Electric and Proctor Silex. Mr. Coffee drip machines were the first of their kind. Looking for an esteemed celebrity to help push his new product to the masses, the company's founder and chairman—Vince Marotta—acquired DiMaggio's unlisted phone number and cold-called the retired baseball icon.

Marotta flew in from Cleveland to meet Joe at San Francisco's Fairmont Hotel. DiMaggio ate lunch while the executive made his pitch. By the end of the meeting, they had a handshake deal. The Yankee Clipper was not the first New York–based athlete to cash in on his fame. Babe Ruth had peddled everything from cigarettes to underwear. And while DiMaggio was convincing television audiences that Marotta's machines made the "best coffee he ever tasted," Joe Namath and Mickey Mantle were hawking a number of products.

DiMaggio's contract required him to record six TV commercials per year, doing them all in one session. He also cut a series of radio ads. The response was overwhelming as Mr. Coffee soon became the industry leader. Explaining Joe's success as a pitch man shortly after his death in 1999, Jed Pearsal—president of Performance Research (a Rhode Island–based marketing firm)—commented, "He was an athlete who commanded respect instead of just attention. Spokesmen were more trusted than they are now . . . and people believed in the products. Now, though, consumers are cynical enough to know that athletes don't really care about the products they are endorsing."

Mr. Coffee was not the only commercial enterprise DiMaggio was involved in. He recorded his first television ad for New York City's

Bowery Savings Bank in 1972. Profits from both ventures netted him more money than he ever made on a ballfield.

In 1983, Joe hooked up with a lawyer named Morris Engelberg, who convinced him to expand into the sports memorabilia trade. Though DiMaggio retired before the renowned Topps Company issued a baseball card for him, his likeness appeared on a number of other brands, including Leaf, Play Ball, and Goudey. By the time Engelberg began booking appearances at card shows for Joe, the market for baseball memorabilia was on the rise. At the height of his career in the sports collectibles industry, DiMaggio was paid up to $100,000 for each appearance and his autographs were selling for around $300 apiece. It was not unusual for him to earn in excess of $300,000 for a few hours of work. Joe was particular about what he would sign. Original art, uniforms, and advertising items were generally off limits along with anything having to do with Marilyn Monroe.

According to biographer Tom Clavin, DiMaggio's brother Dominic was disillusioned by Joe's greed. Although Dom was not above charging money for his own autograph, he donated most of the profits to the Association of Professional Baseball Players of America, which helped out former major leaguers who had retired before pensions were available. Joe's exploitation of the memorabilia market was one of several factors that caused the two brothers to gradually drift apart over the years.

Some of Joe's charitable endeavors weren't particularly charitable. Though he lent his name to the Joe DiMaggio Children's Hospital in 1992, he did so in the midst of a tax dispute with the state of California (which stemmed from profits he had made at card shows). His association with the hospital made it appear as if a portion of his earnings were being used to benefit sick children. But that wasn't the case at all. In his best-selling biography *Joe DiMaggio: The Hero's Life*, author Richard Ben Cramer asserts, "It was all tax true, which is to say it hid the facts. DiMaggio never gave money to the hospital. Well, once he wrote out a check for a hundred bucks . . . but for the most part, Joe wouldn't give anything—not even a signed ball." He did make a few scattered appearances, however. He was on hand for the ribbon-cutting ceremony when the facility opened in 1992. And in 1997, he showed up (along with

Florida Marlins' slugger Jeff Conine) for the opening of "The Visitor's Clubhouse," where families of hospitalized children could stay for free. Benefiting from DiMaggio's name, the hospital continued to grow over the years, adding an oncology unit, a cardiac surgery program, and emergency services. As of 2022, there were more than 650 physicians on staff.

On an interesting side note, Joe's baseball cards still fetch a handsome price nowadays. His 1938 Goudey "Heads Up" card is worth around $200,000 in mint condition. And his 1940 Play Ball card books at roughly $87,000. Signed baseballs are currently valued at $400 to $600.

THE SAN FRANCISCO QUAKE

The 1989 World Series showdown between the Oakland A's and San Francisco Giants was dubbed the "Battle of the Bay." The two cities stand about 12 miles apart, separated by a vast span known to local residents as the Bay Bridge. By 1989, the Giants had been absent from the Fall Classic for more than a quarter of a century, while the A's had not won a championship in over a decade. The celebratory mood of both communities was dampened by a natural disaster.

After winning the first two games at home, the A's made the short trek to Candlestick Park to face the Giants again on October 17. While fans were still settling into their seats, an earthquake shook the stadium. Light towers swayed and pieces of concrete fell from sections of the upper deck, prompting terrified screams from many who were in proximity. The scoreboard shorted out and communications went down. When the rumbling subsided about 15 seconds later, the assembled crowd cheered. Broadcaster Al Michaels referred to it as the greatest opening in the history of television.

The game was postponed as details of the calamity began trickling in. The high-magnitude quake brought down a section of the Bay Bridge along with an elevated stretch of Interstate 880. Thousands of people were injured and more than 60 were reportedly killed. The World Series, which seemed inconsequential at that point, didn't resume until October 27—the longest delay in the history of the event.

DiMaggio was at Candlestick Park sitting in a box with American League president Dr. Bobby Brown when the earthquake hit. He said that it took a few seconds for people to realize what was happening. After the shaking ceased and the cheering began, he thought that everything was okay. But when he heard that there were fires in his neighborhood, he began to worry about his sister.

Joe's home was located in the Marina District, which was among the most heavily damaged sections of the city. He shared the house with his older sister Marie, who he had always felt closest to. Joe lived upstairs while Marie lived on the bottom floor. Although she was well into her eighties, she still looked after her brother. Unable to reach her by phone, Joe left the ballpark and found his neighborhood in shambles. The house directly across the street had collapsed. Several others were in flames. Still looking for Marie, he went to one of the Red Cross stations that had been set up. He eventually learned that she was at a friend's house—shaken up, but essentially okay.

DiMaggio told a reporter, "My home has been pretty badly damaged and right now they won't let me back in. . . . I hear they're going to destroy 60 homes and it could be 14 to 16 weeks before we get our water and power back. The scary thing is that the worst might not be over. We might be getting some aftershocks in the next couple of days."

Joe used his status as "The Greatest Living Ballplayer" to persuade construction crews to begin repairing his home promptly. But he had grown tired of San Francisco by then. Looking to escape the humidity, the high taxes, and the earthquakes (most of which are low in magnitude), Joe purchased a home in South Florida. It was located on a golf course not far from the Children's Hospital that would bear his name.

JOE AND MARILYN TOGETHER AT LAST

In September 1998, the Yankees held a celebration in Joe's honor. Regrettably, his World Series rings had been stolen from a hotel several years earlier and the team wanted to pay him back. He was presented with replica rings during a pregame ceremony at Yankee Stadium. Although he didn't know it at the time, it would be his last official public appearance.

A heavy smoker throughout his life (three packs per day by some reports), DiMaggio was diagnosed with lung cancer and admitted to the hospital on October 12. A tumor was removed from his lung, but not in time to prevent the cancer from spreading. He underwent a number of additional procedures during an extensive inpatient stay.

On November 16—just a few days before his birthday—Joe's blood pressure bottomed out and a priest was summoned to administer last rites. True to his form on the ballfield, he rallied to reach the age of 84. By then, Joe's lawyer and business partner Morris Engelberg had alerted the press that the Yankee Clipper was dying of lung cancer. It was the beginning of a long public vigil.

DiMaggio pleaded with his physicians to be released but later developed a serious intestinal infection accompanied by fever and chest congestion. Staff members were convinced that this was the end, but they were wrong—again. On January 19, Joe was discharged to his home in terminal condition. He received 24-hour nursing services as Engelberg officially became his health care proxy.

Joe held out hope to the very end. The Yankees had invited him to throw out the first pitch on Opening Day. To keep his spirits up, a sign was hung next to his bed, reading: "April 19, Yankee Stadium or Bust!" Joe's final visitors included Yankee owner George Steinbrenner, his adopted grandchildren (Paula and Kathie), and his brother Dominic. The remaining siblings had all passed away by then.

Sadly, Joe didn't make it to Opening Day. He died on March 8, 1999. His brother Dominic arranged for his body to be flown to San Francisco and interred with the family in Holy Cross Cemetery. Respecting Joe's desire for privacy, there was a relatively small gathering at the funeral. Commissioner Bud Selig and AL president Gene Budig were the only baseball personalities present (aside from Dominic). The service was held at Sts. Peter and Paul Church, where Joe had married his beloved Marilyn many years earlier. During a touching eulogy, Dominic mentioned how Joe had accomplished every goal he had set for himself with the exception of finding the right woman to share his life with. But in death, Joe believed he was gaining an eternal partner. According to Engelberg, the Yankee Clipper's last words were, "I'll finally get to see Marilyn."

A testament to DiMaggio's enduring popularity, admirers continued to leave gifts at his grave many years after his passing.
(COURTESY OF NOJUAN ON VISUAL HUNT)

TESTIMONIALS

"In a country that has idolized and immortalized its 20th century heroes from Charles A. Lindbergh to Elvis Presley, no one more embodied the American dream of fame and fortune or created a more enduring legend than Joe DiMaggio. . . . DiMaggio glided across the vast expanse of center field at Yankee Stadium with such incomparable grace that long after he stopped playing, the memory of him in full stride remains ever-green."—**Joseph Durso**

"He was the very symbol of American grace, power, and skill."—**US president Bill Clinton**

"He was a fighter all the way until the very end. That's why he had a 56-game hitting streak. He wasn't going to give in for anything."—**Dusty Baker**

"He was to people all over the world what a baseball player was supposed to be like. . . . I idolized him for what he represented, which was class, dignity, and character. He was a winner, a champion, a true icon."—**Tom Lasorda**

"I never, ever compared myself to him. I thought there never was a greater player in the history of baseball. For me, just to be mentioned in the same breath, boy, I always felt like I was two steps below him."—**Ted Williams**

"He really lived up to his billing. He was the greatest living ballplayer. He just had such a dignity and elegance about him that nobody can match in today's game."—**David Cone**

"Joe was the pride of the Yankees. He was a great, great player and a classy guy."—**Stan Musial**

"I think some people have a hard time understanding how much of a hero he was. The difference between then and now is the coverage on TV. Most of his career, there was no TV, or TV was in its early stages, so what people knew about him was not from a television image. It was the real thing. Once you saw him play and saw the way he carried himself, it was something you didn't forget."—**Dr. Bobby Brown**

"The very mention of his name personifies class, dignity, elegance, and professionalism both on and off the field."—**Tim McCarver**

ASSORTED ANECDOTES

THE CAVEMAN KIDNAPPING CAPER

Because Joe DiMaggio's immediate family was rather large and he captured most of the attention, the lives of some of his siblings are not well documented. Nellie, the oldest child, was born in Isola delle Femmine. Fishing was the primary occupation there, and her father was barely earning enough to live on before he set off by himself to establish a better home in the United States. Nellie was four years old by the time she was reunited with her dad in Martinez, California, which is located in the East Bay region near San Francisco.

When Nellie was in her late teens, she met a 29-year-old crab fisherman named Dominic Tringalli. He became obsessed with her, showering her with gifts and proposing marriage repeatedly. Though Nellie was flattered by the attention, she had no interest in tying the knot. Refusing to accept her polite rejections, Tringalli hatched a nefarious scheme.

On June 18, 1917, Tringalli found two thugs in San Francisco who were willing to help him kidnap Nellie for a modest fee. The plan involved one man to help him grab the girl and another to drive the getaway car. Nothing went as planned from the onset. As Nellie was walking to work the following day with her friend Edna King, Tringalli and one of his hired goons tried to snatch both women off the street. Nellie bit Tringalli's hand while King successfully fought off her would-be abductor. As the vehicle drove away with Nellie inside, King went to find help.

Tringalli's home was located about 50 miles outside of San Francisco, and before the vehicle even reached the outskirts of the city, one of the kidnappers got cold feet and demanded to be let out. The plan unraveled even further after they arrived at Tringalli's San Jose home. Dissatisfied with the $10 he received for his efforts, the driver—a man named R. J. Comolla—went to the nearest police station and alerted authorities about the hostage situation at 265 Sonoma Street.

A warrant was issued as police reached out to Nellie's parents. Her mother accompanied officers to the Sonoma Street address, where Tringalli was taken into custody without major incident. He was transported back to San Francisco to stand trial for his crimes. When the story leaked to the press, the *San Francisco Chronicle* ran a headline that read, "Bold Caveman Tactics Fail to Win Pretty Girl." Tringalli was repeatedly referred to as a "cave man suitor" in later articles.

During the preliminary hearing, Nellie openly stated that she was not in love with Tringalli and would never agree to marry him. She packed up all the jewelry he had given her—an estimated $250 worth (equivalent to more than $5,000 today)—and tried to give it back to him before the subsequent trial. He refused. In the end, Nellie had an unexpected change of heart and dropped all the charges. Apparently, she had no desire to see Tringalli go to prison, she just wanted to be left alone.

As the story goes, the "cave man suitor" never bothered Nellie again. He found another teenager who was willing to marry him without protest—a young woman named Frances. Nellie ended up being wed to a man named Robert Hellquist and they had a son together. In the wake of the kidnapping, Nellie faded back into obscurity. In spite of being the sister of a fabled Yankee icon, she managed to avoid the spotlight until her death in 1983. She was 84 years old at the time of her passing.

FAMILY DYNAMICS

The birth of Dominic in 1917 increased the size of the DiMaggio clan to 11 members. At the time, they were living in a four-room house that consisted of a kitchen, living room, and two bedrooms. The bathroom was an outhouse situated on the banks of the Alhambra Creek. Having clearly outgrown their home, the family moved to San Francisco, establishing tenancy on Filbert Street in North Beach. They relocated to a Taylor Street flat shortly afterward, but it still wasn't big enough to accommodate everyone. Vince, Joe, and Dom shared a bedroom.

The three big-league brothers had distinctly different perspectives on what life was like growing up. Joe remembered his childhood as an outright struggle. Vince said that the family was poor but never went without food and clothing. In Dom's words, the DiMaggios were "not so bad off. We lived comfortably. We weren't wealthy by any means, but that's why America is so wonderful. You can move up in life if you want to work at it and that's what we did." Joe recalled that things were especially bad during the Great Depression. Clothes were passed down from older siblings, and by the time the younger kids got them, there were full of patches. The soles of shoes were often repaired with pieces of cardboard. Forced to use every morsel of food in the house, Joe remembered his mother serving an unappetizing soup made from chicken bones and gizzards.

In the early twentieth century, Americans observed traditional gender roles. The DiMaggio girls helped Rosalie around the house while the boys assisted Giuseppe on his crab boat. The smell of fish and the waves of San Francisco Bay made Joe queasy, but Dom would berate Joe whenever he tried to get out of his fishing duties. Rosalie and Vince were both sympathetic to Joe's plight, which irked Dom even more. Although Tom and Mike—the eldest sons—dutifully embraced a life at sea, both played baseball in the local leagues. Joe once said that Mike had a powerful swing and was the most talented of the clan.

Equipped with a beautiful tenor voice, Vince dreamed of becoming an opera star. He sometimes earned extra money for the family by performing Italian arias on street corners. Pedestrians would toss coins into Vince's hat as they passed, and it wasn't unusual for him to return home with a few dollars in his pocket. Joe and Dom hawked newspapers on street corners. Joe said that Dom always sold more because his outward appearance evoked sympathy from potential customers. Not only was he small for his age, but he wore glasses and ill-fitting clothing.

Giuseppe and Rosalie spoke Italian with a Sicilian dialect. When they arrived in America, they had difficulty mastering the new language and were unable to converse fluently in English. Joe learned enough Italian to understand what his parents were saying to him but had trouble communicating back to them. It was one of several reasons why he became such a quiet person.

Giuseppe was not completely opposed to recreational activities. In fact, he greatly enjoyed the game of bocce. But money was tight and he knew that furnishing his five sons with baseball equipment would be a costly venture. Moreover, he had come from a generation that valued hard labor over fun and games. There was no time for play when there were mouths to feed. Explaining his father's objection to the sport, Dom once remarked, "Baseball violated Dad's code of life, which emphasized the work ethic."

Vince, Joe, and Dom might have been forced to give up the sport altogether had Rosalie not interceded on their behalf. "Dad thought [baseball] was a waste of time," Dom recalled, "but Mother took it from a point of view that we were all young men and we liked to play games and this was a good game, nice and clean."

The boys had to be careful about tearing their clothing or sustaining diamond-related injuries that might arouse their father's suspicion. Whenever Giuseppe found out that they had been playing ball, he chastised them. Occasionally, there were punishments meted out. If Giuseppe found Vince's glove or spikes lying around, he would throw them out. But Rosalie would always rescue them from the trash and hide them in a safe place. Years later, Vince, Joe, and Dom all gave their mother credit for helping them make it to the major leagues.

Joe was actually more drawn to tennis during his younger years. He idolized Maurice McLoughlin and Bill Johnston—champions who had grown up in the western part of the United States. When Giuseppe finally acknowledged that Joe was nauseated by the smell of dead fish, he began suggesting other possible careers. None of them were even vaguely related to the sport that ultimately made his son famous. On an interesting final note, Joe worked on the San Francisco docks briefly and was also employed in a fish cannery after he dropped out of high school. He chose both positions over a job on his father's crab boat.

BASESBALL ON THE WEST COAST

Founded in 1903, the Pacific Coast League is still in operation today. It is considered a Triple A circuit—the highest level of play outside the majors. In the early days, the mild West Coast weather allowed the league to schedule longer seasons, sometimes stretching from late February to early December. In 1905, the San Francisco Seals played 225 games—a PCL record that still stands. The schedule was drastically shortened in the decades that followed. During Joe DiMaggio's era, teams played more than 180 times per year.

The Seals' original stadium—known as the "Old Rec" to local fans— was constructed mostly of wood. Located near the ocean, the bleachers creaked audibly when a strong wind came up out of the west. Oddly proportioned, the wall was 311 feet in left field and 235 down the right field line. A high fence was installed in right field to cut down on cheap home runs.

Women were granted free admission to the "Old Rec" if they were accompanied by male companions. Rows of bleachers were situated beneath the grandstand to accommodate patrons with a taste for alcohol. The cost of entry to the "Booze Cage" (as it was commonly known) entitled ticket holders to a shot of whiskey and two complimentary beers. After prohibition went into effect, team owners turned a blind eye to patrons who brought their own alcohol in flasks.

All three DiMaggio brothers played for the Seals, but Joe and Vince had both graduated to the majors by the time Dominic joined the club in 1937. The PCL consisted of eight teams in those days—six of which were located in California. The two out-of-state franchises were stationed in Seattle and Portland. In addition to the Seals, the city of San Francisco had a second PCL team—the Mission Reds. From 1931 to 1937, the local rivals shared the same ballpark. By then, a new stadium had been built with a larger seating capacity and deeper outfield dimensions.

In addition to Joe DiMaggio, the Pacific Coast League produced quite a few Hall of Famers during the 1920s and '30s. Their profiles appear below.

TONY LAZZERI

Hailing from San Francisco, Lazzeri spent portions of four seasons with the Salt Lake City Bees prior to joining the Yankees. His 60 homers and 222 RBIs in 1925 are PCL records that have withstood the test of time. Though the numbers seem tacky on the surface, it actually took Lazzeri 197 games to generate those totals.

PAUL WANER

Known as "Big Poison" to admiring fans in Pittsburgh, Waner won three batting titles with the Pirates. He began his pro career in San Francisco. A sign of things to come, he hit .401 for the Seals in 1925 with 75 doubles.

ERNIE LOMBARDI

Lombardi forged a 17-year career in the majors with four different teams. His road to the Show began in 1926 with the Oakland Oaks. The big backstop (6-foot-3/230-plus pounds) hit at a robust .370 clip during his minor league days.

EARL AVERILL

Among the best center fielders in the majors during the 1930s, Averill spent a majority of his career with the Cleveland Indians. He got his start with the Seals, gathering more than 200 base hits in three consecutive seasons. His best year in the PCL came in 1928, when he pulverized opposing pitchers for a .354 batting average and 100 extra-base hits.

LEFTY GOMEZ

The wise-cracking Yankee great played for the Seals in 1929, posting an 18–11 record and a 3.44 earned run average—lowest among San Francisco starters. He joined the Saint Paul Saints of the American Association the following year before earning a promotion to New York.

BOBBY DOERR

A longtime teammate of Dom DiMaggio in Boston, Doerr got his professional start with the Hollywood Stars. Traded to the PCL-based San

Diego Padres in '36, he hit .342—the highest single-season mark of his career. This inspired the Red Sox to add him to their roster the following year.

JOE GORDON

Known for his exceptional glovework and surprising power at the plate, this multitalented second baseman came to be known as "Flash" to fans in the Bronx. His professional career began in 1936 with the Oakland Oaks. He joined the legendary Newark Bears squad the following season prior to making his Yankee debut.

TED WILLIAMS

Considered by many to be the greatest hitter in baseball history, Williams spent two years with the San Diego Padres (of the PCL). He was only 17 years old when he made his pro debut. In 1938, he moved to the American Association, hitting .366 for the Minneapolis Millers and drawing a contract offer from the Red Sox.

JOE'S BIGGEST ADVOCATE

DiMaggio's defensive skills (or lack thereof) made life difficult for San Francisco Seals' manager Ike Caveney. Although Joe was a talented hitter, he had proved to be a defensive liability at multiple infield stations. Unsure of what to do with him, Caveney put the untested rookie on the bench at the start of the 1933 campaign.

At the same time, Joe's brother Vince was recovering from an arm injury that made it impossible to produce reliable throws from the outfield. Vince could have been spiteful and jealous of his younger sibling, but he wasn't. In a show of support, he kept raving about Joe's potential to Caveney, who was open to giving the kid a chance. Joe was eventually installed as a right fielder, but things did not go smoothly at first.

Although he had a strong arm, Joe's ability to track flyballs was in need of improvement. One day, as he was settling under a lazy popup, he got distracted. The ball passed between his upraised hands and struck him in the head. Louis Almada, who played for the Mission Reds that season, recalled, "Joe was very sensitive. . . . All the players laughed and he resented that. He had rabbit ears. He heard the players laughing and yelling, 'Get a basket out there!' and 'You'd better put on a catcher's helmet!' Just popping off. He resented that. He was very proud."

Joe's fielding improved with time and Vince was ultimately cut from the roster. But he was never bitter about it. "Don't ever say that I was in any way jealous of Joe and his success in the major leagues," Vince remarked many years later. "He was my brother and I was proud of him."

The sudden loss of revenue was decidedly inconvenient for Vince at the time of his release from the Seals. He had married a woman he met while playing in the Northern California League and was unsure of how he would support her. His fortunes changed dramatically when the Hollywood Stars approached him with a lucrative salary offer. Returning to action in 1934, Vince became one of the most productive power-hitters on the team, ranking third in home runs and extra-base hits. He remained with the Stars until 1936, when a trade landed him in San Diego. At season's end, the Boston Bees (aka the Braves) acquired his contract for two players and cash.

WITH A LITTLE LUCK

DiMaggio's 61-game Pacific Coast League hitting streak is not the longest in baseball history. That distinction belongs to outfielder Joe Wilhoit, who hit safely in 69 straight Western League games during the 1919 campaign. Commenting on what it takes to accomplish such a feat, DiMaggio remarked, "I'm not being over-modest when I say luck was with me during the streak. It has to be with any hitter who puts together a string of consecutive games." Wilhoit's lucky break came in game number 62, when an opposing infielder deliberately chose to hang onto the ball rather than throw him out on a bunt attempt. DiMaggio's luck was derived from an entirely different source.

As word of Joe's streak began to circulate around the league, fans started showing up at the ballpark in large numbers and he began to feel the pressure. Though he wasn't overly superstitious, DiMaggio resorted to using a "lucky" charm. He had developed a bone bruise on his thumb and Seals trainer Bobby Johnson—a former boxer—had covered it with tape to cushion the impact of pitches. The bruise disappeared, but as the hits kept coming, DiMaggio told Johnson to wrap his thumb with "lucky" tape before every game.

At one point during the streak, Joe was held hitless in his first several at-bats against former Yankee hurler Tom Sheehan. Catcher Johnny Bassler (who had enjoyed several productive seasons with the Detroit Tigers during the early '20s) knew that the rookie slugger would be pressing at the plate and, when DiMaggio came to bat in the ninth, Bassler signaled for two curves outside the strike zone. Sheehan obliged, but Joe didn't bite. As fans began to jeer, Sheehan requested a mound conference.

"At this time of my life, I have no desire to be clawed to death by these San Francisco wolves in the stands," said Sheehan, a 39-year-old veteran. "Can't you hear them howling, Johnny? Just what do you suppose they'll do if I bust the kid's streak by giving him a base on balls?"

Bassler agreed that it would be wise for Sheehan to throw strikes from that point forward. DiMaggio worked the count full and then hammered a pitch off the outfield wall. As he pulled up at second base with a double, Sheehan allegedly tipped his cap and said, "Kid, you're a great hitter. You laid off my curve and powdered my fast one."

BUSTING CHOPS

One of DiMaggio's closest friends on the Yankees was pitcher Lefty Gomez. Though Joe tended to be stiff around a majority of his teammates, he and Gomez engaged in friendly banter on a regular basis. The Hall of Fame hurler told biographer Maury Allen about the first time he pitched to DiMaggio and how it became an ongoing joke between the two men.

At the end of the 1934 campaign, Gomez was invited to play in an exhibition game pitting Pacific Coast League alumni against DiMaggio's San Francisco Seals. Gomez had enjoyed one of his finest seasons with the Yankees, winning the first of two Triple Crowns. He had never heard of DiMaggio and was not intimidated at all when Joe made his first plate appearance of the afternoon. Convinced that the kid would be unable to catch up with his celebrated fastball, Gomez laid one right down the middle. DiMaggio swung late but connected solidly, driving the pitch off the right field wall for a double.

The next time Joe came to bat, Gomez exercised a bit more caution, spotting his pitches low and inside. But DiMaggio made the necessary adjustments, pounding a ball off the right field wall again for another double. Gomez admitted to being angry at that point. "I [didn't] like a kid outfielder from the Seals treating the great Lefty Gomez from the Yankees that way," he said facetiously.

Gomez's obvious frustration prompted a mound visit from Earle Mack—son of the great Connie Mack and manager of the PCL alumni squad.

"Do you know who that kid is?" Mack inquired.

"No," the Yankee southpaw grumbled. "Does he know who I am?"

Mack alerted Gomez to the fact that DiMaggio had assembled a 61-game hitting streak the previous year and was on a fast-track to the majors. He advised the flustered veteran to bear down even harder when DiMaggio came to the plate again. Following Mack's advice, Gomez pitched to Joe like it was the seventh game of the World Series the next time around. The effort paid off as he finally retired the 19-year-old slugger on a flyball to deep right field.

After Joe and Lefty struck up a friendship in New York, they got into a habit of razzing one another about the West Coast exhibition game.

"You had a big year with the Yankees. You won 26 games," Joe said during one exchange. "I was just a kid and got two doubles off of you. You couldn't have been so good, Lefty, if a kid like me could get two doubles off of you."

"Yeah, Dago," Gomez countered defensively. "But you couldn't have been too good either. You didn't pull the ball once against me."

COBB THE NEGOTIATOR

DiMaggio hit .398 for the San Francisco Seals in 1935, earning a contract offer from the Yankees. Because the proposal wasn't much higher than his Pacific Coast League salary, he asked Seals manager Lefty O'Doul for advice. O'Doul called upon his old friend Ty Cobb to help negotiate a better deal.

During his 24 seasons in the majors, Cobb had compiled the highest lifetime batting average of all time at .366. Although he carried a reputation as a bully and a curmudgeon, he had mellowed considerably with age, taking an active interest in the development of specific players. Because he lived in proximity to Seals Stadium, he had seen DiMaggio play on multiple occasions. Impressed with Joe's hitting, Cobb had sent the kid several letters, filling them with assorted bits of advice. Not all of his suggestions were terribly practical. (For instance, Cobb told Joe to use lighter bats and avoid participating in outfield practice during the summer months.) But "The Georgia Peach" proved to be extremely helpful when it came to haggling with New York executives.

Cobb advised DiMaggio to reject the Yankees' low-ball offer. He then dictated a letter to GM Ed Barrow, which DiMaggio copied verbatim and signed his name to. Upon receiving the correspondence, Barrow increased his bid, but only slightly. Again, Cobb told Joe what to write and, again, Barrow raised his offer. The third proposal called for an annual salary of $8,500. It came with a note that read, "This is the limit. Don't waste another three-cent stamp. Just sign it. And tell Cobb to stop writing me letters."

After helping DiMaggio maximize his rookie earnings, Cobb later criticized Joe in a piece written for *Life* magazine. "Joe is another modern who made a name for himself without scratching the surface of his talents," the 1952 article read. "And even worse, he was perhaps the outstanding example of how modern ballplayers neglected to train and keep themselves in condition. He hated physical exertion, and as far as I know, never took a lick of exercise from October 'til March."

THE ONE THAT GOT AWAY

During DiMaggio's 13 active major-league seasons, the Yankees failed to win the pennant just three times. They might have won it every year had a prominent Yankee scout been an accurate judge of West Coast talent.

Born and raised in Oakland, Joe Devine appeared in two Pacific Coast League games during the 1915 slate. That was the full extent of his professional playing experience. He spent three years as a minor-league manager before accepting a scouting position with the Pittsburgh Pirates.

In 1931, he returned to managing with the Mission Reds. The club finished near the bottom of the standings in two straight seasons and he ended up being fired. The Yankees signed him as a scout shortly after his dismissal.

Devine had built a reputation as a brilliant evaluator of young prospects. Before recommending DiMaggio to the Yankees (on the advice of assistant scout Bill Essick), he had discovered Joe Cronin and the Waner brothers (Paul and Lloyd). He later added Joe Gordon to his list of Hall of Fame signings (working in tandem again with Essick). In an unfortunate turn of events for the Yankees, Devine completely missed the boat on another all-time great. "You can't scout desire," the veteran talent hawk once said. "There is no man alive who can say just how a player is going to develop." That statement was poignantly accurate in the case of Ted Williams.

Arguably the most gifted batsman in Red Sox history, Williams had plenty of desire, famously asserting, "I wanted to be the greatest hitter who ever lived. A man has to have goals—for a day, for a lifetime—and that was mine, to have people say, 'There goes Ted Williams, the greatest hitter who ever lived.' Certainly nobody ever worked harder at it. It was the center of my heart, hitting and baseball."

A product of San Diego, Williams was tall and rail thin as a teenager (6-foot-3/148 pounds). He hit .430 for Hoover High School in spite of his spindly frame, which would later earn him the famous nickname of "The Splendid Splinter." Upon graduating, he accepted a contract offer from the San Diego Padres.

In 1936, Devine was dispatched by the Yankees to assess Williams' abilities. In his official scouting report, he noted that Williams was a slow runner. He also asserted that the future American League batting champ was a below average outfielder with a mediocre throwing arm. Although Williams impressed Devine to some extent with his hitting, the Yankees terminated negotiations when Ted's mother asked for a hefty signing bonus.

A New York outfield consisting of Williams in left, DiMaggio in center, and Tommy Henrich in right would undoubtedly have been among the greatest in baseball history. It would have given Williams the prize that eluded him throughout his distinguished career—a World Series ring.

THE THREE DAGOS

Things were much different in the game's early days. Sports writing tended to be over the top. And nearly every player was assigned a nickname by a teammate or journalist. Some monikers were flattering. Others were not.

In many instances, nicknames were based on a player's skills. For example, Babe Ruth was known as "The Sultan of Swat" while slugger Jimmie Foxx was "The Beast." Other less fortunate individuals were nicknamed on account of their deficiencies, such as Leo Durocher ("The All American Out") and Luke Appling ("Old Aches and Pains"). Likewise, many players with distinguishing physical characteristics were labeled accordingly. Deaf/mute players (yes, there have been a few) were commonly called "Dummy." Small guys were known as "Rabbit" and portly fellows carried the moniker of "Jumbo."

It logically follows that players with foreign ancestry were saddled with ethnically based nicknames. Though many of these handles are considered pejorative and insulting today, they were perfectly acceptable in the early part of the twentieth century. It was not unusual to see players referred to as "Dutch," "Frenchy," or "Swede."

"Dago," which is now considered a derogatory term for people with Italian or Spanish roots, has seventeenth-century maritime origins. British sailors used it (out of ignorance) to identify foreign-speaking people with olive complexions and dark hair. In the 1800s, the tag became more commonly used in the United States as a disparaging phrase for Italians.

When DiMaggio arrived in New York, the Yankees had Frankie Crosetti and Tony Lazzeri working together around second base. According to a popular story (which may or may not be apocryphal), Lefty Gomez was facing the Browns with one out and a runner on first in the late innings of a close game. He induced a grounder back to the mound, but threw wildly past second base into center field, where Joe D. was stationed. Manager Joe McCarthy was fuming and, although Gomez

DiMaggio is all smiles as he poses with Hall of Fame slugger Jimmie Foxx of the Red Sox.
(COURTESY OF THE LESLIE JONES COLLECTION/BOSTON PUBLIC LIBRARY)

worked his way out of trouble, Marse Joe decided to confront the hurler anyway.

"We should have turned a double play. What were you thinking out there?" McCarthy growled.

"Somebody said 'Throw it to the Dago,'" Gomez explained. "Nobody said which Dago."

Addressing the entire dugout, the Yankee skipper said petulantly, "From now on, you'll specify which Dago, you hear me?"

This drew stifled laughter from players on the bench.

From that point forward, a distinction was made. Lazzeri was "Big Dago" and Crosetti was "Little Dago." DiMaggio became known more plainly as "Dago" or "Daig" for short.

MAKING HIS PRESENCE KNOWN

DiMaggio's first-ever regular season appearance with the Yankees was delayed considerably due to a freak injury. He finally took the field on May 3, joining a lineup that included a quartet of Cooperstown greats. It was among the most highly anticipated debuts in Yankee history. For months, the New York writers had been referring to Joe as the successor to Babe Ruth. One journalist labeled him "the most ballyhooed rookie since the days of [Joe] Kelley and [Marty] O'Toole." (For the record, Kelley and O'Toole spent their entire careers during the Deadball Era.)

The game was played on a rainy Sunday afternoon at Yankee Stadium. The Bombers were perched near the top of the standings while their opponents—the humble Browns—were mired in the AL basement, having won just 3 of 17 games. Adding to the enormous expectations placed upon him, Yankee manager Joe McCarthy inserted DiMaggio into the coveted third slot in the batting order, which had been vacated by Ruth the year before. Describing his spring training experience in '36, the Yankee Clipper said, "I was nearly frightened to death. I took a look at those big fellas, big in size as well as in name. There were guys like Bill Dickey, Lou Gehrig, Red Ruffing, and Lefty Gomez. I just froze."

Though he was probably a bundle of nerves, Joe reached base safely against all four of the pitchers the Browns sent to the hill that day. Facing right-hander Jack Knott in the first inning, he grounded back to the mound. It should have been an easy out, but Frankie Crosetti (who had led off with a triple) created a distraction by bolting toward home. Knott's throw to third sailed wide of the bag and DiMaggio made it all the way to second base. He later scored on a double by Ben Chapman.

The rest of the afternoon went exceptionally well for DiMaggio as he recorded base-hits in the second, sixth, and eighth frames. Recounting Joe's sixth-inning plate appearance, Don Hallman of the *Daily News* wrote, "It was here the fans decided Joe was OK and gave him the hand they had reserved for fellows like Ruth and Gehrig. Rolfe doubled and Joe planted a triple up against the centerfield boards. There wasn't any luck here—that blow would have gone for a homer in a lot of ballparks."

The game was not without its fair share of unfortunate moments. In addition to a brief rain delay, a foul tip off the bat of Gehrig left St. Louis catcher Rollie Hemsley writhing on the ground in pain. He finished the inning, but was replaced with backup receiver Tony Giuliani. By the time the last out was recorded, the Yankees had bowled over the Browns by a score of 14–5. DiMaggio was 3-for-6 with 3 runs scored and an RBI.

The following morning, an article in the *New York Daily News* read, "Now the cheers of New York fans are not handed out to every fellow. In fact, they have subsided almost to a whisper since Babe Ruth packed his duds and went through the gates. But yesterday they rolled in happy volume across the field and back again for a rookie—a $75,000 rookie to be sure, but only a kid stepping up to fill the vacant shoes of Big Boy Ruth."

ALL-STAR FOLLIES

Even the most gifted athletes have bad days on the field. DiMaggio had plenty of them during his career. But of all his epic flops, few compare to the effort he put forth in the 1936 All-Star Game. Describing his horrific performance that day, Dan Parker of the *New York Daily Mirror* wrote, "At every turn, Joe encountered a new pinch. In every pinch, he fell down. . . . McCarthy's prize rookie won the hand-gilded mountain goat antlers in the fourth annual interleague classic." Years later, DiMaggio continued to ruminate over the game, blaming himself for the first American League loss in all-star history. "I was too sure of myself," he said. "Baseball was a cinch for me. Or so I thought. . . . The first lesson to be learned by anybody who wants to play baseball professionally or otherwise is that the game is hardest just when you think it's easiest."

Facing Cardinals' great Dizzy Dean in his first at-bat of the afternoon, DiMaggio produced an inning-ending double play. In the second frame, Gabby Hartnett hit a drive to right field, where Joe was stationed. The Yankee idol charged the ball hoping to make a shoestring catch, but it eluded his glove for a run-scoring triple. His day of infamy was not yet finished. In the top of the fifth, he misplayed a routine single by Cubs' second baseman Billy Herman. Herman ended up on second and later scored. As fate would have it, DiMaggio had a chance to redeem himself in the ninth inning with two outs and the tying run at second base. Completing an exasperating 0-for-5 day at the plate, he popped out, bringing the game to a disappointing conclusion.

The Midsummer Classic was rarely DiMaggio's finest hour as he hit just .225 in 11 appearances. His defensive follies continued in the 1938 All-Star Game. With the National League leading 2–0 in the bottom of the seventh, Frank McCormick of the Reds led off with a single. Dodger shortstop Leo Durocher followed with a sacrifice bunt up the third base line. Jimmie Foxx—normally a first baseman—was stationed at third to accommodate Lou Gehrig. Gehrig was playing very shallow to guard against the bunt. When second baseman Charlie Gehringer failed to cover first, Foxx's throw sailed into right field. DiMaggio chased down the ball and fired wildly to home plate, allowing Durocher to completely circle the bases. Though errors were assigned on the play, it has been widely referred to as the only "bunt homer" in all-star history.

Outfielder Ben Chapman is clowning around with DiMaggio at the 1936 All-Star Game, which took place at Braves Field in Boston. DiMaggio was the only rookie on the All-Star roster that year.
(COURTESY OF THE LESLIE JONES COLLECTION/BOSTON PUBLIC LIBRARY)

BRONX CHEERS

Fans in New York can be notoriously hard on players. Some of the most beloved Yankee greats, Ruth and Mantle included, were booed repeatedly during their careers. DiMaggio was no exception.

On July 1, 1936, DiMaggio was hitting at a robust .363 clip. But after an abominable performance in the All-Star Game, he fell into a funk that reduced his batting average by nearly 30 points. Fans began voicing their disapproval almost every time he came to the plate. Sympathizing with the slumping rookie, Jack Miley of the *New York Daily News* wrote in the colorful language of the era, "All the world is dark and dreary for young Joe DiMaggio. The proud Pisan is plunged in Stygian gloom. For the Great Giuseppe isn't getting his base hits, he's bobbling that ball around in the outfield and some of the Yankee rooters are riding him. The 24-year-old San Franciscan, who was the miracle man of Mulberry Bend until he went into a tailspin up at the All-Star game in Boston two weeks ago, is learning about the fickleness of fans. . . . The cheers have turned to jeers and DiMaggio is dismayed by this change of attitude in the folks he thought were his friends."

After a 2-for-8 showing in a doubleheader against the Browns on July 19, DiMaggio silenced many of his critics by hitting safely in 15 straight games. He finished the season with numbers that would likely have earned him Rookie of the Year honors had the award existed then. But it wasn't enough for some. On the heels of a 6–1 loss to the Giants in the World Series opener, one New York sportswriter published a mock letter to DiMaggio's mother. "Louder, Mama. Speak to him before it's too late," the article read. "You saw what happened to your Bambino Wednesday when there were two on base in the eighth-inning and the rain was in his face and that Hubbell fellow was throwing a wet, wobbling screwball. He hit into a double play and killed a Yankee rally when the ballgame was on fire. That's no way for your Giuseppe to win the World Series, Mama. . . . He's got a honey-smooth swing and a follow through that's as beautiful as poetry, but the Yankees aren't paying him $8,000 a year to fan the air or hit into double plays . . . it's not too late to take Giuseppe off in the corner and talk to him. Tell him to dig his cleats in deeper and forget that this is his first year in the big leagues. . . . Talk to him, Mama, talk to him."

DiMaggio did pick up the pace with a 3-for-5 effort in Game 2. He finished the Series with a .346 average, helping the Yanks eliminate the Giants in six games. But it was not the last time he would be harassed by fans and sportswriters. He was blasted by both during his 1938 contract dispute. And his decision not to enlist in the armed forces during the 1942 campaign invited resounding boos along with scathing commentary from a number of reporters. Through it all, DiMaggio maintained his composure, vowing to play harder while maintaining a cordial relationship with the press. "In a city where the news cycle was fed by several daily newspapers, the dozens of columnists could become a player's best friend or his worst enemy," one biographer observed. "It was a lesson that would be learned by many a New York athlete in the twentieth century, but DiMaggio latched onto it early."

IMPRESSING THE PREZ

Franklin Delano Roosevelt attended many ballgames during his time in office. On October 2, 1936, he made his first and only presidential visit to a stadium outside of Washington, DC. The Giants had opened the Fall Classic with a surprising 6–1 win over the Yankees. Heavily favored to take the Series, the Bombers were looking to get back on track in Game 2 at the Polo Grounds.

Because Roosevelt suffered from paralysis, he had to be driven straight into the ballpark through the center field gate. Players and fans were instructed to remain in their seats after the last out so the nation's 32nd president could make a clean exit. In a brief pregame ceremony, FDR threw out the first pitch.

The Yankees exploded for seven runs in the third and six in the ninth. By the time the Giants came to bat for the last time, they were trailing 18–4. With two outs and Lefty Gomez on the mound, Hank Leiber launched a drive to deep center field. DiMaggio sprang into action, later describing the play as follows: "I went tear-assing after that ball. After about fifty yards, I turned around and put up my glove, and it's a good thing I did, because that ball would have hit me in the nose."

DiMaggio's forward momentum carried him to the steps of the visitor's clubhouse, which was located near the center field exit. With the game officially over, he followed orders and stayed put awaiting the president's departure. FDR's convertible circled the field on the way out and he waved to fans as they gave him a rousing ovation. DiMaggio said that his heart was pounding as the presidential entourage, composed of several vehicles, passed in close proximity. Roosevelt took his hat off, waved it, and smiled before offering a few words of praise for the fine catch Joe had made. The Yankee Clipper later said it was one of the most exciting moments of his career. John Drebinger of the *New York Times* reported that the game "was the most decisive, humiliating defeat ever suffered by a contender in the thirty-one years of World Series warfare and left a crowd of 45,000 stunned and awed at the finish."

MASSACRE IN PHILLY

Because DiMaggio played during one of the most dominant eras in team history, it should come as no surprise that he was involved in a number of Yankee blowouts. The Philadelphia A's captured three consecutive pennants beginning in 1929. But by the time DiMaggio made his major-league debut, the club was in the midst of a rebuilding project. Hall of Famers Mickey Cochrane, Jimmie Foxx, and Al Simmons were all gone before the 1936 campaign, leaving the team to flounder near the bottom of the standings for the remainder of the decade. The Yankees compiled a 64–23 record against the A's from 1936 through 1939. Two of those wins were almost comical in their lopsidedness.

MAY 24, 1936

Only 8,000 fans showed up for a Sunday matinee at Shibe Park, which had a seating capacity of over 30,000. The Yankees were in first place while the A's were mired in seventh. The first inning was not an accurate measure of how things would turn out as Philly built a 2–0 lead off of right-hander Monte Pearson. Over the next seven frames, the Yankees battered five different pitchers for a total of 25 runs on 19 hits. Sixteen walks were issued by Philly moundsmen—more than the collective totals of the entire Yankee staff over the next four games.

DiMaggio went 3-for-7 at the plate with a homer and a double, but the star of the show for New York was Tony Lazzeri, who set a record with 11 RBIs—8 of which came on a pair of grand slams. Recapping his performance, the *New York Times* reported, "Tony Lazzeri hammered his way to baseball fame today with an exhibition of batting unparalleled in American League history as he set the pace in the Yankees crushing 25–2 victory." Prior to Lazzeri, only Jim Bottomley of the Cardinals and Phil Weintraub of the Giants drove in as many runs in a single game. Bottomley still holds the modern record with 12.

JUNE 28, 1939

After Lou Gehrig was permanently removed from the lineup, the Yankees spent the next several months proving that they could contend without him. Never was this more apparent than on June 28, when the New Yorkers annihilated the A's by a score of 23–2 in the first game of a doubleheader at Shibe Park. Gehrig's replacement at first base—Babe Dahlgren—looked highly competent that day, going 4-for-6 at the plate with five runs batted in. DiMaggio scored four times and gathered three RBIs with a pair of homers.

The misery continued for manager Connie Mack as the Yankees followed with a 10–0 win in the second game. Twenty-one thousand fans saw DiMaggio score two more runs while elevating his batting average to .402 on the season. Lefty Gomez was brilliant on the mound, allowing just three hits. The game was played in a brisk one hour and 40 minutes.

MY BROTHER, MY KEEPER

Major-league baseball has seen its fair share of sibling pairings. According to the *Baseball-Almanac* website, more than 400 combinations of brothers have appeared on the diamond over the years. But sibling trios are somewhat rare. And successful threesomes are even rarer. The DiMaggios were the first triumvirate of big-league brothers to play during the modern era. From a statistical standpoint, they were the most productive tandem in history.

After Joe joined the Yankees in 1936, Vince was the next member of the clan to reach the majors, making his debut with the Boston Bees in

'37. An excellent center fielder with a strong arm, he was vulnerable to strikeouts, leading the National League six times in that category. During one particular luckless stretch, Bill McKechnie—Vince's manager in Boston—remarked to a writer, "I can see a foot of daylight between the ball and the bat. I can't understand how someone can swing at a ball so many times without even ticking it once." In spite of all the whiffs, Vince had moderate power at the plate and was a reliable RBI man. But he never stuck with one team for long. He was traded five times over the course of his 10-year career. His best offensive season came with the Pirates in 1941, when he batted .267 with 100 RBIs and 53 extra-base hits. In sharp contrast to Joe, who was quiet and aloof, Vince had the gift of gab. "If Joe could talk like me and I could hit like Joe, we'd both be worth a million bucks," he once joked.

The youngest and smallest of the DiMaggio clan at 5-foot-9, 168 pounds, Dominic looked more like a schoolteacher than a ballplayer. His wire-rim spectacles gave him a bookish appearance and inspired his popular nickname: "The Little Professor." Next to Joe, he was arguably the most talented of the bunch. A patient hitter, his .383 lifetime on-base percentage made him an ideal leadoff man. He demonstrated extensive range, a powerful arm, and a reliable glove in center field—qualities that earned him seven All-Star selections. Describing his unusual defensive style, he told a writer from *Baseball Digest*, "I played center field at a right angle to the plate with my left foot facing the plate and my right foot parallel to the center field fence [meaning that he stood sideways with his back to right field]. It was something I thought of myself. I played outfield that way from the beginning when I played in the sand lots of San Francisco. My feeling was that I got a better jump on the ball that way. I could get a quicker start on flyballs over my head, could come in faster on line drives to short center, and could charge ground balls better." In spite of his stellar play, it was a tough era for the Red Sox. They captured just one pennant during Dominic's 11 active seasons with the club, finishing behind the Yankees in the standings nine times. The Little Professor finally got a taste of World Series action in 1946, reaching base safely in all seven games.

Joe, Vince, and Dom combined for 573 homers and 2,739 RBIs. They banged out more than 4,800 hits while compiling a .297 collective batting average. Although no other sibling trio has ever reached those heights, there are a handful of others worthy of mention.

THE BOYERS

Ken and Clete Boyer arrived in the majors during the 1955 slate. Both were third basemen. When it came to World Series rings, Clete had the edge, winning two with the Yankees. Ken was the family leader in just about every other category, capturing five Gold Glove Awards and making 11 All-Star appearances. In 1964, he was named National League MVP. Cloyd, the oldest of the Boyer clan, broke into the majors with the Cardinals in 1949. A right-handed pitcher, he put up unremarkable numbers over portions of five seasons (20 wins/23 losses/4.73 ERA). Ken and Clete did pretty well by comparison, combining for 444 homers, 1,795 RBIs, and a .267 lifetime batting average.

THE ALOUS

Felipe, Matty, and Jesus Alou were the first sibling tandem to appear in the outfield together. It happened on September 15, 1963, when Giants' manager Alvin Dark penciled the Dominican-born trio into the San Francisco lineup against the Pirates at Forbes Field in Pittsburgh. While all three Alous hit for relatively high averages, there was little power to go around. Felipe had the most pop in his bat, averaging 12 homers per year over 17 seasons. Matty won the NL batting title in 1966, surpassing the .330 mark in four consecutive campaigns. Jesus came away with the most World Series rings, winning a pair of them with the Oakland A's in the 1970s. Together, the three brothers hit at a .291 clip with 269 homers and 1,656 RBIs.

THE MOLINAS

Hailing from Puerto Rico, the Molinas all found their way to the majors as catchers. Yadier (who retired after the 2022 slate) was the most successful by far with 10 All-Star appearances, nine Gold Gloves, and two World Series titles to his credit. Bengie spent 13 seasons with four different clubs, winning one World Series ring and capturing a pair of Gold Gloves. Jose logged 15 years of big-league experience (primarily with the Angels), helping the Angels and Yankees to World Series titles. As a collective unit, the three brothers combined for more than 300 homers and 1,900 RBIs.

MR. GORDON, MEET MR. DIMAGGIO

During DiMaggio's controversial 1938 holdout, he made an arrangement with San Francisco owner Charley Graham to take batting practice with the Seals so he could stay sharp while discussions with the Yankees continued. During one round of BP, DiMaggio was hammering every pitch that left-hander Jimmy Rego delivered. Worried that manager Lefty O'Doul might cut him from the squad, Rego stopped grooving pitches to the Yankee slugger and started using his best stuff. "Jesus, I was throwing hard and shoving the bat right up his ass," the hurler later recalled. DiMaggio—perhaps feeling the pressure of his ongoing contract dispute—got so frustrated, he threw his bat out toward the mound before stalking off the field.

With the country still in the throes of the Great Depression, DiMaggio knew that he was jeopardizing his reputation by turning down a salary that most Americans could only dream about. Worse yet, the Yankees were protected by baseball's reserve clause, which essentially stated that players were property of the teams they had signed with until owners decided to trade or release them. Realizing the gravity of the situation, DiMaggio ultimately decided that the risk of holding out any longer was too great and accepted what the Yankees were offering.

The Yankee Clipper's return to baseball was quite eventful. He entered his first regular season game on April 30 in Washington. With two outs in the bottom of the sixth inning, Taffy Wright of the Senators hit a blooper behind second base. DiMaggio raced in from center field. Myril Hoag came motoring in from right field. Rookie Joe Gordon—who had been called up from the championship Newark squad—ventured far beyond the infield in hot pursuit. All three players converged on the ball. At the last minute, Hoag made the grab and somehow managed to avoid crashing into his teammates. But the 6-foot-2, 195-pound DiMaggio collided with the smaller Gordon, who stood 5'10" and weighed around 180. DiMaggio sustained a minor bruise on his head and remained in the game. Gordon, on the other hand, was carted off the field on a stretcher. He was out of action for a month.

Recounting the incident, DiMaggio later wrote, "Considering that this was my first game since I had come to terms with the Yankees, that I was booed for the first time in my life by fans and that I knocked out our new second sacker halfway through the game, it might be said that I broke in with a bang!"

Playing beside the Yankee Clipper could definitely be hazardous at times. In July 1936, DiMaggio ran into Hoag at full speed while chasing a ball hit by Hall of Famer Goose Goslin. Though both outfielders initially appeared to have escaped serious injury, Hoag was found unconscious in his hotel room two days later. Holes were drilled in his head to relieve intercranial pressure, and doctors believed that he would never play ball again. But in an unexpected turn of events, he successfully rehabbed, returning to the Yankee lineup in April 1937. He continued to play in the majors through 1945, finishing his career with the Cleveland Indians.

Gordon and Hoag were not the only men to incur serious injuries while playing alongside Joe D. In Mickey Mantle's rookie year, he shredded his knee while stopping abruptly to avoid a collision with DiMaggio. Multiple players reported that Joe had a quiet voice that could not always be clearly heard when he called for a ball.

THE LOATHSOME DOWNFALL OF LOU GEHRIG

After Lou Gehrig's farewell speech on July 4, 1939, he was honored again when the American League designated him captain of the All-Star team. There were half a dozen Yankees in the starting lineup that day. DiMaggio reported that he and the other AL stars noticed Gehrig's physical decline in the locker room as he clumsily tried to dress. "He was failing before our eyes," DiMaggio wrote in his memoirs. "He was losing the power of his fingers and his left leg commenced to drag, so that he had to leave the field at a half-trot as he couldn't control his stride at an ordinary walking gait." Out of respect for baseball's reigning "Iron Man," players avoided helping him to spare him the embarrassment.

The Yankees won the World Series in a sweep over Cincinnati that year. But DiMaggio contended that the excitement just wasn't there for him and other players. On the ride back to New York, they tried to manufacture the spirit of celebration, staging a victory parade through the train cars. Things got pretty rowdy until players reached the compartment occupied by Joe McCarthy, who hollered at them to pipe down and act like professionals.

"It wasn't that Joe objected to the celebration, as such," DiMaggio recalled, "but that he'd been sitting there, brooding over the fact that Gehrig was through as a Yankee and was feeling pretty blue about it. Everybody knew then that it wasn't going to be the same without Gehrig. How could it be?"

Gehrig's cherished consecutive games record was finally broken in September 1995, when Cal Ripken made his 2,131st straight appearance. Putting some distance between himself and the Iron Horse, the Orioles' Hall of Fame shortstop eventually extended the skein to 2,632 games. He said that breaking the record was not a conscious effort on his part. "I never really thought about the streak," he told an MLB correspondent. "I never really allowed myself to think about the streak. It was very simple: I wanted to come to the ballpark. I wanted to play. I wanted to help the team win." In 2021, Ripken partnered with MLB to create "Lou Gehrig Day," which helped raise awareness and funds for the cure of amyotrophic lateral sclerosis (ALS).

BAD ADVICE

DiMaggio was known for his quiet nature, rarely saying much of anything to teammates. In a famous anecdote told by International News Service reporter Jack Mahon, DiMaggio was sitting in the lobby of the Chase Hotel in St. Louis one afternoon with Tony Lazzeri and Frankie Crosetti. Mahon kept track of how long the three men went without speaking to one another. An hour and a half went by before DiMaggio suddenly cleared his throat.

"What did you say?" Crosetti inquired.

"Shut up," Lazzeri replied, "he didn't say nothing."

And with that, the three ballplayers lapsed back into prolonged silence.

In spite of his taciturn persona, DiMaggio still possessed leadership qualities. "All you had to do was follow what he did," said Tommy Henrich. "A look from him was enough. He'd stare you down. You'd cringe." Sometimes it was more than a look that inspired teammates. Joe once chewed out Yogi Berra after he complained of being tired and sat out the second game of a doubleheader. Joe insisted on playing in both games, and when he saw Yogi lounging in the clubhouse looking well rested, he snarled, "What's the matter—are you tired? You're 20 years old! What kind of fucking bullshit is this—you can't play in two games?"

Occasionally—and it was a landmark event when it actually occurred—Joe would offer bits of advice to teammates while games were in progress. One day, when the Yankees were facing the Tigers in Detroit, Johnny Murphy was summoned from the bullpen to face Hank Greenberg. Yankee pitchers had been in the habit of feeding the slugger mostly curveballs, which he allegedly had difficulty handling. The bullpens were located behind the center field wall, and as Murphy jogged past DiMaggio, the Yankee Clipper suggested that Murphy try throwing Greenberg a fastball for a change. Hoping to stay on Joe's good side, the four-time AL saves leader figured it might not be such a bad idea.

Born and raised in New York, Greenberg came of age in the Bronx. He was originally scouted by the Yankees, but the presence of Lou Gehrig at first base prompted him to sign with the Tigers. Having missed a golden opportunity, he raised his game to another level whenever he faced the Bombers. He fared pretty well over the years, hitting .333 with 53 homers and 179 RBIs in 190 appearances against New York.

Charged with the unenviable task of facing Greenberg with runners in scoring position, Murphy completed his warmups and got to work. Heeding DiMaggio's advice, he delivered a first pitch fastball. It ended up being a critical mistake as Greenberg drilled a long home run that held up as the game-winning shot.

Years later, Henrich described what happened next. "Game's over. We're in the clubhouse. We're down. . . . DiMaggio is about 10 feet from me and about 15 feet up from me is Murphy. DiMaggio stood up and went to Johnny Murphy and he said, 'I want to tell you something. Don't ever listen to another doggone word that I ever say.'"

CASE OF THE PURLOINED BAT

DiMaggio suffered a major scare during his 56-game hitting streak. On June 29, 1941, the Yankees traveled to Washington for a doubleheader against the Senators. Joe had hit in 40 straight games and was poised to break the modern record set by George Sisler in 1922. His double in the opener tied Sisler's mark. In the first inning of the evening game, Tommy Henrich was on his way to the plate when he heard DiMaggio shouting across the diamond. Joe couldn't locate his favorite bat and wondered if Henrich had done something with it.

Joe was very attached to that particular piece of lumber, naming it "Betsy Ann." He had been using it throughout the streak and worried that he might fall into a slump without it. A frantic search turned up nothing. The bat was gone. Forced to hit without "Betsy Ann," DiMaggio flied out. Two innings later, he switched bats and lined out to short. In the seventh inning, Henrich gave Joe his own bat to use. Averting disaster, the Yankee Clipper lined a clean single to left field, claiming Sisler's record for himself. Still, the loss of his favorite bat vexed him.

"Of course the guy had to pick out the best one," Joe told reporters after the game. "I had three of my bats on the ground in front of the dugout but he got the one I wouldn't take money for . . . the bat was just right for me. I liked the feel of it. I hate to lose it."

About a week later, "Betsy Ann" was delivered by courier to the Yankee clubhouse in a plain brown package. Behind the scenes, one of Joe's assistants—a wise-guy named Jimmy "Peanuts" Ceres—had spent five days looking for the bat. As it turned out, the thief had ties to the Newark underworld (which was Jimmy's domain) and also happened to be a braggart. When the thief's identity was revealed, Jimmy paid the guy a visit with one of his associates. Specific details of how they persuaded the man to return Joe's prized bat have never been disclosed.

It was not the last time DiMaggio would be a victim of larceny. All of his World Series rings—with the exception of the 1936 model he habitually wore—were stolen from his suite at the Lexington Hotel during

This is one of many photos taken during DiMaggio's epic 1941 season. His 56-game hitting streak that year has yet to be surpassed. The closest bid came in 1978, when Pete Rose of the Cincinnati Reds hit in 44 straight games.
(COURTESY OF THE LIBRARY OF CONGRESS)

the 1960s. Although they were never recovered in Joe's lifetime, he was presented with replicas on "Joe DiMaggio Day" at Yankee Stadium in 1998. Interestingly, Joe's lawyer and close friend Morris Engelberg showed up at his funeral wearing the 1936 ring. Questioned about it by family members, Engelberg claimed that Joe had promised the valuable trinket to him as he lay dying.

In 2012, a mysterious 1951 World Series ring turned up at auction. The auctioneers couldn't guarantee that the ring had ever actually belonged to Joe but claimed that it had been shown to the Yankee idol by an executive of the Dieges & Clust jewelry company. DiMaggio apparently rejected the design and the executive kept it for himself. It later passed into the possession of the executive's family. Although Joe's name was etched into the ring, questions still remained about its origin. Authentic or not—it carried a price tag of more than $50,000.

In 2013, another championship ring bearing DiMaggio's name surfaced at auction. This one was a 1950 model that was far too small to have been worn by the Yankee Clipper himself. It had apparently been custom made for DiMaggio's son, who would have been nine years old at the time. Joe Jr. allegedly gave it to a friend in exchange for a favor. It sold for more than $16,000.

Incredibly, more DiMaggio memorabilia was stolen in 2016, when a thief walked into the *Ripley's Believe It Or Not!* museum in Times Square, New York, and replaced an autographed bat and ball with fakes. The estimated value of both items was around $5,000.

IF YOU CAN'T KEEP UP, DON'T STEP UP

In the summer of 1941, rarely a day went by when DiMaggio did not receive top billing in the sports pages. But for a few days in late June, a little-known pitcher from the Philadelphia A's stole Joltin' Joe's thunder.

His name was Johnny Babich and he had an axe to grind. A right-handed flamethrower from Albion, California, he had played with the Kansas City Blues (a New York affiliate) in 1939, compiling a handsome 17–6 record with a 2.55 ERA. After a tryout with the Yankees, he was left unsigned. It was something he never forgot.

The journeyman hurler had an issue with DiMaggio as well. Both men had played in the Pacific Coast League during the 1933 slate. They had faced each other in the midst of Joe's record-setting 61-game hitting streak. In the eighth inning of a scoreless tie, DiMaggio had drilled a fastball off the left field wall, driving in the only run of the game and making Babich a loser.

Babich was confident and boastful—like Dizzy Dean without the talent to back it up. He carried a lifetime earned run average of 5.57 entering the 1940 campaign. Yet somehow he managed to dominate the Yankees that season, winning five of six decisions against them. The losses to Babich had a huge impact on the pennant race as the Bombers ultimately finished two games out of first place. With his reputation as a "Yankee Killer" secured, Babich got carried away with himself during DiMaggio's 56-game hitting streak.

Hall of Famer Phil Rizzuto remembered the incident well. "Babich was another Sal Maglie," he told biographer Maury Allen. "He would knock his mother down. He really threw hard and could intimidate a hitter. He announced in the papers three or four days before we played the A's that he would personally stop the streak. He was going to get Joe out the first time and then walk him the next three times."

The media really played up the story, and according to Rizzuto, DiMaggio was quite upset when he read what Babich had said. The anticipated showdown took place on June 28 at Shibe Park in Philadelphia with close to 14,000 fans in attendance—well above average for the A's that season. In the first inning, Joe D. came to the plate with a pair of runners aboard. He worked the count to 3–1 before popping out to shortstop Al Brancato. Phase I of Babich's plan was complete. Now all he had to do was keep the ball out of the strike zone in DiMaggio's next few at-bats.

The Yankee icon returned to the plate as a lead-off hitter in the third inning. By then, the Bombers had built a 3–0 lead. Babich's first two offerings were way outside, but DiMaggio lunged for the second one, driving it straight through the pitcher's legs. One writer remarked, "If Joe had hit the ball a few inches higher, Babich would have been a hurling soprano." Fueled by all the hype, DiMaggio was not content to settle for a mere single. He went tearing around first base without hesitation and slid safely into second. "The whole bench stood up and cheered Joe and laughed at Babich and called him some pretty good names," Rizzuto recalled. DiMaggio later remarked that the hurler appeared mortified.

After absorbing a 7–4 loss on June 28, Babich logged another dreadful outing against the Yankees a week later, allowing six earned runs in one inning of work. DiMaggio tagged him for a single, extending the hitting streak even further. It would prove to be Babich's last season in the big leagues as he posted a 2–7 record with a stratospheric 6.09 ERA.

He continued pitching in the minors through the 1945 campaign and later spent two seasons as a manager, leading the Stockton Ports of the California League to a championship in 1947.

THE GAME THAT ALTERED BASEBALL HISTORY

At the end of play on July 16, 1941, DiMaggio's hitting streak stood at 56 games. The Yankees were sitting in first place with a comfortable lead over the Indians. In the midst of an extensive road trip, the Bombers had beaten the Tribe 10–3 in the opener of a three-game set at Cleveland Stadium.

Joe's streak had become a national sensation, and more than 67,000 people showed up on July 17 to see if he could keep it going. The Indians sent Al Smith to the mound—a veteran left-hander who had appeared in two World Series with the Giants. The Yankees countered with Lefty Gomez, who had compiled a 7–3 record to that point.

In the first inning, Tommy Henrich put the Yankees on the board with an RBI double. With one out and a runner aboard, DiMaggio hit a hard smash to Ken Keltner at third base. Keltner was among the Indians' most reliable RBI men during the 1940s. He was also a superb defensive player, posting the highest fielding percentage among AL third basemen during three seasons. Although he had already made a name for himself in Cleveland, he would gain enduring fame for his performance on this particular evening. Infielder Johnny Sturm, who was in the lineup for the Yankees, described DiMaggio's first plate appearance as follows: "When Joe got up at bat, Keltner went all the way back to the outfield grass. And right close to the line. He wasn't but two or three feet away from the line. And Joe hit a scorcher. . . . It should have been a hit. [Keltner] just nipped him at first base. It was as close as the thinnest piece of paper. The umpire (Joe Rue) could have called it either way."

The Yankees were leading 1–0 in the fourth when DiMaggio came to bat again, drawing a two-out walk. He ended up being stranded when Joe Gordon flew out to center field. In the bottom of the frame, the Indians tied the score on an inside-the-park home run by Gee Walker. The ball fell between DiMaggio and Charlie Keller in the left-center field gap.

The score was still knotted at one when Joltin' Joe made his third trip to the plate.

Recalling DiMaggio's pivotal seventh-inning at-bat, Sturm remarked, "A lot of times, the guys used to say, 'Hell, why doesn't Joe lay a bunt down?' With Keltner playing that far back, he could walk to first base. . . . But Joe never did." Instead, he hit another hot smash to Keltner, who backhanded the ball and threw across the diamond in time to nail DiMaggio by a narrow margin. "He just took two damn good hits away from [Joe]. They should have been doubles," Sturm said. "I would give Keltner a lot of credit for playing the position the way he did."

The Yankees took a 4–1 lead in the top of the eighth on an RBI single by Gomez and a run-scoring double by Red Rolfe. With the bases loaded and DiMaggio coming to the plate, Cleveland manager Roger Peckinpaugh sent right-hander Jim Bagby to the mound. Joe had a chance to extend his streak in grand fashion, but Bagby—who liked to feed hitters a steady diet of lively fastballs—induced a hard grounder to short. The ball took an awkward hop and hit Hall of Fame shortstop Lou Boudreau in the chest, but he stuck with it, starting a 6-4-3 double play. It was the first time in over two months that DiMaggio had gone hitless. A ninth inning Indians rally fell short as the Yankees held on for a 4–3 win.

DiMaggio admitted to reporters that the streak had frayed his nerves. "I'm tickled to death it's all over. I'm sure proud of the record, but I might as well admit it was quite a strain. Naturally, I wanted to keep it going. But as long as I didn't, I'm happy about the whole thing." Later that day, Joe contradicted that statement, telling members of his inner circle that he was upset about the streak having come to an end.

Keltner and his wife received a police escort from the clubhouse to the parking lot after the game. "Joe had a lot of friends in Cleveland and [the authorities] didn't take any chances," the seven-time All-Star later explained. Although several of his teammates played pivotal roles, Keltner would be the man best remembered for stopping DiMaggio's streak. On the 50th anniversary of the landmark event, he said, "I'm glad I'm remembered for something. . . . Whenever I meet somebody, they always get a knowing look when they hear my name. I didn't feel like a villain. Somebody had to do it. I'm glad he hit them to me."

A few weeks later, when the Yankees were in Washington for a series against the Senators, DiMaggio's teammates threw a surprise party for him. As a token of thanks, they gave him a silver humidor from Tiffany's with his name engraved on it.

THE HEAT OF THE MOMENT

The 1941 World Series was the first of 11 October showdowns between the Yankees and Dodgers during the twentieth century. Though the rivalry remained friendly for the most part, things did get heated at times. During Game 5 of the 1941 Fall Classic, DiMaggio was at the center of an unpleasant incident.

The Yanks were leading 2–1 in the fourth inning when right-hander Whit Wyatt walked Joe Gordon on a borderline pitch. Incensed by the call, Dodger skipper Leo Durocher came storming out of the dugout to confront home plate umpire Bill McGowan. Wyatt slammed his glove down and joined the argument, prompting someone from the Yankee bench to throw a "crying towel" onto the field. This angered Durocher even further and he started shouting at New York players. It took several minutes to settle things down. A bit later, when Joe McCarthy came out to dispute a call, another towel went flying onto the field—this one coming from the Brooklyn dugout.

Tommy Henrich's home run in the fifth gave the Yankees a 3–1 lead and set the Dodgers on edge again. DiMaggio came to the plate next and was treated to a couple of brush-back pitches from Wyatt. Joe later claimed that he heard someone shout from the Dodger dugout, "Stick the ball in the bum's ear, Whit!" After flying out to deep center field, DiMaggio said something to Wyatt on his way back to the bench. Wyatt couldn't make out the words, but he took a run at DiMaggio anyway. Joe followed suit as players from both clubs rushed onto the field to break it up. There was some clutching and shoving, but in the end, no punches were thrown. After the Yankees had put the finishing touches on a 3–1 Series-clinching victory, Wyatt came to the Yankee clubhouse to offer his congratulations. Players shook hands with him as he wished them a pleasant winter.

Though DiMaggio became known for his lack of emotion on the field, the incident with Wyatt was not the only confrontation of his professional career. During his first full season with the San Francisco Seals, he allegedly mixed it up with pitcher Roy Joiner of the Oakland Oaks. Joiner was covering home on a play at the plate and DiMaggio slid in hard. After being called out, Joe got fired up by a nasty remark made by Joiner. According to multiple reports, he took a swing at the veteran southpaw but missed. Joiner's aim was much better as he literally knocked DiMaggio down with a single punch. The benches cleared and order was quickly restored, but not before Joiner had landed another blow and jumped on top of the hapless rookie. It would seem that fighting was not Joe's strongest suit.

CLASH OF THE DIMAGGIOS

Vince DiMaggio spent his entire big-league career in the NL. Because there was no interleague play in those days, his only chance to face his brothers outside of exhibitions would have been in a World Series or All-Star Game. Vince never appeared in a Fall Classic, but he did play on two All-Star squads. In 1943, he gathered three hits and scored two runs in a 5–3 National League loss. He made the team again the following year, appearing as a late-inning replacement for outfielder Dixie Walker. Unfortunately, Joe and Dominic were both serving in the armed forces at the time and didn't play in either game.

Although Joe's Army team faced Dom's Navy unit in the 1944 Service World Series, Joe was unable to participate due to illness. The two rival siblings squared off against each other in major-league action many times over the years. Dominic surprised the entire DiMaggio clan when he blazed a trail to stardom. "The rest of us never thought [Dom] would make a ballplayer because he was short and skinny and wore glasses," Joe wrote in his memoirs. "Charley Graham, owner of the Seals, had been accused of signing Dom for publicity reasons, merely because his name was DiMaggio. Charley then quoted [Lefty] O'Doul to the effect that Dom was a far better ballplayer than either Vince or I had been at that stage in our development."

Dominic had a breakout year in 1939, tearing up the Pacific Coast League with a .360 batting average. He also finished among the league leaders in runs, triples, and stolen bases, capturing the PCL MVP Award. Realizing that he could be a tremendous asset, the Red Sox purchased Dominic's contract for a reported sum of $75,000 before the 1940 campaign. Joe and Dom went head to head 17 times that year. Joe excelled as a cleanup man, gathering 21 RBIs. Dominic capably performed his duties at the top of the Boston batting order, hitting .407 to Joe's .373 while scoring 11 runs. Despite his efforts, the Red Sox lost 11 of the 17 matchups.

There were many more duels between the DiMaggios in the decade that followed. Dominic had more hits than Joe and scored a comparable amount of runs. But Joe's home run and RBI totals were far superior. The Yankees won seven pennants and six World Series between 1941 and 1951. The long-suffering Red Sox made just one visit to the Fall Classic in that span, losing to the Cardinals.

Reflecting on the Yankee–Red Sox rivalry many years later, Dominic told a biographer, "I could actually feel it in the air. I thought everyone could. The adrenaline flowed a little faster." During one particular showdown, Joe (who was vying for the AL RBI crown at the time) hammered a long shot to center field with the bases loaded. Dominic made a fine running grab to extinguish the Yankee threat. "Coming into the dugout after the catch, I half glanced at Joe on his way to center field and I could feel daggers flying my way," the younger DiMaggio recalled. "Joe always gave me terrible looks when I did something like that."

Describing what it was like growing up in his older brother's shadow, Dominic remarked to a writer from the *Boston Globe*, "It's been a struggle all my life. I was always Joe's kid brother. I never encouraged my two sons to get into baseball. I knew it would be twice as hard on them as it was on me. The Joe DiMaggio legend was just too strong."

OUT OF CHARACTER

The ultrareserved DiMaggio was never noted for his sense of humor. But Lefty Gomez saw another side of him. "You had to know Joe to really understand his personality," said the Yankee hurler. "He [was] quiet, but he could be a very funny fellow. I liked to needle him . . . and he could take it. He would never get mad, just look at me and say, 'Aw, Lefty.'" During spring training one year, Gomez handed DiMaggio a suitcase and asked him to carry it back to the team's hotel. It was unusually cumbersome and Joe's arm was aching by the time the task was complete. Curious about what was inside, he opened the case to find that Gomez had stuffed a heavy wooden log in there. Joe found the hurler's prank amusing, later sharing it with a writer from the *New York Times*.

Though DiMaggio maintained a sober image, he could be light-hearted in the right company. One day, after a tough loss to the Indians at Cleveland Stadium, Gomez was feeling dejected. The Yankees were scheduled to play Detroit the following day and, in no mood for company, Gomez planned on spending the train ride alone in his cabin. DiMaggio stopped by and invited Gomez to eat with him in the dining car, but the brooding southpaw refused. In an effort to lift his friend's spirits, Joe resorted to an uncharacteristic display of immaturity, putting his thumb and index finger on his nose and plucking it like a musical instrument. "Don't I sound like a banjo?" he joked.

Unaccustomed to such buffoonery from DiMaggio, Gomez burst out laughing. This drew the attention of Joe McCarthy, who was in a nearby compartment. McCarthy ran the team with a heavy hand. One biographer remarked that he "tended to frown on players who laughed too loud or spoke too loud. He thought they were goofballs who didn't pay strict attention to the game as he wanted. McCarthy thought players should linger in the locker room after games to talk baseball." Wondering what the commotion was about, the Yankee skipper whipped open the door to his cabin and barked at Gomez. His comments amused Joe, who started to laugh. At a loss for words, McCarthy ducked back inside his quarters and slammed the door hard enough to shake the train car.

(NOTE: This story, which appeared in Maury Allen's biography *Where Have You Gone Joe DiMaggio?*, contains a few inconsistencies. The outing Gomez described was most likely the second game of a three-game set played in Cleveland during the '39 campaign. The train ride to Detroit would have taken place the following day on the heels of a 5–1 win. It's possible that Gomez was still ruminating over his tough-luck loss on getaway day. Or the incident could have taken place on a different date. Gomez was noted for embellishing his tales to get laughs. Apocryphal or not, DiMaggio's uncommon display of levity makes for interesting reading.)

UNDER SUSPICION

DiMaggio's salary in 1939 was among the highest in the majors at $27,500. After capturing a batting title with a spectacular .381 mark, team executives naturally assumed he would be asking for a raise. During the offseason, rumors circulated that New York's board of directors had secretly met in the absence of GM Ed Barrow and placed a $30,000 cap on DiMaggio's salary. Questioned by reporters, Barrow denied that such a meeting had taken place and took offense to the mere suggestion of it. "The Board has absolutely nothing to do with determining players' salaries," he blustered. "As in previous years, the job is left entirely to me and nobody knows what the club will offer DiMaggio because I haven't mentioned it to a soul." Rumors of a salary cap persisted even after the Yankee Clipper signed a contract for $32,500.

On April 14, DiMaggio wrenched his knee in an exhibition game against the Brooklyn Dodgers. The leg was slow to heal and he remained out of action for several weeks. While recuperating from the injury, New York writers began publishing reports that he had hired boxing manager Joe Gould as his agent. Gould was renowned for representing former heavyweight champion James Braddock, who had upset Max Baer in 1935 and retained the title for two years.

In the early '40s, Commissioner Kenesaw Mountain Landis still presided over major-league affairs. He had been charged with the task of cleaning up baseball after eight members of the Chicago White Sox conspired with gamblers to throw the 1919 World Series. He remained vigilant throughout his tenure, which came to an end when he died in 1944. A former US federal judge, Landis kept a close eye on sports that were associated with gambling. Any ballplayers with ties to boxing or horse racing were subject to heightened scrutiny.

When rumors of Joe's association with Gould reached the commissioner's office, Landis summoned DiMaggio and manager Joe McCarthy to his headquarters in Chicago. The Yankees had their own concerns entering the May 16 meeting. Worried about the consequences of being linked to gambling activities, team executives wanted an assurance from DiMaggio that a portion of his salary was not being channeled to questionable sources.

The commissioner grilled DiMaggio for the better part of an hour. Joe denied allegations that he had entered into a business relationship with Gould, stating unequivocally, "No one has been authorized to act as my agent. My salary never has been and never will be shared by a manager or agent." (The words would ring false years later when Joe enlisted the services of agent Frank Scott.)

When the meeting was concluded, McCarthy informed reporters of what had transpired. "Joe assured the Judge there is nothing to the report. . . . The club is interested only in whether DiMaggio shares his baseball salary with a manager. We are satisfied with the denial. What money he makes from outside sources such as testimonials, pictures, and radio work is his own business."

The 1940 meeting with the commissioner was not DiMaggio's first. Prior to his 1938 salary holdout, Joe had been warned by Landis about forming a partnership with Gould. Both parties denied having formal business ties. DiMaggio was not penalized in either instance because he had done nothing wrong. But Barrow was inclined to remind players via a clubhouse post of the standard clause in all Yankee contracts that prohibited players from endorsing products deemed to be ethically suspect. This included liquor, beer, and any materials associated with smoking.

ANOTHER HOLDOUT

DiMaggio's landmark performance in 1941 cemented his status as the biggest name in baseball. Not only was he designated AL MVP at season's end, but he was selected as Player of the Year by the New York chapter of the Baseball Writers' Association of America. After being honored at the Hotel Commodore in Manhattan, he met with Yankee executives to discuss his contract for the coming season. He could not have picked a worse time to ask for a raise. The country was in turmoil after the attack on Pearl Harbor and Joe's North Beach neighborhood had been declared a restricted zone. Upon hearing DiMaggio's request for more money, Barrow immediately became defensive, reminding Joe of the national emergency and suggesting that he accept a pay cut. The slugger was so flabbergasted, he walked out of Barrow's office without uttering another word.

Shortly after the meeting, Barrow sent Yankee traveling secretary Mark Roth to DiMaggio's hotel with a contract offer matching his salary from the previous year. Joe was immensely disappointed that Barrow would exploit the war angle to avoid a salary hike. And he resigned himself to fight for what he deserved.

When training camp opened in St. Petersburg, Joe was out of uniform and vacationing in nearby Lido Beach. He informed reporters that he had received a second contract offer of $40,000 but was not satisfied. "I phoned Mr. Barrow and told him I would not sign. All things considered, I feel justified in looking for an increase. I do not consider $2,500 a fair raise." He added that his decision to report to camp would hinge upon Barrow's response. DiMaggio was not alone in his defiance. Five other players, including Hall of Famers Bill Dickey, Joe Gordon, and Red Ruffing, had refused salary offers.

On March 12, Barrow arrived in camp and promptly set up a meeting with DiMaggio. By then, four of the other holdouts had come to terms with the Yankees. Hoping to sign DiMaggio in time for the season opener, Barrow agreed to a substantial raise. Years later, DiMaggio remarked of the incident, "Eventually, I signed for $43,750, but while I was battling for it, the Yankee front office put out a lot of propaganda about guys being in the Army for $21 a month, the insinuation being that I was lucky to be playing ball. I don't think anything ever burned me up as much as that did."

THE ENLISTMENT DEBACLE

By the end of the 1942 campaign, DiMaggio's marriage to Dorothy Arnold was on the rocks. Describing the actress' mindset, one biographer remarked, "As far as she was concerned, that year, 1942, proved to her that DiMaggio would never make the grade as a husband. Of course, he would pose for the cameras with the baby, and reporters would talk about how he doted over young Joe and wasn't afraid to change dirty diapers. But as soon as the cameras turned away, DiMaggio left Dorothy to deal with Little Joe whenever he cried or fussed. As far as he was concerned, the baby was her problem, and if the noise got too bad, Joe would leave, complaining that he couldn't concentrate."

Tired of her husband's lack of support, Dorothy took up residence in Reno, Nevada (the divorce capital of the United States), and enlisted the services of a family lawyer. DiMaggio had spent the '42 campaign under 3-A status—a military classification that placed married men with children low on the priority list for the draft. Realizing that a divorce would put him in line for military duty, he traveled to Reno to straighten things out with Dorothy.

In early January, the Yankees announced that they intended to comply with wartime travel restrictions by holding spring training in a northern location. This prompted Prescott Sullivan, a correspondent from the *San Francisco Examiner*, to seek out DiMaggio for an interview. Though he initially planned to write about how the cold weather might affect Joe's training routine, Sullivan stumbled upon something far more interesting. Upon learning that the slugger had followed his wife to Reno, the veteran reporter found out where Joe was staying and contacted him by phone. The interview began with a nonconfrontational question: "What effect is the absence of spring training in Florida likely to have on your play this year?"

Less than pleased about being interrupted while he was sorting out personal matters, DiMaggio responded tersely, "Spring training won't concern me this year."

"You mean you're quitting baseball?" Sullivan inquired.

"I'm not saying. You can draw your own conclusions."

Seeking clarification, Sullivan followed with a series of intrusive questions. "You mean you're going to announce your retirement? Or do you intend to enlist in the Army or Navy? Are you trying to reconcile with your wife?"

"None of your business," Joe snapped. "I'll be back in town in a couple of days. Then I'll tell you what I'm going to do."

The conversation ended there as Joe slammed the phone down.

Precisely as DiMaggio instructed, Sullivan drew his own conclusions, reporting that the slugger intended to join the military and had traveled to Reno to sort out his nuptial issues beforehand. Responding to the media storm that followed, Joe informed the press that he had been misquoted and had no intention of enrolling in the armed forces. He returned to Reno in mid-January and convinced Dorothy to hold off divorce proceedings. His reluctance to enlist had been a source of marital discord and, hoping to smooth things over, he agreed to delay the inevitable no longer. Smiling for photographers, the couple announced that they were back on good terms. "Everything is straightened out," DiMaggio told reporters. "I'm going to try to get into the armed forces as soon as I can get a few things straightened out."

Joe was widely praised for his decision to join the war effort. But a week later, things were up in the air again. In order to be accepted, he had to submit a formal request to have his 3-A status changed to a 1-A classification (meaning he would be eligible to serve immediately). Unfortunately, enlistments in the North Beach area had been temporarily suspended by the Selective Service System. The only way to expedite Joe's petition was by a unanimous vote of local officials. While awaiting a decision, a correspondent from the Associated Press claimed that Joe had again denied his intentions of signing up for military duty. Even Yankee executives were confused at that point. The matter was finally settled on February 16, when North Beach officials approved Joe's application to enlist in the Army Air Force.

ENEMY ALIENS

Prior to World War II, the US government had adhered to a policy of isolationism. In the wake of the Pearl Harbor attack, media-fueled hysteria built to a fever pitch. Feeling the need to neutralize a perceived threat from within, the Roosevelt administration unjustly labeled thousands of Italian, German, and Japanese immigrants "enemy aliens."

More than 120,000 people of Japanese ancestry were uprooted from their homes and placed in internment camps. Germans were not only subjected to relocation, but they were also forbidden to own specific items (such as flashlights, cameras, and radios) that might be used to communicate with Nazi sympathizers. More than 600,000 Italian Americans were forced to deal with travel restrictions and curfews. Joe

DiMaggio's parents were among the many innocent Sicilians who were made to feel like criminals.

By the time the United States officially entered the war, Giuseppe and Rosalie had been living in America for several decades. Because they couldn't read or write enough English to pass the naturalization exam, neither of them had the proper documentation. Aware of their connection to the famous Yankee icon, General John DeWitt of the Western Defense Command considered arresting the couple to make an example of them. But in the end, he decided that other restrictive measures would suffice. Giuseppe and Rosalie were forbidden to visit DiMaggio's Grotto on Fisherman's Wharf. They were required to carry ID papers on them at all times, and if they wished to travel farther than five miles from home, they had to request a permit. Giuseppe's crab boat—a 16-footer named the *Rosalie D.*—was confiscated along with the vessels of more than a thousand Italians operating on the Pacific Coast.

The mistreatment of "enemy aliens" continued until the end of the war and beyond. Even after hostilities ceased overseas, it took several years to dismantle the internment program. The punitive measures taken against Italian Americans didn't sit well with Joltin' Joe. According to Army officials, he exhibited a "conscious attitude of hostility and resistance" toward his military duties. The Yankee slugger felt that the Army was exploiting his All-Star status for the purpose of public relations. He resented having to play in Army baseball games. And though he was repeatedly hospitalized for chronic abdominal pain, no evidence of an ulcer was detected by military doctors. Major William G. Barrett believed that DiMaggio was fabricating the illness to earn a medical discharge. His suspicions were included in an official report. Joe eventually got the release he had been seeking in September 1945.

Rosalie DiMaggio became an official US citizen in 1944. Giuseppe became naturalized the following year. In 2001, the US Department of Justice formally acknowledged the mistreatment of Italian Americans during the war. The California state legislature waited nine more years to issue a formal apology (of sorts). A 2010 resolution sponsored by Democratic senator Joe Simitian officially expressed "deepest regrets" over actions taken by government officials during the enemy alien ordeal.

THE LEAGUE OF ORDINARY GENTLEMEN

The attack on Pearl Harbor prompted dozens of ballplayers to sign up for military duty in the years that followed. As the war continued to escalate overseas, both leagues were steadily drained of talent. By 1944, there were more than 300 players serving in the armed forces and teams were composed primarily of has-beens, wanna-bes, and never-weres.

There were two specific events during World War II that graphically illustrated the lack of talent in the majors. The first one—which involved the St. Louis Browns—occurred in 1944. From 1903 to 1920, the doleful Browns placed no higher than fourth. After a brief period of improvement in the early '20s, they sank back into mediocrity, finishing in fifth place or lower throughout the 1930s.

. . . And then the impossible happened.

With the war in full swing, the long-suffering Browns finally won a pennant. They did it while Joe DiMaggio and all of the other Yankee stars were fulfilling their military obligations. They did it with just one legitimate star of their own on the roster (shortstop Vern Stephens—a three-time American League RBI leader). And they won it by a slender margin. It took a four-game sweep of the Yankees on the last three days of the regular season to outpace the Tigers (who were bereft of talent themselves) by a single game. On the day the Browns clinched, the Yankees had Bud Metheny, Hersh Martin, Oscar Grimes, Mike Garbark, and Mel Queen in the lineup. None of them went on to accomplish anything significant in the majors.

The Browns' Cinderella story ended with a six-game World Series loss to their intracity rivals—the Cardinals. It was the first time that two teams sharing a stadium (Sportsman's Park) squared off in the postseason since 1922, when the Yankees and Giants had locked horns. It was the one and only World Series appearance for the Browns while they were stationed in St. Louis. A subsequent move and name change (to the Baltimore Orioles) brought them three championships during the twentieth century.

While the Browns' pennant-winning effort in '44 is one of the most unusual stories of the World War II era, stranger still is the tale of Pete Gray.

Gray lost his right arm after falling off of a moving farmer's wagon at the age of six. He taught himself to bat left-handed and had a special glove designed for use in the outfield. Determined to play in the majors, he dropped out of high school and joined a semipro team, slowly working his way up the ladder. In 1944, he fashioned a .333 batting average while stealing 68 bases for the Memphis Chicks of the Southern Association. Looking for some players to fill the holes in their depleted lineup, the St. Louis Browns took a chance on Gray the following year.

Explaining his defensive technique, Gray told a biographer, "I'd catch the ball, stick the glove under my stump, roll the ball across my chest and throw it back in. No big deal." Considering the fact that most players with two arms never become adept enough to play professionally, Gray's ability to overcome his handicap was actually a very big deal.

A newsreel referred to Gray as "The Miracle Man," but after joining the Browns, he appeared less than miraculous. Years later, manager Luke Sewell remarked, "[Gray] didn't belong in the major-leagues and he knew he was being exploited. Just a quiet fellow, and he had an inferiority complex. They were trying to get a gate attraction in St. Louis."

Gray was adept at making contact at the plate, striking out just 11 times in 77 games, but he compiled a substandard .218 batting average. His defensive play suffered as well. Teammate Mark Christman claimed that Gray single-handedly cost the Browns the pennant. According to Christman, Gray was too slow in getting the ball back to the infield on routine singles. "[Hitters] could keep on going and wind up at second base. I know that cost us eight or ten ballgames. . . . We finished third, only six games out."

Gray's lackluster performance resulted in his demotion to the minors, where he closed out his career. He had no regrets, stating that he had attained his dream by aspiring to the game's highest level (albeit at a time when skilled players were in short supply). His story became the subject of a 1986 made-for-TV movie titled *A Winner Never Quits*.

SPRINGTIME IN PANAMA

Prior to spring training in 1946, Yankee players were informed that the team would be holding a special series of workouts in Panama.

Complicating matters further, the new owners (Del Webb, Dan Topping, and Larry MacPhail) decided to hold camp in two Florida locations—St. Petersburg and Bradenton. This was not a welcome proposition to many of the veterans returning from wartime duties, who desperately wanted things to return to normal. Realizing that the public was anxious to welcome players home, MacPhail scheduled dozens of exhibition games against minor-league teams from the South and Midwest. *Herald Tribune* writer Red Smith referred to it as MacPhail's "weird Chautauqua tour."

DiMaggio played well in the spring of 1946 but later admitted that the long layoff from major-league action had done him no good and that he was never the same after the war. Statistics don't actually back that statement up as he averaged 28 homers and 116 RBIs per year from 1946 through 1948. He won an MVP Award in 1947.

DiMaggio didn't usually look to others for advice, but upon joining the club in Panama for the winter workouts, he made a point of watching players closely during batting practice. When Joe Trimble of the *Daily News* asked the Yankee Clipper if he was looking for pointers, he gave an affirmative answer, explaining that he was hoping to improve his ability to identify pitches.

Informal batting practice rules stipulated that a player was allowed to keep swinging until three balls were hit into fair territory. DiMaggio followed Tommy Henrich in the order and it took several pitches for him to produce a couple of fair balls. After his second hit, Charlie Keller approached the cage to retrieve a cluster of discarded bats. Joe mistakenly thought his outfield partner was trying to cut his session short and reminded Keller that he still had a hit coming to him. Keller explained that he was just tidying up and playfully bet a bottle of Coca-Cola that he could drive a ball further than DiMaggio's next fair hit. Upon accepting the friendly wager, Joe promptly slammed a pitch over the center field fence, which was about 375 feet from home plate.

Joe sauntered around the back of the cage to watch Keller take his cuts. The Yankee left fielder's second hit was a towering fly that cleared the fence in right field. After producing a grounder with his last swing, he proposed that the contest had ended in a tie. DiMaggio was satisfied with that result.

JOE VISITS A DYING KID

In July 1946, seven-year-old Patty Ciccarelli was stricken with acute leukemia. He grew increasingly ill in the months that followed. Patty's father, who worked for the Department of Parks, took the boy to two different hospitals for blood transfusions and follow-ups. But the prognosis was grim. Leukemia is a type of cancer that affects the production and function of red blood cells. It can cause swollen lymph nodes, bleeding, weight loss, and recurrent infections. Treatment of the disease was still in its infancy during the 1940s and the survival rate beyond a year or two was extremely low.

Patty was a passionate baseball fan, listening to as many games as he could on the radio. In September 1947, the boy's aunt sent a desperate plea to the Yankees. DiMaggio got the message loud and clear, visiting Patty at his home on Needham Avenue in the Bronx. During the visit, Joe gave the terminally ill third grader an autographed bat and ball. Patty was absolutely thrilled with the gifts. According to a report in the *Daily News*, he referred to himself as "the luckiest kid in the world."

Patty lived long enough to celebrate his eighth birthday. A local business owner offered him a television on loan so he could watch the 1947 World Series. "We knew he was dying," said Patty's uncle, "but we were hoping he'd hold out until he could see the Yankees and DiMaggio in the Series. The kid loved baseball." On September 30—the day the Yankees were due to face the Dodgers in Game 1 at Yankee Stadium—Patty slipped into a coma. He died several hours before the game.

The funeral was held at the Church of the Immaculate Conception in the Bronx. The boy was buried in St. Raymond's Cemetery on Lafayette Avenue. The Yankees beat the Dodgers in seven games. DiMaggio had a pretty good Series, scoring four runs and driving in five more.

THE CATCH THAT FLUSTERED DIMAGGIO

There have been a number of unlikely World Series heroes over the years. David Eckstein, Mark Lemke, Brian Doyle—all were mediocre players who enjoyed a few shining moments on the October stage. The 1947 Fall Classic featured one of the most memorable catches in postseason history. But the man who made the play has faded into virtual obscurity.

A product of the Pirates farm system, Al Gionfriddo played his first full major-league season in 1945, when many of the brightest stars were serving in the military. Though he hit at a competent .284 clip in 122 games, there was little room for him after the regulars returned to action. Traded to Brooklyn in 1947, he appeared in 37 games with the Dodgers. He made the postseason roster in spite of his feeble .177 batting average. Used sparingly in the World Series, he appeared as a pinch-hitter and runner. His moment of glory came in Game 6, when he was inserted as a defensive replacement by manager Burt Shotton.

The Dodgers were leading the Yankees 8–5 in the bottom of the sixth when Gionfriddo took over for Eddie Miskis in left field. Considering the fact that Gionfriddo's lifetime fielding percentage was well below the league average, the decision was a questionable one on Shotton's part. But managers didn't use analytics in those days—they relied on hunches. Fortunately for Brooklyn, Shotton's gambit paid off.

Snuffy Stirnweiss drew a one-out walk for the Yankees off of reliever Joe Hatten. After Tommy Henrich popped out to catcher Bruce Edwards, Yogi Berra singled, bringing DiMaggio to the plate. The Yankee Clipper, who was 1-for-3 on the afternoon, drove one of Hatten's offerings into Gionfriddo's territory. Describing the play in detail, John Drebinger of the *New York Times* reported, "Dashing almost blindly to the spot where he thought the ball would land and turning around at the last moment, the twenty-five-year-old gardener, who had been merely tossed as an 'extra' into the deal that shipped Kirby Higbe to the Pirates earlier this year, leaned far over the bullpen railing and, with his gloved hand, collared the ball. It was a breathtaking catch for the third out of the inning. It stunned the proud Bombers and jarred even the usually imperturbable DiMaggio."

Abandoning his stoic persona, Joltin' Joe kicked the dirt in disgust. He was still visibly upset before the seventh inning began according to multiple sources, pacing restlessly in the outfield. Whether or not his hot smash would have cleared the bullpen fence has been a source of endless debate. Gionfriddo was certain that his catch had saved the game. "The ball hit my glove and a split second later I hit the gate," he recalled. "I knew I had it, but I certainly couldn't have said I was going to get it—because how could any guy say he was on the ball all the way on one like that? It certainly would have gone into the bullpen alley for a home run if I hadn't got it."

Multiple writers observed that Gionfriddo's catch was a rather clumsy one. At the direction of coach Clyde Sukeforth, the diminutive outfielder (who stood just 5-foot-6) was playing too shallow and over-shifted to the left. DiMaggio himself told an assembly of reporters after the game, "Don't write this in the paper, but the truth is that if he had been playing me right, he would have made it look easy." Years later, the Yankee icon gave Gionfriddo full credit for making a fine grab. "Some big guys wouldn't have ever made the catch," he said. "A big guy would have backed off and left it to go over the fence. But this little guy—he always had to work harder than anybody else—he never gave up."

Whether or not the ball would have landed in the bullpen will never be definitively determined one way or the other. Associated Press correspondent Frank Eck believed that DiMaggio's drive would have hit the fence for a triple. Biographer David Jones was in agreement, remarking, "Despite the availability of television replays, which clearly show that the ball would not have left the park, numerous historians, including several DiMaggio biographers, have claimed that Gionfriddo's catch robbed DiMaggio of a game-tying home run. At most, the ball would have landed for a double or possibly a triple." Eric Enders furthered that notion in his 2007 book *The Definitive History of the World Series*: "Though most newspaper accounts of the game said the hit would have been a homer, this was merely an example of the halo granted DiMaggio by the New York media . . . Gionfriddo caught the ball two full steps in front of the fence."

Regardless of where the ball would have ended up, Gionfriddo's timely gem helped the Dodgers to an 8–6 win that day. And it endeared him to fans in his hometown. A few days after the Series was over, he was honored on "Al Gionfriddo Day" in Dysart, Pennsylvania. Sadly, he never played another game in the majors. Demoted to the Montreal Royals of the International League in 1948, he continued in the minors until 1956.

DRUNK AND DISORDERLY

DiMaggio had a long association with mobster Jimmy "Peanuts" Ceres, who proved useful to the Yankee idol on many occasions. Joe disliked driving to Florida but preferred to have his own car with him at spring training. And so Jimmy would drive DiMaggio's Cadillac down to St. Petersburg for him. If Joe wanted to wager on horse racing, Jimmy would place the bets to avoid a confrontation with the commissioner. The problem with "Peanuts" was that he could be brusque and ill mannered. When situations arose that required a bit more finesse, Yankee traveling secretary Frank Scott was a better fit for the task.

During spring training in 1948, DiMaggio found himself in a potentially embarrassing situation at the Soreno Hotel. Built in 1923 and expanded a few years later, the 300-room luxury resort was located on the downtown waterfront in St. Petersburg. It served as the spring home of the Yankees for many years. On the night in question, Joe brought a woman back to his room. Her name was Gregg Sherwood—an actress and chorus girl who later landed a handful of minor TV roles. The two had been casually seeing each other for quite some time. For reasons unknown, DiMaggio grew tired of her company on this particular occasion and tossed her out of his room. The jilted showgirl—who happened to be very drunk—began pounding on the door and shouting for Joe to let her back in. Upon receiving a 2 a.m. phone call from the hotel manager, Scott rushed to the slugger's aid, using his considerable powers of persuasion to convince Sherwood that it was time for her to go sleep in her own bed. The incident was kept under wraps and a PR disaster was averted.

Scott's tenure with the Yankees was troubled. Feeling that he was too close to the players, GM George Weiss fired him shortly after the 1950 World Series. Described by a *New York Times* writer as "a short, feisty, impeccably dressed man," he moved on to a career as a New York sports agent, representing many of the city's biggest stars, including Mickey Mantle, Yogi Berra, Duke Snider, and Roy Campanella. DiMaggio retained Scott's services for several decades.

DOWN TO THE WIRE

A foot injury in the spring of 1949 put DiMaggio out of commission for most of the first half. Strong offensive performances from Tommy Henrich, Yogi Berra, and Bobby Brown kept the team in contention without him. By the time Joltin' Joe returned to action in late June, the Yankees had built a four and a half game lead over the second place Athletics.

DiMaggio hit .350 in July and August as the Yankees entered the final stretch on top of the AL standings. But after a sluggish start, the Red Sox turned up the heat. On September 13, Joe McCarthy's resilient BoSox began an 11-game winning streak that put them ahead of the Yankees for the first time all year. Things went south for New York when DiMaggio fell ill with pneumonia. Nursing a precarious one-game lead, Boston had a chance to clinch the pennant with a win at Yankee Stadium on October 1.

The date had been designated "Joe DiMaggio Day" by the Yankees, and although the Yankee Clipper was extremely ill, he somehow found the strength to play. DiMaggio's mother flew in from San Francisco for the game. Mayor William O'Dwyer was on hand for the preliminary ceremonies along with Cardinal Jim Farley. Joe received a wide array of gifts that included two cars, a speed boat (appropriately named *The Yankee Clipper*), and a college scholarship for his son, which was donated by the Italian newspaper *Il Progresso*. He also got 300 gallons of ice cream.

When Rosalie DiMaggio was introduced, she surprised the crowd by walking right past Joe without a word. She went directly to the Red Sox dugout to greet her other son. The two embraced warmly and Dominic came out to stand beside Joe on the field. Joe put his arm around his younger brother, and although it came across as a gesture of affection, multiple sources have suggested that it was the only thing holding the ailing center fielder up at that point. Choking back tears, Joe delivered a speech, referring to his teammates as "the gamest, fightingest bunch of guys who ever lived." He ended the brief address with one of his most famous lines: "I'd like to thank the Good Lord for making me a Yankee."

The visit to Yankee Stadium turned out to be Rosalie's last trip outside of San Francisco. She had contracted cancer and didn't realize it at the time. In a pregame interview, she was asked by a reporter which team she was rooting for. "I'm pulling for both," she answered. "Only I want Dom to win because Joe wins so much."

Joe had originally agreed to play just three innings, but when the Yankees fell behind by a score of 4–0, he refused to come out of the game. Even in his diminished physical state, he managed to double and score off of Red Sox ace Mel Parnell in the fourth. He added a single in the fifth, moving Tommy Henrich to third base. Henrich ended up delivering a decisive run as the Yankees rallied for a 5–4 win, putting them in a first place tie.

DiMaggio played eight full innings against Boston in the regular season finale. Although he failed to score a run or collect an RBI, his teammates picked up the slack, building a 5–0 lead. On the verge of collapsing from exhaustion, Joe went out to his defensive post in the top of the ninth. With a pair of runners aboard, Hall of Famer Bobby Doerr hit a long fly to center field. On any other day, Joe would likely have made the catch. But his wobbly legs buckled underneath him and the ball dropped in for a two-run triple. Realizing that he might hurt the Yankees' chances if he continued to play, he called for a time out and jogged back to the dugout. Casey Stengel replaced him with Gene Woodling as the Yankees hung on for a pennant-clinching 5–3 win.

Over the next fifty years, the Red Sox finished behind the Yankees in the standings more than thirty times, fueling one of the bitterest rivalries in sports.

THE JOE DIMAGGIO SHOW

DiMaggio had a pretty good year in 1949. He signed a $100,000 contract, earned his seventh World Series ring, and became the star of his own radio program. Broadcast weekly on the CBS network, "The Joe DiMaggio Show" ran until March 1950. The introductory sequence featured the popular song "Joltin' Joe DiMaggio," which was recorded shortly after Joe's 56-game hitting streak in 1941. Sung by Betty Bonney with the accompaniment of the Les Brown Orchestra, the catchy little ditty peaked at #16 on the music charts. The lyrics included a number of details about Joe's landmark achievement, including the date he tied George Sisler's modern record and the city in which the streak ended.

Initial reviews of Joe's radio program were positive. A writer from the *Register-Herald* in Pine Plains remarked, "This column recommends it for good listening if you are a baseball follower. . . . DiMaggio has a voice which could, if he desires, bring him in the ranks of top-notch radio sports announcers when his baseball days are over." Unfortunately, ratings weren't high enough and CBS canceled the show after a few months.

When production ceased at CBS, NBC helped DiMaggio reach a wider audience by continuing the series on both radio and television. It aired on Saturday evenings and featured guest appearances by a variety of prominent sports figures. Joe offered commentary on notable happenings around both leagues. There was also a sports quiz featuring Jack Barry, who went on to a successful career as the host of several TV game shows, including *Tic-Tac-Dough*, *Twenty-One*, and *The Jokers Wild*. Adults and children were selected from the studio audience for the quiz and split into two separate teams. Barry "pitched" the questions while DiMaggio served as the "umpire" in a "three inning game" that followed baseball's standard three out format. Winners received wrist watches while runners-up got subscriptions to *Sport* magazine.

The program included weekly visits from prominent sportswriters, who were invited to tell stories about famous athletes. The stories were scripted and dramatized by a cast of actors. Dan Daniel (of the *World Telegram*), Arthur Daley (of the *New York Times*), and Joe Trimble (of the *New York Daily News*) were among the writers to appear. Casey Stengel, Lefty Gomez, and Phil Rizzuto were the subject of stories (along with many other stars).

The show, which was taped in advance to accommodate DiMaggio's busy Yankee schedule, also had a segment in which Joe answered letters mailed in by listeners—primarily children. But once again, the series failed to generate a large following and the entire production (radio included) was scrapped after just one season on NBC.

It was not the end of Joe's career as a television host. Shortly after "The Joe DiMaggio Show" went off the air, he was recruited to star in a syndicated TV sports quiz program called "Joe DiMaggio's Dugout." Broadcast on Channel 4 out of New York City, it was yet another commercial flop, getting pulled after just a few weeks. Joe went on to do pre- and postgame segments during Yankee broadcasts after his retirement.

THE WILLIAMS-DIMAGGIO DEBATE AND THE TRADE THAT NEVER HAPPENED

Every era of baseball history has generated lively discussion regarding which players are superior to others. Christy Mathewson versus Walter Johnson, Babe Ruth versus Ty Cobb, Mickey Mantle versus Willie Mays. These are just a few of the debates that have raged over the years. In the 1940s, no evaluation of Ted Williams' talents would have been complete without throwing DiMaggio's name into the mix.

In his autobiography *My Turn at Bat*, Williams remarked, "Well, there are hitters and there are *hitters*. It is probably my misfortune that I have been and will inevitably be compared to Joe DiMaggio. We were of the same era. We were the top two players in the league." Additionally, both men grew up in California before exporting their talents to the East Coast.

But the similarities more or less ended there.

Joe sought to master every aspect of the game, while Ted's primary focus was hitting. Joe came off as stoic and aloof, strenuously avoiding the spotlight. Ted was animated and boastful, basking in the attention he received. Joe was leery around reporters but habitually polite. He worked hard to maintain his professionalism. Ted was prickly with most members of the press. And he could be downright uncivilized on the ballfield.

During a 1956 game against the Yankees, Williams dropped a wind-blown fly hit by Mickey Mantle in the eleventh inning of a scoreless tie. As Mantle pulled up at second base, the hometown fans treated Williams to a symphony of boos. Minutes later, they applauded when he made a remarkable catch against the left field wall to end the inning. On his way to the dugout, "Teddy Ballgame" spit directly into the standing room–only crowd. He also flipped fans the bird. Because it wasn't the first spitting incident of the season, BoSox owner Tom Yawkey slapped his prized slugger with a $5,000 fine. Questioned about the incident and the fine, Williams blamed reporters for blowing things out of proportion.

While DiMaggio was clearly the more gentlemanly of the two, Williams' contempt for sportswriters was somewhat justified. In 1947, Joe finished well behind Ted in runs scored, homers, RBIs, and batting average. But the MVP Award went to DiMaggio anyway. As it turned out, one sportswriter deliberately failed to place Williams among his top 10 candidates. The egregious oversight gave Joe D. the edge he needed in voting. Recalling the incident years later, Williams explained, "The writer's name was Mel Webb. He was, as far as I'm concerned, a grouchy old guy, a real grump, and we didn't get along. We'd had a big argument early in the year over something he'd written. . . . I didn't realize until much later that he hadn't even put me on his ballot."

It wasn't the only time Williams was arguably robbed of an MVP Award. In 1941, when DiMaggio assembled his celebrated 56-game hitting streak, Williams became the last major-league player to surpass the .400 mark at the plate, finishing at .406. He also had more runs and homers than Joe along with a far superior on-base percentage. But the Yankees won the World Series that year and Ted received significantly fewer votes.

In the ongoing debate over who was a better player, a convincing argument can be made for either candidate. Joe won nine World Series rings and a pair of batting titles. His hitting streak is considered to be an unassailable record. Ted never won a World Series, but he did capture six batting titles and a pair of Triple Crowns. His record-setting 84-game on-base streak in 1949 (which has yet to be surpassed) is comparable to Joe's 1941 achievement, although it receives far less attention.

Williams offered lavish praise for DiMaggio on multiple occasions during his lifetime. In his 1969 memoirs, the Red Sox idol gushed, "[Joe] was a better fielder than I was. A better thrower. Everything he did was stylish. He ran gracefully, he fielded gracefully, he hit with authority and style." In comparison, Joe was sparing in his praise for Williams. He did say that Ted was among the best left-handed hitters he had ever seen, but he also ridiculed Williams' throwing arm and the way he navigated the bases.

The rivalry between the two players came to a head during the 1949 slate, when the Yankees beat the Red Sox at Fenway Park in a tightly pitched game. With the Bombers nursing a 3–2 lead, Williams smashed a deep drive to center field and ended up with a double. After the game was over, Williams was criticized by writers for not stretching the double into a triple. Even DiMaggio was surprised. "When I picked up that ball and then looked up and saw Williams standing on second, I was stunned," he said to reporters. "I thought [for] sure he'd be resting on third."

Williams promptly fired back, snarling at the Boston press corps, "Nobody said anything when Joe DiMaggio failed to reach second base when he hit the top of the left field wall."

Irritated by the statement, Joe ramped up the dialog, calling Williams a "crybaby." When his comment hit the papers, he attempted a bit of damage control. "It looks like somebody is trying to build up a situation that doesn't exist. I don't want to make any more comments because the thing might get snarled up. These things can get awfully mixed up if they are strung out."

DiMaggio's remarks seemed to satisfy the parties involved. But the debate over who was a better ballplayer continued for many years. Though most researchers consider DiMaggio more versatile, Red Sox owner Tom Yawkey gave the edge to Williams. During the 1947 offseason, Yawkey met up with Yankee GM Larry MacPhail for a few drinks. The prospect of trading Williams for DiMaggio came up in discussion. The two parties initially agreed to cut a deal, but as the story goes, MacPhail backed out when Yawkey asked him to balance the trade by including Yogi Berra in the transaction. Williams lasted thirteen more seasons in the majors, while DiMaggio was done within four years. The loss of Berra would have been devastating for the Yanks and could single-handedly have altered the course of Red Sox history.

POPULAR MISCONCEPTIONS

Few players have been idolized to the extent that DiMaggio was during his lifetime. His hitting streak in 1941 captivated millions of Americans and elevated him to folk hero status. From that point forward, his accomplishments on the field were often exaggerated by newsmen and biographers. There are a number of misconceptions that persist even today. Three of the most flagrant are as follows.

FALLACY #1
DIMAGGIO WAS ROBBED OF HUNDREDS OF HOME RUNS DURING HIS CAREER

Many have said that the deep dimensions of Yankee Stadium kept Joe out of the 500 home run club. Although the fabled Bronx venue had a short porch in right field that was friendly to left-handed batters, the alley in left-center field was a vast 460-foot span. One sportswriter remarked, "In the years he played, [DiMaggio] must have hit 300 balls out in that area that were caught as long flies. . . . If [he] had played in Fenway Park, he would have hit 900 homers." This is a gross exaggeration.

Swinging from the right side of the plate, Joe hit 213 home runs on the road during his career. Only 29 of them came at Fenway Park, which is known for its short left field wall (commonly referred to as "The Green Monster"). Keeping in mind that it took Joe 120 games to reach that total, he would have averaged around 19 long balls at Fenway in a full season had he played for the Red Sox—not much more than he would have amassed elsewhere.

Primarily a pull-hitter, DiMaggio was capable of spraying the ball to all fields. His hitting style—which was marked by incredible bat speed—produced far more line drives than towering flyballs. A majority of Joe's extra-base hits landed in the power alleys. Though he won a pair of home run crowns, he exceeded the 40-homer mark only once. During the three seasons in which he was active between 1942 and 1947, he averaged just 22 blasts per year. The accompanying chart shows where he stands in comparison to some of the most renowned sluggers of his day.

	AT BATS PER HOME RUN	SINGLE SEASON HIGH	CAREER TOTAL
Ralph Kiner	14.1	54	369
Ted Williams	14.8	43	521
Jimmie Foxx	15.2	58	534

DiMaggio connecting for one of his 361 lifetime home runs. This particular shot came at Fenway Park in Boston. The slugger lost several seasons to military duty in his prime and would undoubtedly have hit many more during his career.
(COURTESY OF THE LESLIE JONES COLLECTION/BOSTON PUBLIC LIBRARY)

Hank Green-berg	15.7	58	331
Lou Gehrig	16.2	49	493
Mel Ott	18.5	42	511
Joe DiMaggio	18.9	46	361

FALLACY #2

DIMAGGIO WAS THE CONSUMMATE GENTLEMAN ON AND OFF THE FIELD

Time and again, people who knew DiMaggio painted him as a regal figure, praising him for his elegance, style, and grace. But in many ways, those terms did not accurately describe the Yankee icon.

—DiMaggio had countless one-night stands during his lifetime.

—Marilyn Monroe and Dorothy Arnold both accused Joe of "cruelty" when they sought divorces from him. Joe was said to have physically assaulted Marilyn on at least two occasions.

—DiMaggio had a rocky relationship with his son, Joe Jr., who he never seemed to have enough time for. In later years, the two became estranged.

—Joe had ties to organized crime, regularly associating with known mobsters.

—Although he maintained a close relationship with his older sister Marie, DiMaggio distanced himself from his other siblings as the years wore on.

—Joe could be petty and spiteful. He held grudges over perceived slights. Anyone he felt had betrayed his confidence in some way was at least temporarily cast out of his inner circle.

—DiMaggio insisted on being introduced last at Old-Timers' Day games so he could get the loudest ovation. One year, when Mickey Mantle was granted that honor, Joe said that he would never come back to Yankee Stadium. It was Mantle himself who smoothed things over, instructing team officials to announce his name before DiMaggio's from that point forward.

—Joe charged exorbitant prices to sign autographs at memorabilia shows. To avoid paying taxes, he kept a large portion of his earnings off the books.

FALLACY #3
THE YANKEES COULDN'T WIN WITHOUT DIMAGGIO

The prevailing belief among sportswriters and fans from the late '30s into the early '50s was that "when DiMaggio falls, so will the Yankees." But it was a flawed concept. While it's true that Joltin' Joe won more awards, occupied more newspaper space, and built a larger fan base than any of his New York peers, he was actually just one among a plethora of stars. In fact, the Bombers won the pennant during eleven seasons in which DiMaggio missed almost 400 games.

During his 13 active seasons in the majors, DiMaggio was sidelined for six of the Yankees' regular season openers. He missed three more while serving in the military from 1943 through 1945. Although he prided himself on giving 100 percent to the team, something always seemed to go wrong during the early spring.

Whenever Joe was unavailable, the Yankees turned to a number of heavy-hitters to keep the offense going. In addition to Hall of Famers Joe Gordon, Bill Dickey, and Yogi Berra, less heralded greats such as Charlie Keller, Tommy Henrich, and Red Rolfe all carried their weight during Joe's era. Whenever runs were at a premium, the Bombers could rely upon one of the most talented pitching staffs in the majors to shut down the opposition. Yankee hurlers posted the lowest collective ERA in the American League during six of DiMaggio's active seasons.

Putting things in perspective, Keller once told sportswriter Maury Allen, "It makes good reading how everybody depended on [Joe], but that's not how it was. Everybody went out and did his own job and that's why we won. DiMaggio was the best player, but everybody had to contribute to win."

A TOUGH CUSTOMER

DiMaggio was a firm believer in the popular maxim, "never let them see you sweat." During his rookie year in New York, GM Ed Barrow began to worry that all the media attention would negatively impact Joe's performance on the field. Looking to reassure the 21-year-old slugger, Barrow took him aside and advised him not to let the bright lights of New York rattle him. DiMaggio famously responded, "Don't worry, Mr. Barrow—I never get excited."

Describing DiMaggio's inscrutable persona, teammate Bobby Brown remarked, "You never could tell what Joe was thinking. He was the same whether he hit a home run or whether he popped up. Nothing changed. He didn't have an expression on his face of great dismay, nor would he have an expression on his face that he was exulting." Brown's statement held true when it came to injuries. Joe had an extremely high tolerance for pain and was one of the toughest players of his era.

During a game against the Red Sox, DiMaggio was facing hard-throwing right-hander Tex Hughson, who had no qualms about throwing inside on batters. Hughson hit Joe squarely in the stomach with a high velocity fastball. In the Boston dugout, manager Joe McCarthy said to his players, "Watch him. He won't even rub [it]." True to McCarthy's words, Joe tossed his bat aside in a casual gesture of disgust and walked slowly to first base with an impassive look on his face. He never rubbed the wound. And he refused to come out of the ballgame.

Yankee infielder Jerry Coleman recalled another incident in which DiMaggio was irritated by something that happened on the field. He came into the dugout and kicked what he assumed was an empty equipment bag. Little did he know it was full of baseballs. Though he was obviously in a great deal of pain, he refused to give any indication of it. "We all went, 'ooh!'" Coleman recalled. "It really hurt. He sat down and the sweat popped out on his forehead and he clenched his fists without ever saying a word. Everybody wanted to howl, but he was a god. You didn't laugh at gods."

Joe's high pain threshold was evident throughout his career. He played with torn cartilage, bone spurs, nagging stomach issues, and deterioration of his back and shoulders. He won an MVP Award during a season in which he underwent multiple surgeries. "He didn't show any pressure," said teammate Tommy Henrich. "From what I knew of Joe, he wasn't built that way. He never let us in on his inner thoughts or anything. He never said anything. . . . He was a tough guy on the ballfield."

THE FARTHEST APPLE FROM THE TREE

Things were never easy for DiMaggio's son. Being the only child of one of the most famous athletes in the world came with enormous expectations. Many have said that the odds were stacked against Little Joe from the very beginning.

Joseph Paul DiMaggio Jr. came into the world in October 1941—shortly after the Yankees had clinched a World Series victory over the Dodgers. Though he was well provided for during his childhood, his parents split before his third birthday and he became a source of conflict between the two after the divorce. His mother was trying to put her life back together and his father was too busy to spend quality time with him. Feeling neglected and abandoned, he came of age in summer camps and boarding schools, struggling (and ultimately failing) to maintain his dad's full attention. He grew close to Marilyn Monroe, who was sweet and caring, but his father's unbridled jealousy drove her away.

Joe Jr. tried to make something of himself by enrolling at Yale University. He played football there because baseball would have drawn obvious comparisons to his dad. Unable to cut it on an academic level, he dropped out and joined the Marines. Military culture didn't suit him at all and he returned to civilian life.

Little Joe's uncle Dom set him up with a factory job after he left the military. He was offered a room in his uncle's home but elected to sleep on a cot in the factory instead. He performed well enough at the new job to earn a promotion. Assigned to Baltimore to oversee the startup of a new plant, things took an unfortunate turn when the facility burned to the ground.

Following his parents' example, Joe Jr. married a woman in Baltimore and divorced her—not before adopting her two children. In the years after the marriage ended, he became estranged from them. Joe Sr., on the other hand, continued to treat them like blood relatives, devoting more time to them than he ever had to his own son.

Unable to get his life on track, Little Joe lapsed into alcohol and drug abuse. Damaging the relationship with his father even further, he did a radio interview with Larry King, sharing some revelations about what it was like growing up in the Yankee Clipper's shadow. Though Big Joe was appalled, he continued to offer periodic help and support. At one point, he bought a Peterbilt truck so Joe Jr. could enter the long-hauling business. The vehicle ended up being totaled in a wreck. There were other jobs too, but Little Joe always managed to screw them up.

As the years wore on, Joe Jr. drifted from place to place. In the later stages of his life, he took a job in a junkyard and lived in a trailer. When his dad died in March 1999, he inherited a trust fund worth $20,000 a year. His adopted children, who wanted nothing to do with him by then, received a majority of the remaining estate. Less than six months after his father's passing, Little Joe died from an overdose of methamphetamines, heroin, and crack cocaine—the final chapter of a long-running tragedy.

THE PLAYER REVOLT OF 1947

Many sources have hailed executive Larry MacPhail as a baseball genius. But his glaring personality deficits interfered with his ability to handle the teams he was put in charge of. To his credit, he helped build multiple baseball dynasties, beat cancer twice, and survived a heart attack. On the negative side, he was consumed by ego, greed, and an almost maniacal desire to control the people around him.

After assembling the pennant-winning Dodger squad of 1941, MacPhail obtained a minority share of the Yankees and took over as team president. In 1946, he demonstrated that he was a difficult man to work for when three managers resigned on his watch. In the wake of a public feud with Dodger executives the following spring, he provoked a revolt among Yankee players.

Prior to the start of the 1947 campaign, MacPhail had tried to ship DiMaggio to Washington in exchange for first baseman Mickey Vernon. Adding insult to injury, he had engaged in informal discussions with the Red Sox regarding a possible DiMaggio/Ted Williams swap. When Joe learned that his name was being tossed around in trade talks, he was extremely unhappy.

MacPhail kept players busy in 1947 with a variety of promotional activities. Commenting on the Yankee president's over-the-top marketing strategies, Red Smith of the *Herald Tribune* cheekily wrote, "The Yankees upstairs office is promotion-happy. A seal that can play Beethoven's Fifth on an oboe is more beautiful to L.S. MacPhail than a 20-game pitcher."

At the same time, MacPhail was trying to change the team's preferred method of travel from trains to planes. A number of Yankee players were uncomfortable with flying, but MacPhail pressured them to do so by suggesting that they pay for train fare out of their own pockets. Tommy Henrich, Spud Chandler, and Allie Reynolds were among a group of dissenters who opted to commute by rail during a western road trip in early May.

Displeased with the direction the team was headed and fed up with MacPhail's endless promotional schemes, DiMaggio refused to pose for Army Signal Corps newsreel shots, which the Yankee co-owner had arranged as a favor to one of his military buddies. Several of Joe's team-mates followed suit, including Charlie Keller, Johnny Lindell, and Aaron Robinson. Inspired by the gesture, rookie pitcher Don Johnson skipped out on a dinner appearance MacPhail had scheduled for him. Hoping to stifle any further upheaval, MacPhail issued fines to each player with the heaviest penalty imposed upon DiMaggio.

Skewered by the New York press for his actions, MacPhail tried to talk his way back into their good graces. He denied that Johnson had been sanctioned and hinted that, because the team was not in the habit of collecting fines until season's end, the situation might be resolved by then. In regard to the travel issue, he asserted, "I have never told any player that he could not take the train if he wanted to. No player ever has had to pay his own way and none ever will be required to by this club. . . . The Yankee management has a contract with United Airlines which expires on July 7. Until then, those who desire to fly, can. After that, everyone goes by train. But there will be no penalty against anyone refusing to fly."

MacPhail ultimately rescinded the fines levied against the men who had refused to participate in the newsreel promotion. But his meddling ways united players in their contempt for him.

FAREWELL TO THE BABE

On August 16, 1948, Babe Ruth died of nasopharyngeal cancer. He had been battling the disease for nearly two years. Paying tribute to the man who had helped put the Yankees on the map, a writer from the *New York Times* remarked, "A born showman off the field and a marvelous performer on it, [Ruth] had an amazing flair for doing the spectacular at the most dramatic moment."

Ruth's body lay in state in the rotunda at Yankee Stadium for two days. It was estimated that roughly 80 to 100,000 people came to view the casket, patiently waiting in a line that stretched for several city blocks. American League president Will Harridge and baseball commissioner Happy Chandler were among the dignitaries who paid their respects. Former Tigers slugger Hank Greenberg and New York Giants manager Leo Durocher also made appearances.

More than 75,000 people gathered in the area around St. Patrick's Cathedral on August 19 to say their final goodbyes to the fallen Yankee hero. Thousands more stood in the rain along the funeral procession route. DiMaggio was chosen as an honorary pallbearer while the rest of the team remained in Washington. In a statement to the press, Joltin' Joe asserted, "The Babe must have been more than just a great ballplayer to have so many people think so much of him."

As soon as the services were finished, DiMaggio rushed to the airport to catch a plane to the nation's capital. Team officials had called ahead and the flight was delayed for ten minutes to accommodate Joe's arrival. A pitifully small crowd of less than 5,000 had turned up at Griffith Stadium on a Thursday afternoon to see the Senators take on the Yankees. The game was already in progress when Joe arrived. In his absence, Cliff Mapes had been assigned to center field and placed in the cleanup slot in the batting order. The Yankees were trailing 1–0 by the time DiMaggio logged his first at-bat of the afternoon. He lined a single to center field off of Hall of Famer Early Wynn. Although he was forced out at second base, his presence ignited a six-run Yankee outburst. Allie Reynolds, Snuffy Stirnweiss, Bobby Brown, and Tommy Henrich all collected RBIs in the inning as the Yankee went on to win 8–1.

YANKEE STALKER

While recovering from an injury at the beginning of the 1949 campaign, DiMaggio began receiving love notes from a woman he was not acquainted with. At the same time, letters started turning up at the offices of various New York gossip columnists. They were signed by a woman calling herself "Junior Standish," who claimed to be in a romantic relationship with the Yankee slugger. DiMaggio was familiar with a Broadway dancer of the same name, but had never actually dated her. When a handful of columnists reported that the two had become a couple, DiMaggio and Standish both made public statements to the contrary.

The plot thickened when the mysterious letter writer attempted to make contact with DiMaggio at his hotel. After being turned away, she sent a note threatening suicide if her efforts to meet him were thwarted in the future. Alarmed by this turn of events, Yankee PR man Arthur

"Red" Patterson contacted the police and enlisted the help of a bodyguard to protect Joe.

While police were investigating the matter, another note containing suicidal threats was delivered to DiMaggio's hotel room. Hoping to produce some tangible leads regarding the author's identity, details were leaked to the press. A 30-year-old woman was eventually taken into custody. While being interrogated by the assistant district attorney in Manhattan, she suffered a mental breakdown, screaming hysterically and threatening to kill herself. Police transported her to a Bronx hospital for psychiatric evaluation. Doctors agreed to release her into the custody of her father on the condition that she seek counseling and leave DiMaggio alone. She agreed to the arrangement and never bothered Joe again. Her identity was not disclosed to the press.

Incidents of a darker nature had plagued major-league baseball on prior occasions. A few weeks before DiMaggio's stalker was taken into custody, a 19-year-old office worker named Ruth Steinhagen shot Phillies' first baseman Eddie Waitkus in a Chicago hotel room. The troubled teen, who had developed an unhealthy obsession with Waitkus, ended up in a state psychiatric hospital, where she remained for three years. Waitkus recovered and played six more seasons. A similar scene had unfolded in 1932, when Cubs shortstop Billy Jurges was shot at the Carlos Hotel in Chicago by a showgirl named Violet Popovich. Jurges had broken off a casual relationship with Popovich, prompting her to behave irrationally. The infielder was shot twice—once in the hand and again in the ribs—but returned to action that year. He played in the majors until 1948.

BULLET BOB VERSUS JOLTIN' JOE

Even the greatest pitchers in history had difficulty handling DiMaggio. The Yankee Clipper compiled a cumulative .358 lifetime batting average against Hall of Famers Lefty Grove and Ted Lyons. His ongoing success against Indians' ace Bob Feller was one of the biggest stories of the era.

A teenage phenom with an explosive fastball, Feller ascended to the majors without a shred of minor-league experience in 1936. In his first assignment against the Yankees, he retired DiMaggio on a flyball to left field. But the outs did not come easily after that.

In his next appearance against the Bombers, which took place in July 1937, Feller lost by a score of 5–1. In spite of all the hype surrounding him, multiple Yankee players commented that he should be sent to the minors for more conditioning. DiMaggio, who raked Feller for a double, triple, and home run that afternoon, told a writer from the *New York Sun*, "There are several pitchers in the AL who have showed me more speed than Feller did today. Tommy Bridges of the Tigers for one. Jack Wilson of the Red Sox is another." Upon reading the article, Feller vowed to prove his detractors wrong.

Over the next several seasons, "Bullet Bob" lived up to his billing, becoming one of the premier strikeout artists in the majors. An eight-time All-Star and 20-game winner on six occasions, he hit his peak in 1940, capturing a Triple Crown with 27 wins, a 2.61 earned run average, and 261 punch-outs. He established a modern record (since broken) in 1938 with 18 K's in a game against the Tigers. Even DiMaggio changed his tune, commenting to a writer from the *New York Times*, "I don't think anyone is ever going to throw a ball faster than [Feller] does. And his curveball isn't human." In spite of all his success, the right-handed flame-thrower continued to struggle against the Yankees.

Over the course of his Hall of Fame career, Feller faced the Bombers 79 times, compiling a lackluster 30–37 record with a 4.00 ERA (which was nearly a full point above his lifetime average). While writers of the era produced volumes of copy about the alleged rivalry between Feller and DiMaggio, Joltin' Joe punished the Indians' ace for a .342 batting average with 11 homers. Cleveland catcher Jim Hegan vividly recalled Feller's inability to subdue the Yankee slugger. "Feller tried everything against him—high, low, inside, outside, curve, fast ball. Nothing helped. He just could hit everything that Bob threw up to the plate." One day, Feller tried throwing a change-up, but it proved to be a mistake as DiMaggio deposited it into the upper deck.

Many years after his retirement, Feller said that he actually enjoyed the confrontations with DiMaggio. "I think after awhile the fans and the sportswriters made more of a rivalry out of it than Joe and I did," the hurler said. "I had to get out a lot of other good hitters to beat the

Yankees and he couldn't beat me by himself either. It got so it was more or less like a circus when we faced each other."

While DiMaggio often feasted on "Rapid Robert's" offerings, he had a miserable time hitting against Feller's longtime staff mate Mel Harder. A soft-spoken right-hander from rural Nebraska, Harder made his big-league debut in 1928. He stuck around for 19 more seasons—all of them spent with Cleveland. Harder won no fewer than 15 games in eight consecutive campaigns, making four All-Star appearances in that span. He retired with 223 career wins—second to Feller on the all-time franchise list.

In his prime, Harder had four effective pitches: a curve, sinking fastball, slider, and change-up. In later years, he was immensely proud of the fact that DiMaggio had cited him as one of the toughest pitchers he ever faced. Harder said that he never used a particular pattern against the Yankee idol. He made his selections based on the count, relying primarily on his sinker as an out-pitch. "When I think about it, I really don't know why Joe didn't do better against me," Harder remarked humbly. "Maybe I got him out the first time and he couldn't believe it. He probably figured he should be creaming me with the stuff I had." In 91 encounters, Harder held DiMaggio to a .229 average without a single homer. He was the only pitcher in history to strike Joe out three times in a single game.

TOURING THE FAR EAST

DiMaggio visited Asia on multiple occasions during his lifetime. At the end of the 1950 campaign, San Francisco Seals manager Lefty O'Doul convinced the Yankee Clipper to accompany a team of major-league players on an exhibition tour of Korea and Japan. With the Korean Conflict in full swing, Joe mingled with US soldiers and officers near the battlefront before participating in games against All-Star teams from both countries. One of the highlights of the tour was a home run contest between DiMaggio and Japanese slugger Makoto Kuzuru.

Known as the "Babe Ruth of Japan," Kuzuru played fifteen seasons of professional ball, gathering 230 career home runs. His best season came in 1950, when he slammed 51 homers and drove in 161 runs for the

Shochiku Robins. He was the first player in Nippon Pro Baseball history to reach the 50-homer plateau.

The contest between DiMaggio and Kuzuru took place over the course of several days. Joe didn't bring any bats and was forced to use the ones provided by his hosts, which were shorter, lighter, and made of softer wood. He said that they felt like "Italian sausages" in his hands. The bats definitely made a difference as Kuzuru bested DiMaggio in three consecutive rounds. Finally, on the fourth day, Joe was able to acquire a Louisville Slugger that O'Doul had left behind on a previous tour. Comfortable with the new lumber, he outslugged Kuzuru for the remainder of the contest.

DiMaggio returned to Korea and Japan with O'Doul's All-Star squad the following year. Yogi Berra and Eddie Lopat were also on the team. Japanese fans had voted for the player they most wanted to see beforehand, and Joe came out on top. Upon arriving in Tokyo, city officials threw the major leaguers a ticker tape parade. Millions of people were lined up along the Ginza—the street that runs through Tokyo's central shopping district. DiMaggio remembered the parade being chaotic and frightening as unruly spectators kept jumping on the hood of his car in an effort to get photos of him. The vehicle had to be stopped several times to avoid running over pedestrians. According to the *Baseball-Reference* website, the US All-Stars compiled a record of 13-1-2 during the 1951 tour. Joe reportedly left early to wrap up affairs with the Yankees at home. He returned to the Far East with O'Doul and Marilyn Monroe three years later.

The 1954 visit was a honeymoon of sorts for Joe and Marilyn. Although they were both received warmly, reporters seemed far more interested in Monroe. A mob of admirers hoping to get a glimpse of the "Honorable Buttocks-Swinging Madam" (as she was referred to by the Japanese press) broke the revolving doors at the Imperial Hotel where Joe and Marilyn were staying. Refusing to be kept out, they smashed through plate glass windows and circled the hotel, shouting Monroe's name. At a scheduled press conference, one journalist (utilizing an interpreter) came at her with a series of inappropriate questions.

REPORTER: Do you agree with the 1948 Kinsey report on human sexual behavior?

MONROE: Not fully.

REPORTER: Do you sleep naked?

MONROE: No comment.

REPORTER: When you walk, is it a natural walk?

MONROE: I've been walking since I was six months old and haven't stopped yet.

REPORTER: What kind of fur are you wearing right now?

MONROE: Fox—and not the 20th Century kind.

REPORTER: Do you wear underclothes?

MONROE (appearing irritated): I'm planning to buy a kimono tomorrow.

THE STAND-UP COMEDY OF LEFTY GOMEZ

The Yankees have always demanded professionalism. Under Miller Huggins and Joe McCarthy, players were expected to refine their behavior both on and off the field. DiMaggio fit the mold perfectly. He was disciplined, sober, and emotionally reserved. But he enjoyed a good laugh once in a while. "On a ballclub which approached baseball in as business-like a manner as the Yankees, Lefty [Gomez] was just the touch of comic relief needed," the slugger once declared.

DiMaggio roomed with Gomez during his days in New York, and although they had distinctly different personalities (Lefty was the joker while Joe almost always played the straight man), they developed a lasting friendship. Known for his self-deprecating humor, Gomez was a dominant pitcher in his prime. When injuries affected his explosive fastball, he developed a slow curve to compensate for the loss of velocity. A perennial fan favorite, he was named to every American League All-Star team from 1933 through 1939.

Some of Gomez's most memorable lines were completely improvised. With runners on the corners one afternoon, the colorful southpaw mishandled a one-hopper hit back to the mound. Instead of throwing to the plate, he made a late toss to Tony Lazzeri at second base. Puzzled by the play, Lazzeri asked Gomez why he had done it. "I've been reading in the papers about what a smart player you are," the hurler quipped. "I figured you'd think of something."

Though Lou Gehrig left the Yankees in 1939, he continued to visit the clubhouse periodically. Even in his weakened physical state, he was cheered by Gomez's humor. Players of the era would rub bones against the barrels of their bats to harden the wood for more solid contact. During one of Gehrig's visits, Lefty held up a bone and said to the fading Yankee icon, "Hey Lou! You think those doctors were hard on you? Take a look at what they just pulled out of my left elbow." Gehrig reportedly got a kick out of the joke.

One of DiMaggio's favorite Gomez stories involved slugger Jimmie Foxx of the Red Sox. During a particularly frustrating stretch, the Yankee hurler thought he might solve his pitching woes by wearing glasses on the mound. One day, after Foxx had stepped into the batter's box, Gomez took the glasses off and put them in his pocket. Between innings, DiMaggio asked the hurler if the spectacles were impairing his vision. "I could see with them all too well," Lefty assured Joe. "I happened to look at the plate and there was Jimmie Foxx at bat. He looked as big as a house. If I'd known he was that big I'd have stopped pitching years ago."

LASHING OUT AT THE PRESS

In DiMaggio's final season as a player, he suffered from a variety of ailments and missed over a month of action. Clearly not the player he once was, he compiled the lowest single-season batting average of his career. During one unproductive stretch from late June to early July, he went 9-for-42 at the plate with 6 strikeouts (nearly half of his total from the entire 1941 season). The beat writers who had helped him become a New York legend began criticizing him harshly.

Before the season was underway, Joe had told reporters that it would likely be his last. Joe Trimble of the *New York Daily News* explained the situation in the following words: "Joe, like every other big-league star, yearns for just one more good year. He hopes this will be it so he can step aside and be remembered at his best. He has another purpose, too. The name DiMaggio has commercial value, and he doesn't want to cheapen it. The big Yank would like to carve a career in radio and television when he's through as a player. He'll hurt his chances if he hangs on until he's a joke afield and at bat."

In the middle of a 10–4 loss to the BoSox that bounced the Yankees out of first place, Yankee manager Casey Stengel removed Joe from the game. Joe was highly embarrassed, snarling at reporters afterward, "There's nothing wrong with my legs or anything else. I was taken out and if you want to know anymore about it, see Stengel." They already had. Before the game, Stengel had informed members of the press, "Four or five of these players are dead tired. I'd like to take them out. Good thing they are getting a vacation next week. I hope they'll come back fresh."

Things remained unsettled between DiMaggio and Stengel in the weeks that followed, prompting columnist Milton Gross of the *New York Post* to comment nastily, "I did recognize a profound difference in the personal climate which surrounds DiMaggio and the Yankees this season. It is a frigid one, all because Joe, who always was a strange man, difficult to understand, is now living in a shell that is virtually impenetrable." Joe had no immediate response, but his brother did. Acting completely out of character, Dominic angrily chastised New York writers, complaining that Joe was being skewered without legitimate cause.

On August 9, Joe blasted a triple and a homer against the Senators, helping the Yankees to a 6–4 win. After the game, he struck back at the reporters who had been denigrating him periodically throughout the season. "You're darn right that I wanted to make you writers look bad," he said. "I'll always try to make you look bad. Just because I have a bad day, you guys want to fire me. Some of you guys are the ones who had me washed up in 1946. But here I am, five years later. How are you going to explain the hits I made today? Are you going to fire me every time I have a bad day?"

There were plenty of bad days to come. During the next home series versus Washington, he gathered just 3 hits in 13 plate appearances. He followed with a 1-for-9 effort in a two-game set against the last place Browns. By season's end, he had failed to lead the Yankees in a single statistical category.

THE CHILL OF OCTOBER

In 1985, Yankee owner George Steinbrenner made an infamously nasty remark about slugger Dave Winfield, telling members of the press, "I let Mr. October [Reggie Jackson] get away and I got Mr. May, Dave Winfield. He gets his numbers when it doesn't count." Though the same could not be said of DiMaggio, the World Series was not always the Yankee Clipper's finest venue. He played in ten Fall Classics during his career and exceeded the .300 mark at the plate in only four of them. Some of his October outings were especially forgettable. In 1951, he went hitless in 12 consecutive at-bats against the Giants. In 1941, he waited until Game 3 to record his first base hit of the Series. His performance in 1949 was the worst by far.

It was a rough regular season for DiMaggio as he was sidelined with foot issues until the end of June. Although he made his 11th consecutive All-Star appearance, it was the first time in his career that he was not actually voted in. Lou Boudreau, manager of the American League squad, added Joe to the roster by special appointment. Near the end of the season, the Yankee slugger contracted a case of pneumonia. He was in rough shape by the time the third installment of the Yankee-Dodger postseason rivalry unfolded.

Coming off one of the closest pennant races in team history, the Yankees appeared to be a team of destiny. "Stengel prepared us for the 1949 World Series quite simply," recalled outfielder Gene Woodling. "He said, 'Go get 'em.'" The Series opened at Yankee Stadium and featured a tight pitching duel between Don Newcombe and Allie Reynolds. DiMaggio was stifled by Newcombe's offerings throughout, failing to hit the ball beyond the infield. He was due to bat in the ninth when Tommy Henrich delivered a walk-off homer, giving the Yanks a 1–0 win.

Facing left-hander Preacher Roe in Game 2, DiMaggio stranded a runner with a flyball out in the first inning. He followed with a strikeout and a groundout before reaching safely on an infield single in the bottom of the ninth. His teammates failed to drive him home as Brooklyn evened the Series with a 1–0 win.

DiMaggio's weak hitting continued in Game 3 at Ebbets Field. Facing right-hander Ralph Branca—who would famously yield a pennant-clinching home run to Bobby Thomson of the Giants a couple of years later—DiMaggio contributed virtually nothing to the Yankee cause. He did, however, pad Branca's strikeout totals with a pair of whiffs. His 0-for-4 showing dropped his cumulative Series average to .091.

Game 4 pitted Newcombe against junk ball artist Eddie Lopat. DiMaggio faced three different Brooklyn pitchers that day, failing to hit safely off of any of them. He did draw a pair of walks though, one of which was intentional in spite of his ongoing October slump. The intentional pass came with runners on second and third and no outs in the top of the fifth. Bobby Brown followed with a bases clearing triple as the Yankees prevailed 6–4. DiMaggio's run was his first of the Series.

Entering Game 5 with a miniscule .071 batting average, DiMaggio finally snapped out of his funk. In the first inning, he picked up an RBI on a sacrifice fly. After a lineout in the top of the third, he cracked a solo homer to deep left field off of reliever Jack Banta. It gave the Yankees a comfortable 6–1 lead. By the time the Bombers clinched with a 10–6 win, DiMaggio's cumulative batting average stood at a meager .111.

THE RIFT BETWEEN JOE AND TOOTS

During DiMaggio's heyday with the Yankees, one of his favorite nighttime hangouts was Toots Shor's. Originally located on West 51st Street, the popular eatery attracted a variety of celebrities. Heavyweight champion James Braddock, Pulitzer Prize–winning novelist Ernest Hemingway, and actor Jackie Gleason were among the many stars who frequented the place. On one particular evening during the 1940s, Bing Crosby, Babe Ruth, and boxer Jack Dempsey (a very odd pairing to say the least) received a round of applause as they moved from the restaurant's circular bar to the dining room, where they shared a meal together.

The establishment's namesake—Bernard "Toots" Shor—grew up in a tough Philadelphia neighborhood. His mother was struck and killed by a car when he was 15. His father committed suicide a few years later. Toots attended college and business school before taking a job as a traveling clothing salesman. A big man with a lively personality, he worked as a bouncer at several New York City nightspots before opening his own restaurant in 1940.

Although Toots was accommodating to celebrities, he had no qualms about mouthing off to them. One night, when Louis Burt Mayer—cofounder of MGM Studios—complained about having to wait too long for a table, Toots assured him that the food would be of much better quality than some of the "lousy" MGM pictures he had stood in line for. There was an unspoken code of etiquette in the restaurant. Wives were not especially welcome, but neither were married men accompanied by mistresses. Suit jackets and ties were mandatory. Toots habitually referred to his friends as "crumb bums," while people he didn't care for were known as "pieces of raisin cake." According to Toots, the menu was "nuttin' fancy." It offered standard American fare such as lobster, shrimp, and steak entrees served with sides of green vegetables and potatoes.

Toots took an instant liking to DiMaggio, who he considered one of the most prominent figures in sports. Toots kept a table reserved for Joe in the front corner of the dining area. The Yankee idol would sit with his back to the wall so he could keep an eye on everyone who entered. No one ate at his table without an invitation, and members of the wait-staff went out of their way to keep unwanted guests at a comfortable distance. DiMaggio wasn't much of a drinker and would mostly just sip coffee all night.

Toots once assembled a group of All-Stars to play against another team representing the famous 21 Club. Toots' squad included DiMaggio and Carl Hubbell along with boxing greats Rocky Marciano and Joe Louis. The exhibition, which took place at the Polo Grounds, was won handily by Shor's team.

Over time, the relationship between Joe and Toots turned sour. There are competing theories as to how this came about. Multiple sources claim it was because Toots called Marilyn Monroe a "whore" in a private conversation with Joe. Others have contended that he insulted Marilyn right to her face. A less popular hypothesis alleges that the falling out was caused by Joe's failure to show up at a charity dinner Shor had invited him to. There is no disputing the fact that Joe became chillier toward Toots after he began paying special attention to Mickey Mantle. When Mantle first joined the Yankees in '51, *Look* magazine published a story about Joe's personal life. It included quotes that DiMaggio believed could only have come from Shor. Joe, who valued privacy over all other things, was immensely displeased. According to a number of reports, Toots eventually told DiMaggio that he was no longer welcome in his establishment.

Whatever the cause of the rift, DiMaggio carried a grudge against Shor into his twilight years. In the 1970s, after Toots had lost his restaurant and suffered a stroke, Mantle, Whitey Ford, and Yogi Berra sent money to him. Joe refused to contribute. When Toots paid a surprise visit to the Yankee clubhouse during an Old-Timers' Day celebration, he was warmly welcomed by a majority of the players in attendance. DiMaggio, on the other hand, retreated to the trainer's room when he saw Toots hobbling across the room with the use of canes.

In 1971, Shor landed himself in hot water for tax evasion, and his restaurant (which had been moved to a 52nd Street location) was temporarily closed by authorities. By the time it reopened on East 54th Street a year and a half later, he had lost most of his celebrity clientele. Sadly, Shor was virtually penniless when he died in 1977. That same year, his 52nd Street restaurant became a disco called "New York New York."

THE INFAMOUS WRONG DOOR RAID

Throughout his marriage to Marilyn Monroe, DiMaggio was possessive, jealous, and highly suspicious of other men. Shortly after the couple split, Marilyn moved into the Brandon Hall Apartments on Hollywood's Sunset Strip. She had become friendly with a fellow actress named Sheila Stewart, who lived nearby. Joe believed that Stewart was helping facilitate an affair between Monroe and Hal Schaefer—a vocal coach who worked with both actresses. When DiMaggio shared his concerns with longtime pal Frank Sinatra, the world-famous crooner recommended that he enlist the help of private detectives to keep tabs on Marilyn. Joe agreed it was a good idea.

On an early November night in 1954, DiMaggio was having dinner with Sinatra at the Villa Capri in Hollywood. While the two celebrities were enjoying some Italian cuisine, Barney Ruditsky—the man who ran the detective agency Joe had hired—called to inform them that Marilyn's white Cadillac had been spotted by one of his associates (a private eye named Phil Irwin) outside of Stewart's home. The retired Yankee slugger instructed Ruditsky to meet him on site.

DiMaggio and Sinatra assembled a raiding party before hurrying to the West Hollywood apartment complex, which was located on the corner of Waring Avenue and Kilkea Drive. Shortly after 11 p.m., members of the group broke open the door to an apartment they believed was occupied by Monroe and Schaefer. They were in for a surprise. The unit was actually being leased by a 39-year-old secretary named Florence Kotz. Kotz later described the home invasion as follows, "I was terrified. The place was full of men. They were making a lot of noise and lights flashed on. I saw one of them holding something up to me. I thought it was a weapon."

It wasn't a weapon—it was a camera with a flashbulb. After Kotz let out a series of blood-curdling screams, the intruders realized they had made a colossal mistake and fled in haste. Kotz reported that they broke a number of glasses in her kitchen on their way out. According to multiple sources, Monroe (who was in one of the adjacent apartments, possibly with Schaefer) was alerted by Kotz's screams and managed to leave the scene undetected.

The Los Angeles Police Department investigated the incident as an attempted burglary. Because the apartment had been dark and the camera flashes had blinded Kotz, she was unable to identify the intruders. There were no other tangible leads, so the episode was largely forgotten until September 1955, when *Confidential Magazine* picked up the story from an anonymous source and published the details. The cover of the popular tabloid featured a picture of Monroe with a teaser line that read, "From a Detective Report: The Real Reason for Marilyn Monroe's Divorce."

The article prompted Kotz to sue DiMaggio and Sinatra for damages. Sinatra's lawyer negotiated a quiet out of court settlement and it appeared as if the case was closed. But a group of movie executives refused to let the matter rest. *Confidential Magazine* had been publishing sordid features about Hollywood stars since 1952 and had built a large following. At its peak, the saucy periodical attracted more readers than *Time* magazine. Concerned that the salacious stories were damaging the reputation of their clients and negatively impacting box office returns, multiple studio heads appealed to the state of California for help.

In February 1957, a state committee chaired by Republican senator Fred Kraft of San Diego launched an investigation into the ethical practices of *Confidential Magazine*. At the same time, a Los Angeles grand jury was assembled. There were multiple inquiries, and details of the so-called wrong door raid were again brought to light. Sinatra, Ruditsky, and DiMaggio were threatened with perjury charges after offering testimony, but all three walked away clean. In the end, *Confidential Magazine* was forced to stop publishing scandalous articles. With less juicy material to print, the magazine eventually went out of business.

At one time, Ruditsky's agency had been the most popular in Hollywood. But the negative publicity generated by the botched Monroe investigation damaged his reputation immeasurably. During the state senate inquiry, it was discovered that he was operating without a license. He retired shortly afterward, commenting that private detective work was a "dirty, filthy, rotten business."

THIRD TIME'S A CHARM
Before the aches and pains of advancing age made it impossible to do so, DiMaggio played in Old-Timers' Day games at Yankee Stadium every year. The 1965 celebration was especially memorable. After the Bombers lost the 1964 World Series to the St. Louis Cardinals, Yogi Berra was fired as manager and replaced with St. Louis skipper Johnny Keane. Berra received a rousing ovation when he was introduced as an old-timer the following year, while Keane was robustly booed.

DiMaggio led off the second inning for the AL retirees. With former Cincinnati hurler Bucky Walters on the mound, Joltin' Joe hit a foul pop to catcher Jim Hegan. Hegan, who had spent his peak seasons with the Indians before finishing his career in the National League, deliberately dropped the ball. Given a second chance, DiMaggio hit another foul to Hall of Famer Monte Irvin. Stationed at third base, the former New York Giants and Newark Eagles star followed Hegan's example and intentionally dropped the ball.

DiMaggio would never have been extended such courtesy during his playing days. Taking advantage of it in his retirement, he deposited a pitch into the lower deck in left field. The crowd gave him a standing ovation as he rounded the bases. Acknowledging their cheers, he tipped his cap as he crossed home plate. The game featuring the active Yankees that day was equally eventful as Whitey Ford faltered on the mound, staking the Indians to a 5–1 lead. The Bombers later rallied for a 7–6 win, pushing the deciding run across the plate in the bottom of the ninth.

THE MEANING BEHIND MRS. ROBINSON

Among the most popular folk-rock duos of the 1960s, Paul Simon and Art Garfunkel began writing songs together when they were in grade school. By the time they embarked upon solo careers during the 1970s, they had won ten Grammy Awards. Some of their highest charting hits included "Bridge Over Troubled Water," "The Sound of Silence," and "Mrs. Robinson." The latter song, which contains multiple lines about Joe DiMaggio, deeply offended the Yankee idol until he understood the meaning of the lyrics.

Released in 1968, "Mrs. Robinson" was written in reference to Eleanor Roosevelt, who Simon greatly admired. The tune was actually titled "Mrs. Roosevelt" until the popular duo changed the name to make it fit the Academy Award–winning movie it was being featured in (*The Graduate*, starring Dustin Hoffman and Anne Bancroft). "Mrs. Robinson" was a smash hit for Simon and Garfunkel, peaking at #1 on the *Billboard* charts and remaining there for several weeks. The four-minute musical masterpiece, which is a bitter social commentary, suggests that DiMaggio faded from the spotlight at a time when the American public needed him most. When the retired Yankee slugger heard about the lyrics, he believed that Simon was making him out to be some sort of deadbeat and threatened to sue.

As fate would have it, the two American icons had a chance encounter in Lattanzi's restaurant on West 46th Street in New York. Simon, who was a lifelong Yankee fan, had heard about Joe's beef with the song. Upon spotting the legendary Hall of Famer at a nearby table, he worked up the courage to say "hello." DiMaggio invited him to sit down and immediately started talking about Simon's lyrics.

"What I don't understand," said Joe, "is why you ask where I've gone. I just did a Mr. Coffee commercial. I'm a spokesman for the Bowery Savings Bank and I haven't gone anywhere."

"I don't mean it that way," Simon explained. "I mean, where are these great heroes now?"

When DiMaggio realized that Simon considered him a hero and that the song was actually about how much he meant to people, he was flattered. The two shook hands and remained in each other's good graces from that day forward. Interestingly, Simon was forced to explain himself to Mickey Mantle while taping an episode of *The Dick Cavett Show*. Mantle, who was actually Simon's favorite player while growing up, asked the singer why he hadn't used his name in place of DiMaggio's. Simon explained that Mickey's name had the wrong number of syllables.

In 1999, Simon was asked to perform "Mrs. Robinson" on Joe DiMaggio Day at Yankee Stadium. In a subsequent interview on MSG's "The Game 365" show, Simon described the strange ordeal as follows: "Can you imagine, just the irony of it? I write this line I don't know where it comes from, about a ballplayer I know is really famous, but he's not my favorite guy—and I end up, number one, writing one of the main obituaries, and then singing the song in center field at Yankee Stadium. I mean, our attachment was so powerful because of that song."

DIMAGGIO'S ACHILLES HEEL

Not only did DiMaggio sacrifice three seasons to military duty in his prime, but he lost a significant amount of playing time due to injuries. In 1946, he began experiencing chronic pain in his heel. Surgery was performed in the offseason to remove a bone spur, but the incision site became infected and a skin graft was required to repair it. Joe missed a total of 36 games in '46 and '47. In 1949, the pain in his heel returned, forcing him to sit out for two months (and bringing the grand total of games missed on account of foot issues to more than 100). The heel injury became so renowned that it was actually referenced in Ernest Hemingway's Pulitzer Prize–winning novella *The Old Man and the Sea*.

In 1990, Joe (in his late 70s by then) was still experiencing discomfort from old baseball-related injuries. He consulted with a foot and ankle specialist named Dr. Rock Positano, who later became a close personal friend. Upon examining Joe, Positano noted that the retired slugger had an arthritic left big toe—the result of repeatedly fouling balls off of his foot. It was also confirmed that the initial bone spur surgery in 1947 had been bungled. Doctors used the wrong kind of incision for the procedure and additionally removed a majority of the fat that provides padding for the bone. Joe played the rest of his career with virtually no natural cushion to protect his heel. He was essentially running on bare bone. Positano later learned that the hand-me-down shoes passed to Joe from his older brothers (some of which were not even the correct size) had created preliminary foot and ankle problems long before the slugger's professional career even began.

DiMaggio made it somewhat difficult for Positano to arrive at a diagnosis and determine a course of treatment. Fearing that the scans might turn up at a memorabilia show with a high price tag attached to them, the Yankee icon refused to have X-rays taken. Positano recommended special orthopedic bracing designed to reduce inflammation in Joe's foot while easing the tension in the tendons and ligaments near his heel. Within a couple of weeks, DiMaggio reported dramatic improvement. He was able to move around with minimal pain for the first time in quite a while.

AN AWKWARD DINING EXPERIENCE

DiMaggio's Yankee teammates considered it a privilege to have dinner with him. Joe usually ate with his own elite circle of friends, and few of his Yankee peers—aside from Lefty Gomez and Billy Martin—had the courage to even ask him to a restaurant. Long after Joe retired, Hall of Fame shortstop Phil Rizzuto admitted, "I am still in awe of him fifty years after playing on the same team. That's how much I still respect and fear him. I never ate with him when we were playing together."

DiMaggio was extremely uncomfortable around strangers throughout his lifetime. In his later years, he avoided dining out with people unless he had properly vetted them first. One day, a good friend of Joe's made the mistake of inviting a colleague to dinner without giving the Yankee idol advance notice. It turned out to be an uncomfortable experience for everyone involved.

Clearly unhappy with the situation, Joe ate in virtual silence, avoiding eye contact and refusing to engage directly with the unannounced guest—an esteemed Manhattan plastic surgeon named Dr. John Hunter. After Hunter excused himself to use the restroom, Joe said irritably to his friend, "You didn't have the courtesy to ask my permission for him to come along and eat with us. What makes you think you can invite a total stranger to break bread with me?" Joe's buddy tried to explain that he had known Hunter for many years, but Joe was having none of it. "I don't care how long you've known him or what kind of friend he is. You didn't clear it with me first."

DiMaggio was still annoyed by the end of the evening. When the meal was complete and the check had been paid, Joe's dinner companions dropped him off at his apartment. The retired Yankee slugger got out of the car without offering a "goodnight." When Hunter issued a sincere curbside apology, Joe slammed the door and walked briskly away. A week later, DiMaggio tried to atone for his boorish behavior by sending an autographed ball to Hunter. Joe's friend had the good sense to never surprise him with an unapproved dinner guest ever again.

JOE IN HIS BIRTHDAY SUIT

DiMaggio was photographed thousands of times during his career. Nearly all of those photos are tasteful. But in 2009, the one he would not have wanted anyone to see finally surfaced.

The photo—a full frontal shot of Joe standing naked in the showers at Yankee Stadium—appeared in a San Francisco art gallery exhibit. It later passed into the possession of an auction house and went up for sale. The auctioneers provided the following description of the graphic picture: "Obviously aware of being photographed in such a state, [DiMaggio] is seen smiling for the camera—a young Joe, perhaps still in the 1930s, still in his purest youth. We are not sure how the photo made it to this point, but it is 100% authentic, first generation, and vintage." An unidentified man—only partially in the frame—is standing shoulder to shoulder with Joe in the shot.

At least one source claimed that the photo was a sham. Morris Engelberg, attorney for the DiMaggio estate and one of Joe's most trusted advisors, commented to reporters, "I could never imagine Joe DiMaggio, this private individual, ever letting anyone take a photo of him in the nude with someone next to him. When Joe DiMaggio went to the bathroom in a restaurant, I always had to escort him. And I made sure no one took a picture of him at the urinal." Engelberg's comments about Joe being intensely private are indisputable. The self-conscious Yankee idol strenuously avoided situations that might cause him embarrassment throughout his career. And it would indeed have been highly out of character for him to allow such a photo to be taken.

The *New York Post* published Engelberg's comments under a facetious headline reading, "Lawyer: That's Not Joltin' Joe's Penis." Speculating on the identity of the man standing next to DiMaggio, a writer from the *San Francisco Chronicle* comically reported, "A similar photo of Mantle recently surfaced. Collect the entire set. Bonus mystery: Next to DiMaggio in the photo is an unidentified guy. Is it a Yankee teammate? A coach? A stadium peanut vendor? Maybe it's Engelberg letting down his guard." Though the *New York Daily News* couldn't verify the picture's authenticity, a correspondent claimed that it had been taken in 1939.

Genuine or fraudulent, the one of a kind photo was acquired for more than $17,000 by John Rogers—owner of the Rogers Photo Archive. Composed of more than 40 million images, Rogers' private collection is among the largest in the world.

THE DIMAGGIO EFFECT

Decades after DiMaggio logged his last at-bat for the Yankees, he was still hailed as a demigod whenever he was in New York. One of Joe's closest friends observed, "People would trip over themselves, walk into doors, and miss curbs at seeing Joe DiMaggio. I called it 'The DiMaggio Effect.' It didn't matter if you were a famous star, a billionaire, or the guy next door, the 'Effect' would hit everyone in the same way." When DiMaggio walked into restaurants, a hush would fall over the room. People would often form a line near his table to greet him. And when he got up to use the restroom, male diners would sometimes follow him. One woman actually stole a potato off of Joe's plate just to get his attention. On another occasion, the Yankee idol was mobbed by autograph seekers in St. Patrick's Cathedral during a Catholic mass. Some members of the congregation tried to get him to sign prayer books and missals they had snatched from pews.

While he was an active player, sportswriters waxed poetic about DiMaggio's marvelous feats in the outer expanse of Yankee Stadium. Long after he retired, he was still being compared to the all-time greats. There was no Gold Glove Award in DiMaggio's day, but contemporary statistician Bill James claimed that Joe could have won eight of them. Even Whitey Ford—who had the privilege of playing alongside Mickey Mantle—ranked DiMaggio as the greatest center fielder in Yankee history. "I have a dilemma," Ford wrote. "Who is the Yankees' greatest center fielder? My heart says Mickey Mantle, my buddy, my teammate, my running mate. My head says Joe DiMaggio."

DiMaggio had a small handful of detractors. Hall of Famer Tris Speaker once bristled at having his abilities compared to Joe's. "Him?" the former Indians and Red Sox great grumbled, "I could name fifteen better outfielders." While it's true that DiMaggio was a superb defensive player, he was not quite as exceptional as some writers have made him out to be. During the 12 seasons in which he made at least 116 appearances, he led American League center fielders in errors three times. On a positive note, he was also the statistical leader in putouts, assists, and double plays on several occasions.

Like any outfielder, Joe suffered from occasional lapses. In a game against the Tigers at New York, the Yankees were trailing 7–2 in the top of the ninth with Hank Greenberg at bat and a runner on first. Greenberg launched a deep drive toward the alley in center field. Tommy Henrich later described the play as follows: "At the crack of the bat, [Joe] sees the ball take off and he's got a doggone good idea where the ball is going and when it's coming down. That's what Joe did. He turned around. He ran as fast as he could to the center field fence and when he got within one full stride—that would be about seven or eight feet—over his left shoulder, he turned his head to the left and there is the ball. And he got his glove up and caught the ball. And that is the first time he looked for that ball since the crack of the bat. I call that the best one I ever saw." A correspondent from the *New York Times* agreed, referring to it as the greatest catch in the history of Yankee Stadium. DiMaggio must have thought so too. He got so caught up in the moment, he forgot that there were only two outs and started jogging back toward the dugout. Had he remained focused, he might have thrown out Earl Averill on his way back to first base. Joe's mental error allowed the rival outfielder to scramble back in plenty of time. "It was just about the only time I saw him make a mistake," Greenberg later recalled. "I was glad it happened. Just proved he was human."

DiMaggio was definitely human. In another story told by Lefty Gomez, the Yankee Clipper was playing very shallow against slugger Rudy York of the Tigers. Gomez retired York on a ground ball, but between innings, he advised Joe to play deeper next time. DiMaggio told Gomez not to worry because his abilities were equal to (if not greater than) Tris Speaker's. When York came to the plate again, DiMaggio positioned himself fairly close to second base. Gomez motioned with his glove for Joe to move back, but the headstrong outfielder ignored the instructions. Sure enough, York blasted a deep shot that sailed over DiMaggio's head for extra bases. After the Yankees lost the game, DiMaggio apologized. "I'm sorry about that ball," he said to Gomez. "I should have caught it. But I'm still going to make them forget Speaker." The wise-cracking hurler retorted, "I know you should have caught it too, and if you keep playing shallow like that, you'll not only make them forget Speaker, you'll make them forget Gomez."

ENHANCING THE LEGEND

While compiling notes for a DiMaggio biography that was released in the mid-70s, sportswriter Maury Allen sat down with Joe's old friend Toots Shor in the hope of getting some inside stories. By then, Shor had lost his business and was no longer on speaking terms with DiMaggio. Even so, the renowned restaurateur had many flattering things to say about the Yankee Clipper. "Joe was the kind of guy that made everybody around him better," Shor asserted. "The players were better for having played with him and everybody was better for just knowing him. . . . He was more concerned about his teammates and other people than he was about himself."

According to Shor, DiMaggio brooded over every Yankee loss and blamed himself regardless of how he played. He could be moody and inconsolable at times. One day, before a game against the Red Sox at Yankee Stadium, Joe made plans to have dinner with Toots and his brother Dom. But after Dom made a pair of spectacular catches in center field, robbing Joe of two extra-base hits, Joe abruptly canceled those plans.

The bond between DiMaggio and Shor was genuine. Joe became friendly with members of Shor's immediate family. And he would sometimes stay with them at their house in Monmouth, New Jersey. After particularly tough losses, Joe and Toots would walk through the neighborhood surrounding Shor's restaurant—not talking much, just looking at the items in the store windows. Shor said that the walks were therapeutic for DiMaggio and almost always lifted his spirits.

Joe wasn't a habitual drinker, but according to Shor, he could hold his own when he set his mind to it. One night, DiMaggio went out on the town with Shor and actor Jackie Gleason. Though Joe's companions were notorious lushes, he outlasted them both. While Gleason and Shor had the luxury of sleeping it off, Joe had to get up early for a game. Shor showed up at the stadium the next day, and shortly before the first pitch he ran into Red Sox player-manager Joe Cronin, who was a personal friend. "I just saw your friend, Joe," said Cronin. "He had his head down. You guys must have worked him over pretty good last night." Despite his presumed hangover, DiMaggio smashed a two-run triple in his first at-bat.

Of all the stories involving DiMaggio, Shor most enjoyed telling the one about how he allegedly cost the slugger thousands of dollars. It happened before the 1949 campaign. After leading the American League in homers and RBIs in '48, Joe was looking for a significant salary increase. The Yankees were willing to meet his demands by including an attendance bonus in his contract. But Shor—along with a few other members of Joe's inner circle—convinced the Yankee icon to ask for a straight $100,000 contract. Joe's demands were met, but he ended up losing a bundle when the Bombers lured nearly 2.3 million fans through the turnstiles. Shor claimed that the attendance bonus would have netted DiMaggio an additional $20,000 and that the slugger razzed him about it for a long time afterward.

THE GRUDGE

From the time that Mickey Mantle made his first appearance in spring training with the Yankees, he was hailed as the next great Yankee star and the successor to Joe DiMaggio. A vain, sensitive man, DiMaggio couldn't help being insulted by all the hype. When his numbers came crashing back to earth during Mickey's rookie year and the pain of multiple injuries became too heavy to bear, Joe knew he would have to step aside. It wasn't easy for him, and from that point forward he harbored a grudge against Mantle.

The ongoing rivalry between the two men was one-sided. Mantle grew up idolizing DiMaggio. When he first arrived in New York, he was so star-struck by the Yankee Clipper that he could scarcely even hold a conversation. Mickey always harbored a deep respect for Joe. "Heroes are people who are all good with no bad in them," Mantle once proclaimed. "That's the way I always saw Joe DiMaggio. He was beyond question one of the greatest players of the century."

In spite of Mantle's reverence for him, DiMaggio hung onto his bitter feelings to the very end. A close friend of Joe's recalled an elevator ride up to the owner's box at Yankee Stadium in 1994. The elevator stopped between floors and Mantle got on. Joe shot Mickey a disapproving look and refused to say hello. By then Mantle had become accustomed to Joe's standoffish behavior and refused to give in. "An eternity passed in those minutes," Joe's friend later wrote. "Both men were avoiding eye contact, looking anywhere but at each other. Joe was waiting for The Mick to blink and acknowledge him first. It was a pecking order thing or the ballplayer's version of chicken." It was Mantle who finally broke the awkward silence, offering a greeting. DiMaggio officially ended the standoff with a polite reply.

DiMaggio had formed strong opinions about how players should behave on and off the field. During his playing days, Mantle had violated Joe's principles with his incessant drinking and carousing. DiMaggio later became jealous when Mantle made a big splash in the memorabilia trade. Even today, Mantle's baseball cards and autographs fetch a higher price than DiMaggio's.

When Joe found out that Mickey was dying of cancer in 1995, he told one of his friends that he didn't feel sorry for the former Yankee great because he had failed to take proper care of himself. In the wake of Mickey's passing, a special day was held at Yankee Stadium in his honor. Joe agreed to make an appearance but outright refused to deliver a speech. He simply walked onto the field, basked in the applause, and left abruptly afterward. He was conspicuously absent from Mantle's funeral. When reporters asked him for a tribute statement, Joe made sure to point out that Mantle had been demoted to the minors in his rookie year. "I was surprised by how rigid and bitter he allowed himself to appear," said one of DiMaggio's confidants. "It didn't do much to enhance his reputation. . . . He should have been bigger than that. He expected others to rise above their grudges."

HAIL TO THE CHIEF!

In his lifetime, DiMaggio mingled with a wide variety of dignitaries. It seemed that everybody wanted to meet him, including assorted heads of state. The Yankee slugger established connections with a number of world leaders over the years. But not all of those connections were particularly amicable.

FRANKLIN DELANO ROOSEVELT

FDR was an avid sports fan. In January 1942, he drafted his famous "green light" letter, which stated that baseball was a valuable recreational asset and should continue operating during the war. Roosevelt attended nearly a dozen games while he was in office and once remarked that he would go to the ballpark more often if he didn't have to hobble up and down the stairs in front of crowds. A disorder of the immune system (which may have been Guillain-Barre syndrome) left him paralyzed from the waist down. He navigated in a wheelchair more often than not but was able to stand with canes and move around in public with help from aides. FDR saw DiMaggio play more than once and had the opportunity to meet the Bronx idol. Their brief encounter was an amicable one. Roosevelt was one of the few Democratic presidents Joe approved of.

DWIGHT D. EISENHOWER
In 1953, DiMaggio visited the White House with boxer Rocky Marciano. "Ike" engaged in friendly banter with both men. Multiple photos exist of Joe smiling as Marciano clowned around with the president, showing him the fist that had famously KO'd heavyweight champ Jersey Joe Walcott the previous year.

HARRY TRUMAN
The 33rd US president saw DiMaggio play on four occasions during his time in office. He was the first Commander in Chief to attend a night game. Truman brought good luck to the Yankee center fielder. Joltin' Joe reached base 11 times by hit or walk with Truman in attendance.

JOHN F. KENNEDY
Because Jack and Bobby Kennedy both reportedly engaged in trysts with Marilyn Monroe, DiMaggio absolutely despised them. To the day he died, Joe was convinced that the two brothers had played a role in Marilyn's death. Voicing his opinions to a friend, the Yankee icon once said, "If any of those Kennedys had shown up [at Marilyn's funeral] I would have taken a baseball bat and bashed their faces. All of those sons-of-bitches killed Marilyn." On "Mickey Mantle Day" at Yankee Stadium in September 1965, DiMaggio escorted Mantle's mother to the dignitary lineup on the infield. After being introduced as an honored guest, Bobby Kennedy began working his way down the line with handshakes. When DiMaggio saw him coming, he flashed the senator an icy glare and ducked out of line to avoid engaging with him.

RICHARD NIXON

Nixon claimed that he attended his first baseball game on July 4, 1936, in Washington and saw DiMaggio hit a home run. He carried a deep respect for the Yankee Clipper after that. In 1972, Nixon compiled a list of all-time All-Star teams from two different eras. DiMaggio appeared on the AL squad representing the time period of 1925–1945. The president's fantasy outfield tandem also included Babe Ruth, Al Simmons, Goose Goslin, and Harry Heilmann. DiMaggio had a chance to spend some time with Nixon at an event in 1985 and Joe maintained a friendship with Nixon's former Secretary of State Henry Kissinger. Joe and Henry watched several World Series games together. Although DiMaggio hated signing baseballs without being paid for it, he autographed a number of them for Kissinger. Nixon's successor, Gerald Ford, awarded DiMaggio the Presidential Medal of Freedom.

RONALD REAGAN

In 1987, DiMaggio was invited to attend a White House dinner honoring Russian leader Mikhail Gorbachev. Asked how he would like to be introduced, the retired Yankee slugger answered humbly, "just Joe DiMaggio." After introductions were made, Reagan told Gorbachev that Joe was one of the greatest ballplayers of all time. DiMaggio was rarely star-struck, but he had brought a baseball into the White House for the purpose of having both luminaries sign it. The two men honored his request.

GEORGE H. W. BUSH

In July 1991, George Herbert Walker Bush invited DiMaggio and Ted Williams to the White House, where they were honored for "contributions to baseball and sportsmanship" on the 50th anniversary of their landmark 1941 seasons. Bush and Williams had trained together as fighter pilots during World War II. They remained friendly over the years, fishing and golfing together periodically. After the ceremony, Joe and Ted flew on Air Force One with the president to Toronto for the All-Star Game.

BILL CLINTON

DiMaggio's experience with the Kennedys soured him on Democratic presidents. Joe became a staunch conservative over time, and according to multiple sources he was not particularly fond of Bill Clinton. In 1995, he declined an invitation to meet the president at Camden Yards in Baltimore. At a *Time* magazine dinner in 1998, Clinton extended another request for Joe to sit with him at the presidential table. Because Joe had already accepted an offer to dine with Henry Kissinger and his wife, he sent his regrets through a friend. The icing on the cake—Joe rejected phone calls from the president while he was undergoing treatment for lung cancer. This time, it wasn't Joe himself who declined—it was Joe's health care surrogate, Morris Engelberg. Explaining the decision, Engelberg remarked, "My reasoning was that when Joe was healthy, he wouldn't speak with Clinton, so he certainly wouldn't do it under those circumstances." Though some have tried to downplay DiMaggio's behavior toward Clinton, it's pretty clear that he went out of his way to maintain a distance from the nation's 42nd Commander in Chief.

On an interesting final note, DiMaggio was awarded the Ellis Island Medal of Honor in 1986. The award is considered one of the nation's most prestigious prizes and recipients are read into the Congressional Record every year. The 1986 ceremony was the first of its kind. In addition to DiMaggio, the list of winners included Muhammad Ali, Rosa Parks, and none other than future US president Donald Trump.

CASHING IN ON JOE'S FAME

Because DiMaggio's name was a marketable commodity, he was taken advantage of repeatedly during his lifetime. One of the prime offenders was Barry Halper—vice president of baseball operations for the Yankees during the early '90s and one of the world's most prolific memorabilia collectors. Halper was known to enhance his collection through bribery. He once obtained a Lou Gehrig jersey by sweet-talking the Iron Horse's widow after he had sent her a case of expensive scotch. He later sold the jersey for more than twice the value of the liquor. Keenly aware of what DiMaggio's signature was worth on the open market, Halper struck up a superficial friendship with the Yankee icon. Over time, Joe began to realize that every dinner outing with Halper was followed by an autograph request. And he came to resent it. One night, after wining and dining the retired slugger, Halper opened the trunk of his car and asked Joe to sign an extensive array of photos. Though DiMaggio had been in the habit of complying out of courtesy to his so-called friend, he finally put his foot down and refused.

DiMaggio received many invitations to Halper's home in Livingston, New Jersey. During one particular visit, he was ambushed by a photographer from *USA Today*. Halper had told Joe that the visit would be private, and although DiMaggio was highly irritated, he found himself without a means of escape because his driver (a man hired by Halper) had conveniently left as soon as Joe was dropped off. Pictures taken of DiMaggio that evening ended up being published.

In 1991, Halper approached the organizers of the Columbus Day Parade in New York without DiMaggio's permission and told them that Joe was interested in serving as Grand Marshal. Putting it bluntly, the Yankee Clipper was pissed off. Though he had turned down many prior invitations to participate in the popular Italian American celebration, he reluctantly decided to accept the honor this time around. When Halper showed up at a reception in Cardinal John O'Connor's residence on the day of the parade, Joe told him in no uncertain terms to leave.

According to DiMaggio's lawyer Morris Engelberg, Joe became convinced that Halper had secretly purchased the eight World Series rings that were stolen from his room at the Hotel Lexington in the 1960s. Though no legal action was ever taken, the shady collector landed himself in hot water after Joe's death when he tried to sell original contracts that DiMaggio and a number of other baseball greats had signed with the Hillerich & Bradsby Bat Company. Corporate executives, who were under the impression that the documents had been unintentionally destroyed, were highly surprised to see the items up for auction. When Louisville Slugger representatives reached out to Halper's lawyer for an explanation, they were informed that the memorabilia mogul had acquired the contracts from a dealer in the late '70s. Rather than face a lawsuit, Halper returned the documents (worth thousands each) to the original owners.

Halper managed to gather one of the largest and most diverse treasure troves of baseball collectibles on the planet. In addition to the game used jerseys of numerous deadball greats, he acquired a variety of unique items, such as Ty Cobb's dentures, the glove Lou Gehrig used during his last season with the Yankees, and an uncut strip of T-206 tobacco cards containing one of the most valuable pieces of cardboard in existence—the ultrarare 1909 Honus Wagner card. In 1998, Halper sold a significant portion of his collection to major-league baseball. Many of the items were donated to the Hall of Fame. A few years after Halper's death, his reputation was tarnished when a Cooperstown spokesman told a *New York Post* reporter that a Halper-owned jersey allegedly worn by Shoeless Joe Jackson was a fake. The authenticity of several other items came into question in subsequent reports. Lending some credibility to DiMaggio's theory regarding his World Series rings, Halper was also accused of purchasing stolen items.

STEINBRENNER'S FAILED MURDER PLOT

Born into a wealthy family, Yankee owner George Steinbrenner lived a life of privilege. After making a fortune as CEO of the American Ship Building Company, he assembled a group of financiers to purchase the Yankees from CBS. He had previously tried to acquire the Cleveland Indians, but his offer was declined. Although the Yankees won seven World Series titles during Steinbrenner's tenure, his time with the club was wrought with controversy. Fickle and tempestuous, he went through more than a dozen managers between 1973 and 1990. His favorite target was Billy Martin, who he fired several times. In 1974, "The Boss" was suspended for making illegal contributions to President Richard Nixon's reelection campaign. Another suspension followed in the early '90s after he paid a Bronx gambler to dig up dirt on Hall of Fame outfielder Dave Winfield.

Despite his problems with other Yankee personalities, Steinbrenner was particularly fond of DiMaggio. He believed that Joltin' Joe was a good luck charm, and when the Yankees made the playoffs in 1996, he made sure that the Yankee Clipper attended all of the home games. He even let Joe sit in the owner's box. During one of their many conversations about baseball, Steinbrenner asked DiMaggio what kind of salary he would require to play for the Yankees in the modern era. DiMaggio jokingly told George that he would have to make him a partner.

Steinbrenner wanted to commission a statue of DiMaggio to be put in center field at Yankee Stadium. He also sought to have a DiMaggio statue erected in Central Park. In order to complete both projects, he needed Joe's permission. The retired Yankee slugger stubbornly rejected the proposal, commenting, "As long as I am still walking, there is no way I will have anyone build a statue of me in this city. When I'm dead, they can do whatever the hell they want." Joe had declined similar offers from New York City officials, who reportedly wanted to rename East 56th Street and the Major Deegan Expressway in his honor.

Shortly after Steinbrenner's statue proposal, DiMaggio was invited to Yankee Stadium to watch a game in the owner's box. George always went to great lengths to make Joe feel comfortable. All of the Yankee idol's favorite beverages and snacks were readily available. On this particular occasion, Steinbrenner had added a new Philly cheesesteak vendor. He raved about the quality of the sandwiches and insisted that Joe sample one. DiMaggio was very particular about what kinds of food he would eat but eventually agreed. After finishing his sandwich, Joe complained of stomach discomfort and asked his companion to bring him home immediately.

Joe's friend ignored multiple traffic laws getting him back to his apartment in haste. Upon arriving, Joe rushed off to the bathroom in obvious discomfort. "I don't know what the hell Steinbrenner fed me," he said from behind the bathroom door, "but I think he's trying to kill me so he can put up that statue of me in center field."

This statue of the Yankee Clipper (unveiled in 1991) stood in the Piazza DiMaggio across the street from the Italian American Sports Hall of Fame in Chicago's "Little Italy" neighborhood. It was moved when the museum relocated to the city's Northwest Side. The decision to uproot the statue greatly displeased many local residents.
(COURTESY OF CATCHPENNY ON VISUAL HUNT)

Appendix I

DiMaggio's Lifetime Hitting Stats

REGULAR SEASON

G	AB	R	H	2B	3B	HR	RBI	BA	BB	OBP
1,736	6,821	1,390	2,214	389	131	361	1,537	.325	790	.398

POSTSEASON

G	AB	R	H	2B	3B	HR	RBI	BA	BB	OBP
51	199	27	54	6	0	8	30	.271	19	.338

ALL-STAR GAME

G	AB	R	H	2B	3B	HR	RBI	BA	BB	OBP
11	40	7	9	2	0	1	6	.225	3	.279

Appendix II

Interesting Facts about DiMaggio's 56-Game Hitting Streak

—The streak began on May 15 in a 13–1 loss to the White Sox at Yankee Stadium.

—DiMaggio hit .408 with 91 hits in 223 at-bats during the streak. He collected 16 doubles, 4 triples, 15 homers, and 55 RBIs over 56 games.

—Prior to the streak, DiMaggio's cumulative batting average was .304. On the day the streak ended, he was hitting .375.

—DiMaggio faced four Hall of Fame pitchers during the streak.

—The All-Star Game took place during the streak. Joe hit safely in that game as well (going 1-for-4), although it didn't count toward his total. Joe and Dominic were the first set of big league brothers to appear on the same All-Star team.

—DiMaggio extended the streak in his final at-bat of the day more than half a dozen times.

—The Yankees went 41-13-2 during DiMaggio's streak. They were five and a half games out of first place when it began. When it ended on July 17, they were sitting in first place with a seven-game lead.

—Before DiMaggio, the longest major-league hitting streak ever assembled belonged to Willie Keeler, who hit in 44 straight games for the Baltimore Orioles in 1897. In Keeler's era, foul balls were not yet counted as strikes.

—The longest hitting streak since DiMaggio's was assembled by Pete Rose of the Reds. He tied Keeler's old record of 44 in 1978.

—DiMaggio broke Keeler's record in style, drilling a two-run homer off of Red Sox ace Dick Newsome.

—DiMaggio hit safely in 16 straight games after his 56-game streak ended.

—Prior to DiMaggio, the longest hitting streak by a Yankee was 33 games, which was accomplished by first baseman Hal Chase in 1907.

—DiMaggio faced St. Louis pitcher Bob Muncrief several times during the streak. The right-handed swingman could have ended Joe's streak one afternoon had he chosen to intentionally walk the Yankee slugger in his final at-bat. Muncrief opted to face DiMaggio instead, giving up a hit. Asked about the decision after the game, the hurler replied, "That wouldn't have been fair—to him or to me. He's the greatest player I ever saw."

—DiMaggio was named AL MVP at season's end. He won the award in spite of Ted Williams' .406 batting average and 69 game on-base streak.

—According to multiple sources, DiMaggio lost out on a lucrative endorsement deal with Heinz 57 Ketchup when his streak ended at 56.

Appendix III

Career Milestones

FIRST MAJOR-LEAGUE AT-BAT: May 3, 1936, versus St. Louis Browns

FIRST MAJOR-LEAGUE HOMER: May 10, 1936—two-run shot off of George Turbeville of the A's

FIRST WORLD SERIES TITLE: October 6, 1936—13–5 win over the Giants at the Polo Grounds

FIRST AMERICAN LEAGE MVP AWARD: 1939

FIRST BATTING TITLE: 1939 (.381)

FIRST TIME HITTING FOR THE CYCLE: July 9, 1937, versus the Senators at Yankee Stadium

CAREER HOMER #100: August 25, 1938—two-run shot off of Denny Galehouse of the Indians

SECOND BATTING TITLE: 1940 (.352)

SECOND MVP AWARD: 1941

SECOND TIME HITTING FOR THE CYCLE: May 20, 1948, versus the White Sox at Comiskey Park

CAREER HIT #1,000—May 11, 1941, versus the Red Sox

CAREER HOMER #200: April 22, 1942—solo shot off of Bill Beckmann of the A's

CAREER RBI #1,000: August 26, 1946, versus the Tigers at Yankee Stadium

THIRD MVP AWARD: 1947

CAREER DOUBLE #300: May 18, 1948—off of pitcher Cliff Fannin of the Browns

CAREER HOMER #300: September 16, 1948—solo shot off of Fred Hutchinson of the Tigers

CAREER HIT #2,000: June 20, 1950, versus the Indians at Cleveland Stadium

LAST HOMER: October 8, 1951, off of Sal Maglie of the Giants (Game 4 of World Series)

LAST RBI: October 9, 1951, off of Al Corwin of the Giants (Game 5 of World Series)

LAST WORLD SERIES TITLE (Ninth of Career): October 10, 1951–4–3 win over the Giants at Yankee Stadium

APPENDIX IV

Major-League Records Held

CONSECUTIVE GAMES WITH A HIT, 56, 1941

STRIKEOUT TO HOME RUN RATIO, CAREER, 1.02

MOST HOME RUNS IN FIRST 2 SEASONS, 75, 1936–1937

FASTEST PLAYER TO REACH 200 RBI IN HIS CAREER
(201 games)

FASTEST PLAYER TO REACH 300 RBI IN HIS CAREER
(297 games)

FASTEST PLAYER TO REACH 400 RBI IN HIS CAREER
(396 games)

FASTEST PLAYER TO REACH 500 RBI IN HIS CAREER
(505 games)

FASTEST PLAYER TO REACH 600 RBI IN HIS CAREER
(604 games)

FASTEST PLAYER TO REACH 700 RBI IN HIS CAREER
(693 games)

FASTEST PLAYER TO REACH 800 RBI IN HIS CAREER
(803 games)

MOST RBI IN FIRST 2 SEASONS, 292, 1936–1937

MOST RBI IN FIRST 3 SEASONS, 432, 1936–1938

MOST RBI IN FIRST 4 SEASONS, 558, 1936–1939

MOST RBI IN FIRST 5 SEASONS, 691, 1936–1940

MOST RBI IN FIRST 6 SEASONS, 816, 1936–1941

MOST RBI IN FIRST 7 SEASONS, 930, 1936–1942

MOST RBI IN FIRST 10 SEASONS, 1,277, 1936–1948

MOST RBI IN FIRST 12 SEASONS, 1,466, 1936–1950

MOST RBI IN FOUR CONSECUTIVE GAMES: 18, August 28–September 1, 1939 (tied with Jim Bottomley, Lou Gehrig, Tony Lazzeri, Sammy Sosa, and Alfonso Soriano)

Appendix V

Timeline of Major Events

1914: DiMaggio is born on November 25 in Martinez, California. He is the eighth child of Giuseppe and Rosalie DiMaggio.

1930: DiMaggio drops out of Galileo High School at the age of sixteen. He tries his hand at several menial jobs before pursuing baseball as a career.

1932: Joe's older brother Vince signs a contract with the San Francisco Seals. He convinces team executives to give Joe a trial at shortstop.

1933: In his first full season with the Seals, DiMaggio compiles a 61-game hitting streak—a Pacific Coast League record that still stands.

1934: In November, DiMaggio's contract is sold to the Yankees. The deal stipulates that Joe will spend one more season with the Seals.

1936: DiMaggio makes his Yankee debut on May 3, going 3-for-6 against the St. Louis Browns. He becomes the first rookie to play in an All-Star Game. The Yanks win the pennant and Joe gets his first World Series ring.

1937: DiMaggio leads the American League with 46 homers—the highest single season total of his career. His 167 RBIs are also a personal high.

1938: DiMaggio engages in a salary dispute with the Yankees. Bronx executives stand their ground and Joe caves to pressure, accepting what they are offering. Upon returning to action, he is booed by fans in New York. This continues throughout the first half of the season.

1939: DiMaggio wins a batting title and is named NL MVP. In November, he marries actress Dorothy Arnold. The Yankees sweep the Reds in the World Series, winning their fourth straight championship—a new record.

1940: DiMaggio wins his second straight batting crown. Despite his efforts, the Yankees finish in third place, two games behind the Tigers and Indians.

1941: Lou Gehrig dies. Joe assembles his fabled 56-game hitting streak and is named AL MVP in spite of Ted Williams' .406 batting average. The Yankees beat the Dodgers in the World Series. Joe's wife gives birth to their son, Joe Jr.

1943: Joe reluctantly enlists in the US Army. He spends a majority of his time in the service playing baseball, never getting anywhere near a combat situation.

1944: Dorothy Arnold divorces Joe, citing "cruelty."

1945: Joe gets a medical discharge from the Army due to his chronic reports of acute stomach discomfort.

1946: Joe McCarthy resigns as Yankee manager. He is replaced by Bill Dickey, who also resigns. DiMaggio returns to action but has a mediocre season, hitting below .300 for the first time in his career as the Yanks finish in third place.

1947: Bucky Harris is named manager of the Yankees. DiMaggio wins his third MVP Award. The Yankees beat the Dodgers in the World Series.

1948: DiMaggio tears up the American League, leading the circuit with 39 homers and 155 RBIs. It's not enough as the Yankees fall to third place.

1949: Joe signs the first $100,000 per-season contract in big-league history. Casey Stengel takes over as manager of the Yankees. An injury limits DiMaggio to 76 appearances. His father dies while he is recovering. Joe ends up hitting .346 and helping the Yanks win the first of five straight World Series titles.

1950: Joe's mother dies of cancer on June 18. Joe has his last great offensive season with 32 homers, 122 RBIs, and a .301 batting average.

1951: Mickey Mantle joins the Yankees. He is being hyped as the next great Yankee and a successor to DiMaggio, which irritates Joe. Joe has his worst season ever at the plate, but the Yankees beat the Giants in the World Series. It is DiMaggio's ninth championship. In December, Joe officially announces his retirement.

1952: Joe enters into a committed relationship with Marilyn Monroe.

1954: Joe and Marilyn tie the knot on January 14. The tumultuous marriage ends in divorce just nine months later.

1955: DiMaggio is inducted into the National Baseball Hall of Fame.

1968: Joe signs on as coach and advisor for the Oakland A's.

1969: Joe resigns from his on-field duties with the A's and moves to the front office. He is designated "The Greatest Living Ballplayer" in a nationwide poll celebrating MLB's 100th anniversary. The Yankees add a DiMaggio plaque in center field next to Ruth and Gehrig.

1972: DiMaggio becomes spokesman for the Bowery Savings Bank of New York.

1973: DiMaggio serves as a spokesman for Mr. Coffee products.

1980s: Joe enters the sports memorabilia trade, becoming one of the most sought after Hall of Famers and charging up to $100,000 for a single appearance.

1992: The pediatric wing of Memorial Regional Hospital in Hollywood, Florida, is renamed the Joe DiMaggio Children's Hospital.

1998: Joe receives a cancer diagnosis. A malignant tumor is removed from Joe's lung.

1999: Joe dies in his sleep. He is 84 years old at the time of his passing.

Appendix VI

Awards and Honors

AMERICAN LEAGUE ALL-STAR: 1936–1942, 1942–1951

AMERICAN LEAGUE MOST VALUABLE PLAYER: 1939, 1941, 1947

WORLD SERIES CHAMPION: 1936–1939, 1941, 1947, 1949–1951

AMERICAN LEAGUE BATTING CHAMPION: 1939, 1940

ASSOCIATED PRESS ATHLETE OF THE YEAR: 1941

INDUCTED INTO NATIONAL BASEBALL HALL OF FAME: 1955

VOTED "GREATEST LIVING BALLPLAYER" IN NATION-WIDE POLL OF FANS AND SPORTSWRITERS: 1969

PRESIDENTIAL MEDAL OF FREEDOM: 1977

ELLIS ISLAND MEDAL OF HONOR: 1986

HONORARY DOCTORATE DEGREE COLUMBIA UNIVERSITY: 1990

MAJOR-LEAGUE ALL-CENTURY TEAM: 1999

APPENDIX VII

DiMaggio's Annual Yankee Salary and How It Compared to the Average American Income

YEAR	YANKEE SALARY	AVERAGE US WAGES PER YEAR
1936	$8,500	$1,713
1937	$15,000	$1,780
1938	$25,000	$1,730
1939	$27,500	$1,730
1940	$32,500	$1,725
1941	$37,500	$1,750
1942	$43,750	$1,880
1946	$43,750	$2,500
1947	$43,750	$2,850
1948	$65,000	$2,950
1949	$100,000	$2,950
1950	$100,000	$3,210
1951	$90,000	$3,510

Appendix VIII

DiMaggio's Miscellaneous Career Batting Splits

LONGEST MAJOR-LEAGUE HITTING STREAKS

YEAR	LENGTH	DATES
1941	56 Games	May 15–July 16
1940	23 Games	July 4–July 30
1937	22 Games	June 27–July 21
1950	19 Games	September 7–September 26
1936	18 Games	May 17–June 5
1939	18 Games	August 16–September 2
1942	18 Games	July 4–July 31

LONGEST MAJOR-LEAGUE ON-BASE STREAKS

YEAR	LENGTH
1941	83 Games
1937	52 Games
1940	40 Games
1949	39 Games
1938	35 Games
1951	32 Games

FAVORITE BALLPARKS

STADIUM	G	R	HR	RBI	AVG.	OBP
Sportsman's Park (StL)	127	131	45	156	.389	.464
Griffith Stadium (Wash)	125	110	30	118	.352	.420
Fenway Park (Bos)	120	95	29	113	.334	.410
Comiskey Park (Chi)	117	104	30	102	.335	.397

FAVORITE OPPONENTS

TEAM	G	R	HR	RBI	AVG.	OBP
St. Louis Browns	252	241	67	260	.364	.438
Boston Red Sox	253	193	46	223	.334	.415
Washington Senators	257	206	58	250	.336	.408
Chicago White Sox	236	192	58	203	.324	.390

CAREER WITH BASES LOADED

60-for-181   .332 BA   27 Extra-Base Hits   200 RBIs   (13 Grand Slams)

FAVORITE MONTH TO HIT IN

(JULY)   469-for-1294   .362 BA   183 Extra-Base Hits   315 RBIs   .435 On-Base Percentage

Appendix IX

DiMaggio's Ranking among Franchise Leaders

(Does not include active players.)

EXTRA-BASE HITS	SLUGGING %	BATTING AVG.
Lou Gehrig 1,190	Babe Ruth .711	Babe Ruth .349
Babe Ruth 1,189	Lou Gehrig .632	Lou Gehrig .340
M. Mantle 952	*J. DiMaggio* .579	Earle Combs .325
J. DiMaggio 881	M. Mantle .557	*J. DiMaggio* .325
Derek Jeter 870	Reggie Jackson .526	Bill Dickey .313

DOUBLES	TRIPLES	TOTAL BASES
Derek Jeter 544	Lou Gehrig 163	Babe Ruth 5,131
Lou Gehrig 534	Earle Combs 154	Lou Gehrig 5,060
B. Williams 449	*J. DiMaggio* 131	Derek Jeter 4,921
D. Mattingly 442	Wally Pipp 121	M. Mantle 4,511
Babe Ruth 424	Tony Lazzeri 115	*J. DiMaggio* 3,948
J. DiMaggio 389		

HOME RUNS	RBIs	ON-BASE PLUS SLUGGING
Babe Ruth 659	Lou Gehrig 1,995	Babe Ruth 1.195
M. Mantle 536	Babe Ruth 1,978	Lou Gehrig 1.080
Lou Gehrig 493	*J. DiMaggio* 1,537	*J. DiMaggio* .977
J. DiMaggio 361	M. Mantle 1,509	Charlie Keller .928
Yogi Berra 358	Yogi Berra 1,430	Jason Giambi .925

INTENTIONAL BASES ON BALLS

M. Mantle 148
D. Mattingly 136
Lou Gehrig 114
J. DiMaggio 111
Bill Dickey 101

Bibliography

"Alleged Nude Photo of Yankee Legend Joe DiMaggio Up for Auction." CBSNews.com, June 13, 2011.

Allen, Maury. *Where Have You Gone Joe DiMaggio? The Story of America's Last Hero.* New York: EP Dutton, 1975.

Anderson, Dave, and Bill Pennington, ed. *The New York Times Story of the Yankees.* New York: Black Dog and Leventhal, 2021.

"Babe Ruth, Baseball's Great Star and Idol of Children, Had a Career Both Dramatic and Bizarre." *New York Times*, August 17, 1948.

Bak, Richard. *Casey Stengel: A Splendid Baseball Life.* Dallas, TX: Taylor Publishing, 1997.

Baseball-almanac.com.

Baseball as America: Seeing Ourselves Through Our National Game. Washington, DC: National Geographic, 2005.

Baseball-reference.com.

Bob Feller 1937 Game by Game Pitching Logs. Baseball-alamanac.com. https://www.baseball-almanac.com/players/pitchinglogs.php?p=fellebo01&y=1937.

Bradlee, Ben Jr. "Two Unmatched MLB Stars, Opposite in Many Ways." *Boston Globe*, December 3, 2013.

Brown, Curt. "Rivalry Still Vivid for Former Red Sox Star." *The Standard Times*, August 18, 2006.

"Browns Bid for DiMaggio. But Yankees Refuse $150,000 for Hold-Out." *New York Times*, April 19, 1938.

Bush, Anthony. "Dorothy Arnold." SABR Biography Project. https://sabr.org/bioproj/person/dorothy-arnold/.

Casey Stengel Quotes Page. Baseball-almanac.com. https://www.baseball-almanac.com/quotes/quosteng.shtml.

Catano David. *I Remember Joe DiMaggio: Personal Memories of the Yankee Clipper by the People Who Knew Him Best.* Nashville, TN: Cumberland House, 2001.

Charyn, Jerome. *Joe DiMaggio: The Long Vigil.* New Haven, CT: Yale University Press, 2011.

Churchill, Winston. *The Gathering Storm, Vol. 1.* Boston: Houghton Mifflin Harcourt, 1948.

Clavin, Tom. *The DiMaggios: Three Brothers, Their Passion for Baseball, Their Pursuit of the American Dream.* New York: HarperCollins, 2014.

Coffey, Alex. "Cal Ripken Breaks Lou Gehrig's Record." The National Baseball Hall of Fame and Museum (Official Website). https://baseballhall.org/discover/inside-pitch/cal-ripken-breaks-lou-gehrigs-consecutive-games-record.

Cohen, Stanley. *Yankees 1936–39, Baseball's Greatest Dynasty: Lou Gehrig, Joe DiMaggio and the Birth of a New Era.* New York: Skyhorse Publishing, 2018.

Corbett, Warren. "Vince DiMaggio." Society for American Baseball Research Biography Project. https://sabr.org/bioproj/person/vince-dimaggio/.

Costello, Rory. "Al Gionfriddo." Society for American Baseball Research Biography Project. https://sabr.org/bioproj/person/al-gionfriddo/.

Cramer, Richard Ben. *Joe DiMaggio: The Hero's Life.* New York: Simon and Schuster, 2000.

Daily News Legends Series. *Joe DiMaggio: An American Icon.* Champaign, IL: Sports Publishing LLC, 1999.

DeGregorio, George. *Joe DiMaggio: An Informal Biography.* New York: Stein and Day, 1981.

"Dimag, Daz Among 6 Feted at Hall of Fame." *Daily News,* July 26, 1955.

"DiMaggio Agrees to $25,000 Term. Ruppert Wins Salary Battle—Pay Starts When Joe Shows He's Ready to Play." *New York Times,* April 21, 1938.

DiMaggio, Dom, with Bill Gilbert. *Real Grass, Real Heroes: Baseball's Historic 1941 Season.* New York: Zebra Books, 1990.

"DiMaggio Had 'Defective Attitude' Toward Military in World War II: Report." *New York Post,* August 3, 2010.

DiMaggio, Joe. *Lucky to be a Yankee.* New York: Rudolph Field, 1946.

Dorothy Arnold Page. Internet Movie Data Base. https://www.imdb.com/name/nm00036419/.

Dowd, Katie. "The Untold Story of the San Francisco Kidnapping of Joe DiMaggio's Sister Nellie." *San Francisco Chronicle,* August 27, 2019.

Drebinger, John. "Dodgers Capture 1st World Series, Podres Wins, 2–0." *New York Times,* October 5, 1955.

Drebinger, John. "Dodgers Set Back Yankees by 8–6 For 3–3 Series Tie." *New York Times,* October 6, 1947.

Drebinger, John. "Yanks Crush Giants, 18–4, a World Series Record. Fans Cheer Roosevelt and Remain Until He Leaves." *New York Times,* October 3, 1936.

Drebinger, John. "Yanks Win Series from Cubs by 4–0; 8–3, in Final. Club First to Take 3 World Titles in a Row—McCarthy, Pilot, Shares Record." *New York Times,* October 10, 1938.

Durocher, Leo, with Ed Linn. *Nice Guys Finish Last.* Chicago: University of Chicago Press, 1991.

Durso, Joe. "Joe DiMaggio, Yankee Clipper, Dies at 84." *New York Times,* March 9, 1999.

Durso, Joseph. "Joe McCarthy, Yanks' Ex-Manager Dies at 90." *New York Times,* January 14, 1978.

Enders, Eric. *The Fall Classic: The Definitive History of the World Series.* New York: Sterling Publishing, 2007.

Engelberg, Morris, and Marv Schneider. *DiMaggio: Setting the Record Straight.* St. Paul, MN: MBI Publishing, 2003.

Ferguson, Harry. "Dear Mrs. DiMaggio." *Daily News*, October 2, 1936.

"56 Game Hitting Streak by Joe DiMaggio." Baseball-almanac.com. https://www
.baseball-almanac.com/feats/feats3.shtml.

Ford, Whitey, with Phil Pepe. *Few and Chosen: Defining Yankee Greatness Across the Eras.*
Chicago: Triumph Books, 2001.

Freedman, Lew. *DiMaggio's Yankees: A History of the 1936–1944 Dynasty.* Jefferson,
NC: McFarland & Company, 2011.

Frommer, Harvey. "Summer of '41: Joe DiMaggio's Epic 56-Game Hitting Streak." Base-
ballguru.com (Blog). https://baseballguru.com/hfrommer/analysishfrommer271
.html.

Gaffney, Dennis. "Joe Directs Marilyn's Funeral." PBS American Experience. https://www
.pbs.org/amaericanexperience/feattures/dimaggio-joe-directs-marilyns-funeral/.

Garraty, John A., and Mark C. Carnes, eds. "Barney Ruditsky." In *American National
Biography Volume 19: Rousseau-Simmons.* New York: Oxford University Press, 1999.

Goldstein, Richard. "Frank Crosetti, 91, a Fixture in Yankee Pinstripes Is Dead." *New
York Times*, February 13, 2002.

Greene, Nelson "Chip." "April 17, 1945: Pete Gray: One-Armed Outfielder, Makes MLB
Debut for St. Louis Browns." Society for American Baseball Research Games
Project. https://sabr.org/gamesproj/game/april-17-1945-pete-gray-one-armed
-outfielder-makes-MLB-debut-for-st.louis-browns/.

Greene, Nelson "Chip." "Charlie Keller." Society for American Baseball Research Biography Project. https://sabr.org/bioproj/person/charlie-keller/.

Hallman, Don. "DiMag Hits 3, Yankes Win, 14–5." *Daily News*, May 4, 1936.

Haupert, Michael. "MLB's Annual Salary Leaders Since 1874." Society for American
Baseball Research. https://sabr.org/research/article/mlbs-annual-salary-leaders
-since-1874/.

Heymann, David C. *Joe and Marilyn: Legends in Love.* New York: Atria/Emily Bestler
Books, 2014.

Huber, Mike. "May 24, 1936: Tony Lazzeri's Two Grand Slams and 11 RBIs." Society for
American Baseball Research Games Project. https://sabr.org/gamesproj/game/may
-24-1936-tony-lazzeris-two-grand-slams-and-11-rbis/.

Italie, Hillel. "They Called It a Case of Old Age." *Los Angeles Times*, April 30, 1989.

James, Bill. *The New Bill James Historical Baseball Abstract.* New York: Free Press, 2003.

Joe DiMaggio Bio Page. Gary Bedingfield's Baseball in Wartime (Blog). https://www
.basebaballinwartime.com/player_biographies/dimaggio_joe.htm.

Joedimaggio.com (The Official Site of Joe DiMaggio).

Joe DiMaggio Quotes Page. Baseball-Alamanc.com. https://www.baseball-almanc.com/
quotes/quodim.shtml.

"Joe DiMaggio: 1914–1999/REACTION/An Awesome Player to Players of Any Era."
San Francisco Chronicle, March 9, 1999.

Joe Gordon Page. National Baseball Hall of Fame and Museum (official website). https:
//baseballhall.org/hall-of-famers/gordon-joe.

"Joe's Dating Marilyn—Last Night Anyway." *Daily News*, June 2, 1955.

Johnson, Greg. "Even as an Endorser, DiMaggio Had an Instinct for the Home Run." *Los Angeles Times*, March 9, 1999.

"Joltin Joe DiMaggio by Ben Homer and Alan Courtney (Lyrics)." Baseball-Almanac. com.

Joltin' Joe DiMaggio by Les Brown (baseball-almanac.com).

Jones, David. *Baseball's Greatest Hitters: Joe DiMaggio: A Biography*. Westport, CT: Greenwood Press, 2004.

Klapisch, Bob. "Quake Jolts DiMaggio." *Daily News*, October 19, 1989.

Kostya, Kennedy. *56: Joe DiMaggio and the Last Magic Number in Sports*. New York: Sports Illustrated, 2011.

Krell, David. "The Death of Babe Ruth." David Krell.com, December 28, 2016.

Lariccia, Tony. "Hall of Famers Bob Feller and Joe DiMaggio Created a Rivalry for the Ages." *Cleveland Plain Dealer*, May 20, 2018.

Leerhsen, Charles. *Ty Cobb: A Terrible Beauty*. New York: Simon and Schuster, 2015.

Lefty Gomez Quotes Page. Basebal-Almanac.com. Lefty Gomez Quotes | Baseball Almanac (baseball-almanac.com).

Lefty O'Doul Page-BR Bullpen. https://www.baseball-reference.com/bullpen/Lefty _O'Doul.

Lisi, Clemente. "DiMaggio's Dying Words: 'I'll Finally Get to See Marilyn.'" *New York Post*, August 8, 2000.

Litsky, Frank. "Frank Scott, 80, Baseball's First Player Agent." *New York Times*, June 30, 1998.

"Marilyn Weds Joe DiMaggio." *Daily News*, January 15, 1954.

McCann, Dick. "Cards Win, 4–2, Take Series." *Daily News*, October 6, 1942.

McGowen, Roscoe. "Brooks Agrees DiMaggio's Drive Snared by Gionfriddo Was Headed for the Bullpen." *New York Times*, October 6, 1947.

McGowen, Roscoe. "Dodgers Stress Luck of Rivals." *New York Times*, October 6, 1941.

McMurray, John. "Joe McCarthy." Society for American Baseball Research Biography Project. https://sabr.org/person/joe-mccarthy/.

Miley, Jack. "Give DiMaggio a Break." *Daily News*, July 19, 1936.

Miller, Jennifer Jean. "How Bill Clinton Latched onto the Legacy of Joe DiMaggio Though Joe DiMaggio Never Liked Bill Clinton." Inside Scene.com (Online News site). insidescene.com/2016/06/how-bill-clinton-latched-onto-the-legacy-of-joe-dimaggio-though-joe-dimaggio-never-liked-bill-clinton/.

Muratore, Elizabeth. "DiMaggio's 56-Game Hit Streak One of MLB's Most Hallowed Records." MLB.com, February 24, 2022.

Neft, David S., et al. *The Sports Encyclopedia: Baseball 2000*. New York: St. Martin's Griffin, 2000.

Nitz, Jim. "Ken Keltner." Society For American Baseball Research Biography Project. https://sabr.org/bioproj/person/ken-keltner/.

O'Neill, Edward, and Henry Lee. "Death Stills a Yankee Fan, 8." *Daily News*, October 1, 1947.

Ostler, Scott. "Shower Photo Shows the Full DiMaggio." *San Francisco Chronicle*, June 17, 2011.

Ostler, Scott. "Sibling Rivalry? The DiMaggios Had No Peers." *The San Francisco Chronicle*, July 15, 2015.

Owen, Russell. "DiMaggio the Unruffled. Portrait of a Ballplayer Who Just Keeps Hitting 'Em." *New York Times*, July 13, 1941.

Parr, Patrick. "Japan Yesterday: Mrs. and Mr. Marilyn Monroe Honeymoon in Japan." *Japan Today.com* (online news), August 23, 2018. https://japantoday.com/category/features/lifestyle/Mrs-and-Mr-Marilyn-Monroe-honeymoon-in-Japan.

"Paul Simon Told DiMaggio Lyric Meant No Disrespect." *Chicago Tribune*, March 9, 1999.

Peary, Danny. *We Played the Game: Memories of Baseball's Greatest Era*. New York: Black Dog & Leventhal, 1994.

Pietrusza, David, et al. *Baseball: The Biographical Encyclopedia*. Toronto, Ontario, Canada: Sport Media Publishing, Inc., 2003.

Ponder, Jon. "Wrong Door Raid: The Celebrity Scandal That Irked Sinatra, Made a Fool of DiMaggio—All at Marilyn's Expense." Playground to the Stars.com (Historical Website), December 7, 2010. www.playgroundtothestars.com/2010/12/wrong-door-raid/?msclkid=a53584aab83411ecb5887e7a234eed2a.

Positano, Rock (Dr.), and John Positano. *Dinner with DiMaggio: Memories of an American Icon*. New York: Simon and Schuster, 2017.

Posnanski, Joe. "The Greatest Living Yankee." NBC Sports World, September 25, 2015. https://sportsworld.nbcsports.com/the-greatest-living-yankee/.

Powers, Jimmy. "Powerhouse." *Daily News*, October 1, 1938.

Ray, James Lincoln. "Mickey Mantle." Society for American Baseball Research Biography Project. https://sabr.org/bioproj/person/mickey-mantle.

"Reunion Tales Irk Mrs. DiMaggio." *Daily News*, November 22, 1944.

Ring, Dwayne. "Joe Devine." Society for American Baseball Research Biography Project. https://sabr.org/bioproj/person/joe-devine/.

Rogers, Thomas. "Charlie Keller, 73, an Outfielder and Slugger for Yanks in the 40s." *New York Times*, May 24, 1990.

Schudell, Matt. "The Brothers DiMaggio." *The Washington Post*, May 9, 2009.

Schwartz, Larry. "DiMaggio's 61-game Pacific Hitting Streak Ends." ESPN.com, November 19, 2003. https://espn.com/classic/s/moment010726-dimaggio-pacificrecord.htlml.

Seidel, Michael. *Streak: Joe DiMaggio and the Summer of '41*. New York: McGraw-Hill, 1988.

Smith, Jack. "'Quite a Strain,' Joe Admits, Glad It's Over." *Daily News*, July 18, 1941.

Statscrew.com.

Stout, Glenn. *Yankees Century: 100 Years of Yankees Baseball*. New York: Houghton Mifflin, 2002.

Swide, Joe. "The 1937 Newark Bears: The Greatest Team in Minor League Baseball." Ebbets Field Flannels (Blog). https://www.ebbets.com/blogs/news-and-history/newark-bears.

Swift, E. M. "Yanked About By the Boss." *Sports Illustrated*, April 11, 1988.

"The Joe DiMaggio Show." Martin Grams Blog, February 27, 2012. https://martingams
.blogspot.com/20212/02/joe-dimaggio-show.html.
Thorn, John, ed. *The Complete Armchair Book of Baseball: An All-Star Lineup Celebrates
America's National Pastime.* Edison, NJ: Galahad Books, 1997.
Trimble, Joe. "Clipper Shrewd Quitting While He's Still on Top." *Daily News*, March
25, 1951.
Trimble, Joe. "Dimag Flips First Pitch, A's Flip Yankees, 4–1." *Daily News*, March
14, 1968.
Trimble, Joe. "DiMaggio, Vance, Hartnett, Lyons in Hall of Fame." *Daily News*, January
27, 1955.
Vaccaro, Mike. "Case of Joe DiMaggio and the Stolen Bat." *New York Post*, June 3, 2007.
Wancho, Joseph. "Bill Dickey." Society for American Baseball Research Biography Project. https://sabr.org/bioproj/person/bill-dickey/.
Weeks, Jonathan. *Baseball's Most Notorious Personalities: A Gallery of Rogues.* Lanham,
MD: Scarecrow Press, 2013.
Whitman, Mike. "Lou Gehrig's Streak Ends in Detroit." Society for American Baseball Research Games Project. https://sabr.og/gamesproj/game/may-2-1939-lou
-gehrigs-streak-ends-in-detroit/.
Williams, Ted, with John Underwood. *My Turn at Bat: The Story of My Life.* New
York: Pocket Books, 1970.

INDEX

MacPhail, Larry (Dodgers/
Yankees executive), 41, 47, 48,
53, 55, 138, 148, 155, 156
Maglie, Sal, 123, 194
Mahon, Jack (writer), 118
Majeski, Hank, 67
Manhattan Merry Go Round
(film), 23
Mantle, Mickey, 55, 62–63, 64, 81,
84, 85, 143, 145, 172, 176, 198
1951 World Series injury, 66,
117, 168
Mapes, Cliff, 157
Maranville, Rabbit, 72
Marciano, Rocky, 167
Martin, Billy, 173, 186
Martin, Hersh, 136
Mathewson, Christy, 145
Mayo, Eddie, 20
Mays, Willie, 81, 83, 84, 145
McCarver, Tim, 91
McCann, Dick, 45
McCarthy, Joe (Yankees manager),
viii, 16, 17, 25, 28, 29, 30, 31,
47, 105, 106, 107, 108, 118,
129, 131, 143, 162, 198
resignation from Yankees,
48, 57
McCormick, Frank, 109
McDougald, Gil, 64
McKnight, Marian, 74
McLoughlin, Maurice (tennis
player), 96
McQuinn, George, 50
Medwick, Joe, 41

Melton, Cliff, 23
Merriweather, Lee, 74
Metheny, Bud, 136
Michaels, Al (broadcaster), 87
Miely, Jack (writer), 110
Miller, Arthur (and Marilyn
Monroe), 77
Miskis, Eddie, 140
Mize, Johnn, 46, 61, 64
Molina brothers (Bengie, Jose,
Yadier), 115–16
Monette, Val, 75
Monroe, Marilyn:
childhood and early career,
68, 71
death of, 77–79
disputes with J. DiMaggio,
69, 78, 151
funeral, 79–80
meeting J. DiMaggio, 67–68
marriage to J. DiMaggio,
70–72, 199
reconciliation with
J. DiMaggio, 78
relationship with DiMaggio's
son, 154
touring Japan with
DiMaggio, 161–62
wrong door raid, 168–70
Morgan, Joe, 83
Mr. Coffe, 85, 172
Mullin, William, 41
Musial, Stan, 44, 91
Myer, Buddy, 17
Muncrief, Bob, 192